LIBERTARIANISM
TODAY

LIBERTARIANISM TODAY

Jacob H. Huebert

 PRAEGER

AN IMPRINT OF ABC-CLIO, LLC
Santa Barbara, California • Denver, Colorado • Oxford, England

Library of Congress Cataloging-in-Publication Data

Huebert, Jacob H.
    Libertarianism today / Jacob H. Huebert.
        p. cm.
    Includes bibliographical references and index.
    ISBN 978-0-313-37754-9 (hard copy : alk. paper) — ISBN 978-0-313-37755-6
(ebook)
    1. Libertarianism. I. Title.
    JC585.H855   2010
    320.51′2—dc22   2010005196

ISBN: 978-0-313-37754-9
EISBN: 978-0-313-37755-6

14   13   12   11   10   1   2   3   4   5

This book is also available on the World Wide Web as an eBook.
Visit www.abc-clio.com for details.

Praeger
An Imprint of ABC-CLIO, LLC

ABC-CLIO, LLC
130 Cremona Drive, P.O. Box 1911
Santa Barbara, California 93116-1911

This book is printed on acid-free paper ∞

Manufactured in the United States of America

Contents

Acknowledgments

I'm grateful to the many people whose speaking, writing, and encouragement helped me reach the point where I could write a book about libertarianism. Thanks especially to Anthony Gregory, Allison Harnack, Jeffrey Herbener, Stephan Kinsella, Manuel Lora, and Thomas Woods for providing helpful comments on drafts of various parts of the book. Thanks also to my editor, Vince Burns, for giving me this opportunity and for patiently and pleasantly guiding me through the process.

1

What Is Libertarianism?

Is libertarianism an idea whose time has come?

Maybe not. In 2008, Americans elected a president who openly urges a bigger, more invasive government. The federal government is taking over businesses and dominating industries in unprecedented ways, spending trillions of taxpayer dollars along the way. Across the country, innocent men, women, and children are being brutalized by increasingly militarized police supposedly waging war on terror, drugs, and crime. American troops remain in Iraq, Afghanistan, and over a hundred other countries around the globe. Every day, in nearly every way, government only gets bigger and more inhuman.

On the other hand, libertarians do have some cause for hope—more now, perhaps, than at any other point in our lifetimes. Libertarianism used to be of interest only to a scattered handful of students and activists; the movement was so small that it seemed like everyone in it knew everyone else in it. Today, libertarians are not a majority, but they are innumerable and they are everywhere.

The biggest sign of hope has been the presidential campaign of Ron Paul, the Texas Congressman and physician who sought the Republican nomination in 2008. He did not win or even come close, but something in his candidacy, which focused on the libertarian themes of peace and freedom, touched a nerve with a lot of people.

The Paul campaign's success on the Internet and at the grassroots level is well known, but it is worth a brief review to show how many people supported him and how intense their support was. In November 2007, Paul received donations of over $4 million online in one day through a "money-bomb" organized by a supporter, music promoter Trevor Lyman, not by the campaign. The next month, supporters broke *that* record by donating another $6 million in one day. Paul ultimately racked up more donations than any other Republican contender for the fourth quarter of 2007, with nearly $20 million. The donations were not from the usual political players, but from ordinary people across the country, many of whom had never before made a campaign contribution to anyone, donating an average of just $100 each.

The outpouring of online support was so overwhelming that the official campaign was not quite ready for it—no libertarian candidate had ever been so well funded. But as the campaign worked to catch up, eager supporters took it upon themselves to make their own campaign signs and hold their own rallies. They thought of innovative ways to attract attention, from unfurling "Ron Paul" banners at nationally televised events to renting a blimp with "Google Ron Paul" emblazoned across the side. They also took to the Internet to make sure that Paul won as many online polls as possible (and he won most of them); they sent e-mails to news networks urging them to cover Ron Paul; and they made sure that Ron Paul would not go unmentioned in the comment section appearing below any news story related to the election. Some traveled to New Hampshire and Iowa on their own dime to campaign, led in part by a Google engineer who left his lucrative position to volunteer full-time. The septuagenarian candidate also drew crowds of enthusiastic young people at college campuses, and people from all social and economic backgrounds everywhere else. And though Paul did not win the Republican nomination, he did win over 1.1 million votes and some convention delegates. Not bad, especially when compared to one-time front-runner (and Paul critic) Rudolph Giuliani's less than 600,000 votes and zero delegates.

Paul drew all this support because he presented a clear, credible alternative to the other options in both parties. While Paul decried the growth of government and its destructive foreign and monetary policies, other politicians from both parties not only did not care about this, but wanted to go further in the wrong direction. Some people who considered themselves conservative came to Ron Paul after they saw their party embrace "big-government conservatism," lead the country into war on false pretenses, create a domestic police state, and spend like Lyndon Johnson. Some people who considered themselves liberal found their way to Ron Paul, too, as the Democrats failed to live up to their occasional anti-war rhetoric and also failed to seriously challenge the police state, corporate welfare, the monetary system, and other programs that benefit the elite in business and government at the expense of ordinary people.

Ron Paul's campaign was unique partly because it was all about ideas. In the wake of the campaign, a surge of newcomers to the libertarian movement have sought more information on these ideas—and the information has been available as never before. Less than two decades ago, libertarians had to scrounge for literature, getting what they could from a limited selection in a few catalogs and whatever happened to be on their local library or bookstore shelf. Today, an enormous library of libertarian literature, including hundreds of full-length books and countless scholarly and popular articles, is available online for free.

Education of oneself and others has always been libertarians' foremost activity, but libertarians today are fighting back by other means, too. Some are moving to New Hampshire in hopes of creating a "free state" there by influencing local and state governments. Some are going to court to challenge laws that restrict freedom, and in some very high-profile cases, they are winning. Some are creating alternatives to government programs, such as the homeschooling movement.

Another reason why libertarians may have an unusually good opportunity to see their ideas advance now is because there is an economic crisis and, if libertarians are correct, the government's attempts to fix it will only make things worse. This may open more people's minds to question the policies that led to the crisis, the hundreds of billions of dollars spent keeping troops in Iraq and around the world, and the countless other ineffective, oppressive programs we may no longer be able to afford. Libertarian economist Milton Friedman observed that in a time of crisis, when the people and government are desperate to solve a problem, "the actions that are taken depend on the ideas that are lying around,"[1] and what once seemed politically impossible may become politically inevitable. Perhaps that time has come for libertarian ideas.

WHAT IS LIBERTARIANISM?

Before we say much more about libertarianism, we should define what libertarianism is and briefly look at the history of the libertarian movement.

The Libertarian Idea

This is the basic libertarian idea: that people should be free to do "anything that's peaceful," as libertarian thinker Leonard E. Read put it.[2] That means, in the words of libertarian theorist and economist Murray Rothbard, that "no man or group of men may aggress against the person or property of anyone else."[3] Or, to rephrase it one more time, anyone should be free to do anything he or she wants, as long as he or she does not commit acts of force or fraud against any other peaceful person. Libertarians call this the "non-aggression principle."

In everyday life, people understand and follow this basic libertarian rule. If you want something and it belongs to someone else, you have to persuade him or her to give or sell it to you—you cannot just steal it or threaten to hit the other person over the head if they refuse to part with it. If you do not like the books your neighbor is reading, or the religion he is practicing, or most anything else he is doing in the privacy of his own home, too bad—you cannot go force other people to do what you want them to do.

Libertarians extend this rule to the political realm. If one person cannot steal money from another, then the government (which is made up only of individual people) should not be allowed to forcibly take money from people, even if it is called taxation. If one person cannot kidnap another person and force him into slavery, the government should not be allowed to do it, either, even if it is called a draft (or "national service"). If one person cannot go into his neighbor's house and force him to give up bad personal habits, then the government should not be allowed to do it, even if it is called a war on drugs. And so on.

Libertarians do not just morally object to the government doing these things; they also see government as incompetent. And they view politicians as nobody special. After all, why would having the skills it takes to be elected—the ability to give empty speeches pandering to the lowest common denominator, to kiss babies, and the like—make a person an expert on everything, capable of "running the economy," or otherwise directing people's lives? Why would succeeding in politics make someone an expert on *anything* other than politics itself? Libertarians also recognize that politicians are not altruistic, but are self-interested like everyone else. And as endless scandals demonstrate, the types of people who want power over others tend to be of *lower* character than the rest of us. Plus, the free-market economic theory to which libertarians subscribe says that government intervention in people's voluntary exchanges will make people worse off and that central planning of the economy by anyone, regardless of their motive, is certain to fail.

Viewed through this libertarian lens, most politicians and bureaucrats are not public servants at all. Instead, through their legalized killing and stealing, they constitute the world's largest and most successful criminal gang. Their gang is so successful, of course, because most people do not think of it as criminal. We are trained from a young age to respect it and view it as necessary, so most of us acquiesce without thinking.

Many people will find this libertarian view of government strange, but libertarians find it strange that people would view the State in any other way.

After all, by one scholar's estimate, governments killed 170 million of their own people in the twentieth century.[4] Then there are the many others killed in wars. Then there are the countless people whose deaths by government are unseen—those who die, for example, because the government denies them the freedom to choose a potentially life-saving medical treatment or to procure an organ for transplant. Libertarians tend to think that if more people were aware of the ways in which government kills and steals on a massive scale, they would be less likely to assume that government is a benevolent institution.

Taken all the way, the libertarian idea means that no government is justified—any government is a criminal enterprise because it is paid for by taxes and people are forced to submit to its authority. Many libertarians (including this author) *do* go that far. But many others (Ron Paul is one) stop just short of this and are willing to accept a minimal "night watchman state," as philosopher Robert Nozick put it, to provide for common defense, police, and courts because they believe only government can effectively provide these services. But even those small-government libertarians (or "minarchists," as they are sometimes called) believe that government cannot be trusted and must be watched vigilantly because it is so likely to exceed its boundaries.

Having said all that, not everyone defines libertarianism in exactly the same way. The definition just reviewed is a primary definition that has guided the modern libertarian movement, though, and it is the definition we will apply in this book. And for the most part, we will not concern ourselves much with the difference between no-government libertarians and minimal-government libertarians. Nor will we concern ourselves with how many exceptions to the basic libertarian rule one can make before that person no longer "counts" as a libertarian. But we will say now that a given policy can only be called libertarian if it calls for reducing or abolishing the power of government over individuals, and that any policy that maintains or increases the government's power is anti-libertarian.

Libertarianism and Morality

To accept libertarianism, at least in its purest form, one has to agree with the non-aggression principle—the idea that it is wrong to defraud or use aggressive force against another person. Why would someone accept that idea? Libertarians do so for different reasons. Some believe in the non-aggression principle because they believe people have natural rights, either given by God or somehow inherent in man's nature. Others do because their religion tells them that murdering and stealing are wrong. Others do, not because they believe in "rights," but simply because they believe that following the non-aggression principle will lead to the greatest good for the greatest number.

It should be clear, then, that libertarianism is not a complete moral philosophy or a philosophy of life. It is just a political philosophy, and one can come to libertarianism from a variety of angles. As Murray Rothbard put it:

> [L]ibertarianism per se does not offer a comprehensive way of life or system of ethics as do, say, conservatism and Marxism. This does not mean in any sense that I am opposed to a comprehensive ethical system; quite the contrary. It simply means that libertarianism is strictly a *political* philosophy, confined to what the use of violence should be in social life.[5]

That means libertarianism has nothing to say about how one should live one's life within the broad limits of peaceful activity. For example, libertarianism says that it is wrong to forcibly prevent someone from using marijuana, but it has nothing at all to say about whether you should use marijuana or should abstain. Libertarianism says that you should be free to have voluntary sexual relations with any other willing adult, but it has nothing to say about whether you should be chaste, promiscuous, or something in between. Instead, each individual has to bring his or her other philosophical or religious views to bear on such questions. The point may be simple enough, but as we will see in the next chapter, it is lost on some people (including, unfortunately, some libertarians) who conflate libertarianism and libertinism.

LIBERTARIAN ECONOMICS

There really is no such thing as "libertarian economics." Economics is just a science that studies production, consumption, exchange, and related topics. Economics can explain what effects certain policies will cause, but it does not dictate what ends we should want. Nonetheless, economics is extremely important to libertarians because libertarians believe that economics shows that liberty—that is, a free market that protects private property rights and voluntary exchange—makes people better off, and that government restrictions on liberty make people worse off.

Voluntary Exchange and Private Property

Critics sometimes deride libertarians for saying that various problems should be "left to the market." But when libertarians refer to "the market," they just mean individuals freely making voluntary exchanges with each other. In a voluntary exchange, the trading partners necessarily make each other better off because each person gives up something he or she values less for something he or she values more. What is rarely said, but true, is that the people who want to interfere with "the market" actually want to use physical violence (or the threat of it) to stop others from making voluntary exchanges—that is, from making choices that they believe will make themselves better off. These meddlers in the market want to forcibly substitute what they think people *ought* to want for what people *actually* want. Libertarians oppose this.

Libertarians observe that on a mass scale, voluntary exchange in the market makes society *much* better off. As Adam Smith famously observed, people pursuing their own self-interest unwittingly benefit society in the process. The successful businessman in a free market can make money only by persuading large numbers of people to give him their money in exchange for what he is offering and then pleasing them enough that they will want to come back for more. Contrary to the popular perception, consumers in a free market are not at the mercy of businesses, but businesses are at the mercy of consumers. In a free market, only those businesses that are best at providing what consumers want, at the best price possible, will succeed. Similarly, a worker will earn money in proportion to the value of the service he provides to his fellow man.

In the nineteenth and early twentieth centuries, a relatively free market gave rise to a dramatically improved quality of life for the average person in America. Wages increased—for example, worker's earnings went up by about 60 percent just between 1860 and 1890—and the variety of goods available greatly expanded.[6] Entrepreneurs such as Henry Ford made previously unimaginable luxuries such as automobiles available to the ordinary working person. Since then, countless miracles that were unimaginable to even the wealthiest people of centuries past—airline flights, televisions, computers, air conditioners, and so much else—are now available to ordinary people, even relatively poor people, who cannot imagine life without them.

Libertarians emphasize that such an explosion of wealth could never have come about through central planning. This is so in part because no one could possibly have the knowledge to organize such a system. In his classic essay entitled "I, Pencil,"[7] Leonard E. Read illustrated this point by observing how many different people have to act to bring a single pencil into existence. Trees must be cut for the wood—but before that saws must be made, and all the different parts of saws. And ropes. And loggers have to get to the trees. And loggers probably drink coffee—which itself takes countless thousands of individuals to produce and deliver. Then there is the paint to cover the pencil, the graphite inside the pencil, the metal that holds the eraser, and the eraser itself. All these components have an "ancestry" that involves thousands of people across the world voluntarily coordinating their actions. No single one of them knows all he or she would need to know to produce the pencil from scratch, and none of them needs to know. And, of course, no central planner could have arranged any of this, and none needed to. No one has or could have the knowledge that would be needed to put this system together. Econo-mist Friedrich Hayek called the market's ability to voluntarily organize in this way "spontaneous order." Libertarians favor this and oppose command and control.

Capitalism versus the Status Quo

America's economy is often called free-market or "capitalist," but that is not true. The U.S. economy is hampered by countless interventions: trade bar-riers, corporate welfare, wage controls, price controls, regulation, occupational licensure, antitrust laws, compulsory unionism, taxes, and so much else. So when libertarians defend free-market capitalism—or certain capitalist aspects of America's past or present economy—one should not assume that libertar-ians are defending the status quo. Instead, libertarians would say that *to the extent* we have had a relatively free market, we are better off. Libertarians point to annual "economic freedom indexes" compiled by the Fraser Institute (a Canadian think tank) and by the *Wall Street Journal* and the conservative Heritage Foundation, which consistently show that the countries with the most economic freedom tend to have the highest incomes and economic growth, while those with the least economic freedom—think Cuba and North Korea—are the least well off.[8]

Because we do not have a true capitalist economy, but have an economy that is still relatively free in some important respects, libertarians view many players in our current economy as being part hero and part villain. For exam-ple, most libertarians see Wal-Mart as heroic for providing consumers with a wide array of goods at low prices. Wal-Mart became as successful as it did largely because it was better at serving consumers than its rivals. But libertar-ians see Wal-Mart as villainous when, for example, it persuades a local govern-ment to use eminent domain to take property to build one of its stores. In our current mixed economy, few businesses are "pure"—so libertarians do not defend big business per se, but only those aspects that are compatible with genuine free-market capitalism.

Schools of Thought

Libertarians advocate free-market economics—that is, they promote eco-nomic ideas that show why free markets are beneficial and government inter-vention is harmful. Do libertarians choose their ideas about economics to support their preconceived political ideas? Maybe some do, but for many, an understanding of free-market economics is what leads them to libertarianism in the first place. That is, they see the failures of government intervention and the wealth created by the market, learn the causes and effects, and form their political ideas accordingly. For many people, free-market economics reinforces what their intuition, moral views, and observations already suggested.

Of course not all economists, and not even all free-market economists, agree about everything. But there are important economic questions on which nearly all economists, regardless of their political stripes, agree, which support libertarian positions. For example, the overwhelming majority of economists agree that, other things being equal, minimum-wage laws create unemployment, price controls cause shortages, and people are better off under free trade than under protectionism. On other questions, free-market economists stand apart from the rest of their profession. Free-market economists see government spending (including so-called "stimulus" spending) as harmful to the economy. Some economists argue that there is such a thing as "market failure," where people participating in markets do not do what economists think they should do, but free-market economists would argue that this is a myth, and that most so-called "market failures" are actually the result of *government* failure. Then there is the issue of money. Unlike most economists, free-market economists (at least those of the "Austrian School," about which more below and in Chapter 3) believe that the market can provide money just as it provides everything else.

Among free-market economists, there are two main schools of thought: the Austrian School and the Chicago School. The Austrian School, which arose in the late nineteenth and early twentieth centuries, is so named because its founder, Carl Menger, and many of its early adherents, such as Ludwig von Mises and Friedrich Hayek, spent at least part of their careers living and working in Vienna. The Chicago School, which arose in the mid-twentieth century, is so named because its leading thinkers, such as Milton Friedman and George Stigler, were part of the University of Chicago's economics department.[9]

We cannot possibly do justice to the differences between the two schools in this brief overview. The fundamental difference, however, is one of *methodology*— that is, it is a disagreement about how economists should go about studying the economy.

Applying a method called *praxeology*, Austrian economists look at individual action as the basis for understanding economics. Austrians observe that people act to express their preferences and achieve goals, and from this premise Austrians are able to reason about all manner of economic phenomena. Austrians emphasize that our preferences and the utility we enjoy from things are subjective; they exist in our heads, cannot be measured, and cannot be compared between people. The only way to know, then, what maximizes people's utility is to observe what people freely choose.

In contrast, the Chicago School looks not to individuals, but to mathematical models and relationships between statistical aggregates, and then bases its theories and predictions on what these seem to show. For the Chicagoans, if there appears to be a statistical correlation between two things, then economists can claim that there is a relationship between them—even if there is no apparent *logical* connection between them that we can trace back to individual actors. Austrian economist Richard Ebeling illustrates this point with a reductio ad absurdum: to a Chicagoan, "if a strong correlation was found between the anchovy catch off the coast of Peru and business-cycle fluctuations in the United States, this would be considered a good predictive theory, regardless of any real causality between these two measured events."[10] Also, unlike the Austrian School, the Chicago School's methodology allows economists to assume that we *can* measure and compare different people's utility.

These theoretical differences between the Austrian and Chicago Schools are enormous, but economists of both schools tend to agree that free-market policies lead to prosperity. Because they believe that voluntary exchange maximizes utility across society (and for other reasons), Austrians find very few cases, if any, where government intervention could create greater prosperity. Chicago economists also generally disfavor government intervention for a different reason: because statistical evidence tells them that free-market policies make people better off. The Chicago view, however, allows for more exceptions than the Austrian view. If statistics suggest to a Chicago economist that an intervention would make people better off, then he or she may favor it. Austrians, on the other hand, would say that their economic theories cannot be proven or disproven with statistics. Instead, Austrians rest their conclusions on logic, extrapolating from fundamental premises about the nature of human action; so if other economists' statistics suggest Austrian conclusions are wrong, then those statistics must be incorrect, incomplete, or based on unrealistic assumptions.

The most significant policy disagreement between Austrian and Chicago economists pertains to monetary policy. Austrians tend to believe that money should be left to the free market to avoid inflation and business cycles; Chicagoans tend to believe that government must control the money supply. Chicagoans are also more likely to see "market failure" that can be solved by government than Austrians are, and to see a need for other government interventions such as antitrust laws.

Because their methods are closer to the mainstream, and their conclusions allow a greater role for government, Chicago School economists have had more influence than Austrian School economists. Chicagoans are also more numerous. On the other hand, the Chicago economists' inconsistent support for laissez-faire makes them less appealing to the most principled libertarians, and opens their defense of the free market to more compelling criticisms.

THE LIBERTARIAN MOVEMENT

Libertarian ideas have ancient roots, but the "libertarian movement" is a relatively recent phenomenon. Before we spend the rest of the book talking about libertarian ideas today, we should quickly review the history of libertarianism so far.

Origins of Libertarian Thought

One can find hints of libertarian thought in a variety of ancient sources, from the Bible to Lao Tsu. One starts seeing the bigger seeds of libertarian thought in writings by Cicero and Thomas Aquinas on natural law. According to natural law theory, the law is not whatever the government says it is, but instead is something "higher" that exists before government, and which binds kings and other rulers just like everyone else. Spanish Scholastic scholars also had much to say on individual rights and economics that resembles modern libertarian thought. So did the "Levellers," a group that argued for individual rights in seventeenth-century England.

Libertarians were the original liberals. Liberalism arose in the seventeenth century as a political philosophy that gave primary importance to individual liberty. John Locke is widely regarded as the first true liberal. Like many or most libertarians today, Locke believed that each person owns his or her own body and for that reason has a natural right to life and liberty. By mixing their labor with previously un owned parts of the Earth, people can create property, in which they have property rights. For Locke, government could only be justified as something people consented to as a means of protecting their natural rights. There are nuances in Locke's thought that are beyond the scope of this book, but that is the essence of Locke's contribution: a system of individual, libertarian natural rights that came to be known as "liberal" thought.

Why "liberal"? Because "liberal" was the most obvious term for a political philosophy that maximizes individual *liberty*. Unlike today's liberalism, this type of liberalism, now known as "classical liberalism," did not call for government to fund any sort of welfare state or to impose one group's social values on another. It simply called for individuals to have equal rights—that is, equal, maximum liberty—before the law.

Liberalism caught on in America as the country's founding generation, notably including Thomas Paine and Thomas Jefferson, took up Locke's ideas. The Declaration of Independence forcefully states the liberal idea that people have "unalienable Rights," including "Life, Liberty and the pursuit of Happiness," and that people may cast off any government that is "destructive of these ends."

Liberal ideas enjoyed great success in England, France, and the United States, and led to great prosperity for the Western world, but by the late nineteenth century, liberal thought had mostly fizzled for a variety of reasons. Over time, the people calling themselves "liberals" became like the liberals we know today: socialists or welfare statists. By the early twentieth century, liberals of the old school were few and far between. As we will see in the next chapter, only a handful remained to oppose the onslaught of Franklin Delano Roosevelt's New Deal, and they mostly faded away after World War II.[11]

The Foundation for Economic Education

Franklin Roosevelt's New Deal permanently enlarged the federal government and inspired a new generation of libertarians to stand against the intellectual tide, lest liberty be lost forever.

One of the instigators of this new movement was Leonard E. Read, a former head of the Los Angeles Chamber of Commerce. With the backing of a number of business leaders and the leading libertarian intellectuals of the day—most notably economist Ludwig von Mises and *New York Times* and *Newsweek* writer Henry Hazlitt—Read established a nonprofit think tank (as one might call it today) in 1946 called the Foundation for Economic Education (FEE) in a mansion in Westchester County, New York, just north of New York City.

FEE was the most important institution in the early decades of the modern libertarian movement. Its approach to advancing its ideas was unusual for its time and would be unthinkable to most think tanks today. Instead of activism, FEE focused exclusively on helping people educate themselves. Following the example of libertarian journalist Albert Jay Nock, Read believed that a person should focus first and foremost on improving the one unit of society over which one has true control: one's self. By educating oneself in libertarian principles and free-market economics, one could share the "freedom philosophy," as Read called it, with others who were interested, and gradually the ideas would spread. Liberty was not something that could be imposed from the top down; it would have to come from widespread support among a "Remnant," that small group of people keeping the ideas alive and slowly spreading them. Some accused FEE of preaching to the choir by limiting its reach like this, but in those dark days for liberty and libertarianism, the choir needed the attention, and needed to be built up slowly but steadily on a firm foundation.

This approach meant that FEE did not use mass marketing or mass media to spread its message. Nor did it send people to Washington to lobby Congress. Instead, it published a monthly magazine, *The Freeman*, with short articles written for the intelligent layman that explained the basics of liberty and free-market economics. The magazine was sent to people who asked for it and to schools; it was not available on any newsstands. (It is still published and can be read for free at http://www.thefreemanonline.org.)

FEE published books, too, most notably reviving the work of nineteenth-century French political economist Frederic Bastiat. Bastiat's book, *The Law*, explains the libertarian view that when government takes from one group to give to another, this is nothing but "legal plunder." Bastiat's essays on economics illustrated free-market principles, often using wit and satire. In "What Is Seen and What Is Not Seen," Bastiat demolished the idea so often expressed by pundits and politicians that disasters and wars are good for the economy because they create jobs. Of course, people only see the job that is created; they do not see the things the money would have been spent on and the jobs that would have been created if the wealth-destroying disaster had never occurred. In "The Candlemakers' Petition," Bastiat ridiculed economic protectionism with a fictional demand by candlemakers for the government to block their major competitor, the sun, so everyone would be forced to buy candles to see.

FEE's approach may seem small-scale and simple, but its impact was huge. Generations of young people (including this author) received their introduction to libertarian ideas through copies of *The Freeman* passed along by a friend or relative. Leonard Read and other FEE staff members toured the country giving lectures (only where invited, never as "missionaries") and persuaded people who became supporters of the cause and in turn introduced others to the ideas. FEE's students would also go on to find new ways to advance the cause and grow the movement.

Ludwig von Mises and Austrian Economics

We mentioned Ludwig von Mises and Austrian economics above. We should say more about who Mises was and why he is important.

Mises was an economist who was born and lived most of his life in Austria. He did not begin his career as a dogmatic libertarian, and he never accepted the idea of natural rights. Instead, he was an economist searching for truth about which policies make for economic prosperity. This work led him to a number of conclusions that are important for libertarianism. One conclusion was that laissez-faire capitalism (economic liberty) is the only means for a society to become prosperous. Another conclusion—explained in his 1922 book, *Socialism*—was that central planning of an economy was destined to fail because the planners could not engage in economic calculation without a market price system, and economic chaos would result if they tried. Another important insight of Mises was that "middle of the road" interventionist policies cannot last—any government intervention in the economy is certain to create new problems, which the government can respond to by either repealing the bad policy, or heaping new policies on top of it (which in turn will fail, and so on).

When the Nazis came to power, Mises, who was of Jewish ancestry, fled Austria to Geneva and eventually to New York City. Though he was once a leading intellectual light of Europe, his ideas had long since fallen out of fashion when he arrived in America, and he struggled to find a teaching position. With the help of libertarians who knew of him and his plight, especially Henry Hazlitt, Mises found a position at New York University.

At NYU, Mises taught a weekly seminar, which was attended not only by enrolled students but also by area libertarians. Among the young attendees who would go on to play a major role in the world of free-market economics and libertarianism was Murray Rothbard, who would become one of the movement's leading economists and political theorists.

Mises remained prolific to a late age, writing books and articles, most notably including his 1949 treatise, *Human Action*, a comprehensive case for the free market as the foundation of civilization. Though mostly ignored by the mainstream economics profession after his move to America, Mises's work found its way to students of free-market economics—including, eventually, to Ron Paul, whose views on economics were largely shaped by Mises, Rothbard, and one of Mises's students from his Vienna days, Friedrich Hayek.

Hayek, like Mises, worked in the Austrian School tradition, and in the late 1920s and 1930s he built on Mises's work to study business cycles—why economies have booms and busts. (More about this and its relevance to our recent economic woes in Chapter 3.) Hayek eventually moved to the London School of Economics, and in 1944 he published *The Road to Serfdom*, which, thanks to a prominent *New York Times* review by Hazlitt, received considerable mainstream attention and even a *Reader's Digest* condensed edition. In that book, Hayek argued that central economic planning leads inevitably to tyranny, as it had in Hitler's Germany and the Soviet Union. The book was not purely libertarian—Hayek allowed for more government than most libertarians would—but against the backdrop of a world that considered fascism and socialism to be the way of the future, it was radical.

Hayek eventually came to America as well and taught for some time at the University of Chicago before returning to Europe. Hayek's later work focused less on economics and more on topics such as the philosophy of science and political philosophy. Though Hayek was never a pure libertarian, he was close, and came closer in some respects over his lifetime. Because of his influence and undeniable genius, Hayek remains an inspiration to libertarian intellectuals, even if his challenging, German-influenced prose makes him less accessible to laymen, and his less-than-pure libertarianism makes him less interesting to radicals.

Murray Rothbard, whom we have mentioned, was a radical by any measure and saw no legitimate role for government. His impact on libertarianism came at least as much through his deliberate attempts to build the movement as through his prodigious output as an economist, political philosopher, and historian. Unlike Mises and Hayek, who were utilitarians, Rothbard did believe in natural rights and systematically explained his rights-based libertarian political ideas in books such as *For a New Liberty* and *The Ethics of Liberty*.

Rothbard intentionally sought to build a libertarian movement that he hoped would see results sooner rather than later. He insisted on purity among libertarians, considering it essential to have a "cadre" that would not waver on principle. He brought together all the key strands of libertarian thought up to that time into one consistent system that integrated anti-imperialism, individualist anarchism, Austrian economics, natural-rights theory, and Jeffersonian decentralism. Though Rothbard emphasized purity, he also sought political alliances that libertarians could use to achieve real-world success. He became involved in the Libertarian Party and played a role in the foundation of the Cato Institute and the Ludwig von Mises Institute—about which more below.

No discussion of modern libertarian economists would be complete without a mention of Milton Friedman. Unlike Mises, Hayek, and Rothbard, Friedman was a member of the Chicago School, not the Austrian School. Still, Friedman mostly advocated the free market, even though he did not support monetary freedom, which many libertarians consider crucial, and even though he was more open to government intervention in general than the likes of Mises or Rothbard. And Friedman was influential—policymakers consulted him, for better and for worse, and he played a role in convincing Richard Nixon to end the draft. Also, his book *Capitalism and Freedom* introduced many to free-market economics.

Ayn Rand and Objectivism

Ayn Rand is another central figure in twentieth-century libertarianism. She is best known for two big, important novels, *The Fountainhead* (1943) and *Atlas Shrugged* (1957), and for the philosophy of Objectivism that she espoused in them and in nonfiction works such as *The Virtue of Selfishness* (1964). Unlike libertarianism, Objectivism is a complete philosophy of life, not just a political philosophy. Rand's individualistic philosophy emphasized the ideas that reality is what it is (she rejected the supernatural); that a person should learn about the world by using reason; that a person's own life should be his or her highest value (that is, a person should be rationally selfish); and that laissez-faire capitalism is the only political system consistent with humans' nature as rational beings.

Rand was a bestselling author in her time, and her work remains highly popular. As of 2007, her books were selling three times the number sold in the early 1990s. In the first half of 2009, *Atlas Shrugged* sold 25 percent more copies than it had sold in all of 2008, presumably because the book's vision of a country and its economy falling apart as government planners take over major industries appeared to be coming true. Two organizations, the Ayn Rand Institute (which was founded by Rand's chosen "intellectual heir," Leonard Peikoff and is hostile to non-Objectivist libertarians) and the Atlas Society (a group more friendly to libertarians) continue to promote Rand's ideas, and a scholarly *Journal of Ayn Rand Studies* has been published semi-annually since 1999.

Ayn Rand was once one of the primary paths by which people discovered libertarian ideas—maybe the leading path. (A satirical memoir on the libertarian movement of the 1960s was called *It Usually Begins With Ayn Rand.*) Many Rand readers followed her recommendation to read Mises, which in turn led them to a larger libertarian world. Despite Rand's novels' continued popularity, Rand is probably not quite the leading "gateway drug" to libertarianism she once was. In the 1950s and 1960s, there were not many other paths available, especially in bookstores and libraries. Now, information on libertarianism abounds on the Internet, and most of it has nothing to do with Rand or Objectivism. In addition, many people who are receptive to libertarianism are repelled by some aspects of Rand's work—for example, her insistence that others share her preferences in art and music, her hatred for religion, and her philosophy's selfish ethics.

Libertarians in Politics

Many voters know the word "libertarian" only from the Libertarian Party (LP), whose candidate they make sure not to vote for on their presidential ballot every four years. Like FEE and the later Ron Paul movement, the LP arose in response to especially bad times for liberty; founder David Nolan decided to form it after President Nixon abolished the gold standard and imposed wage and price controls in 1971.

The LP's founders didn't delude themselves with the idea that they would win elections for high office anytime soon. Instead, they saw the Party as another way to get the word out. Many libertarians, including Leonard Read, disapproved of this approach because political campaigns by their nature tend to be more about slogans and getting votes than communicating substantive ideas. Others such as Rothbard were initially skeptical but eventually became involved, at least for a time.

The LP ran its first presidential candidate, philosopher John Hospers, on just two states' ballots in 1972. Though the ticket received fewer than 3,000 popular votes, it oddly received an electoral vote from a libertarian member of the Electoral College who defected from Nixon. (Tonie Nathan, the Libertarian VP candidate, became the first woman to receive an Electoral College vote.) That elector, Roger MacBride, became the Libertarian presidential candidate in 1976 and performed better, with 0.21 percent of the popular vote.

The 1980 Libertarian ticket consisted of corporate lawyer Ed Clark and oil billionaire David Koch. Koch and his brother, Charles, had begun funding libertarian causes in the 1970s. With Koch putting more than $2 million of his own money into the campaign, the ticket received nearly a million votes and over one percent of the total.

That campaign has been the peak of Libertarian Party success to date. Subsequent presidential campaigns, including Ron Paul's 1988 campaign on the Libertarian ticket, have received closer to 0.5 percent of the popular vote, sometimes less. (Paul joined the Libertarian Party only for the purpose of his presidential run; he has served in Congress as a Republican from 1976 to 1977, 1979 to 1985, and 1997 to the present.) In 2008, the Libertarian Party nominated former Republican Congressman Bob Barr and seemed to change its focus—about which we will say more in Chapter 11.

Libertarian Institutions

The Koch brothers and some other libertarians, including Edward Crane (chairman of the Libertarian Party for much of the 1970s) and Rothbard, wanted to advance libertarianism on multiple fronts, so they founded the Cato Institute in 1977. Unlike FEE, Cato would deliberately engage in the public-policy discussions of the day, but unlike other policy outfits, it would be based in San Francisco, not Washington, DC. At first, Cato published a magazine, *Inquiry*, which avoided using the word "libertarian" and attempted to appeal to people on the left and right who had some libertarian sympathies. Cato also published scholarly work by the likes of Rothbard.

Before long, Cato began to shift its emphasis. To appeal more to the mainstream, it moved away from Austrian School economics toward the Chicago School. After Ronald Reagan's election, it moved its headquarters from San Francisco to Washington, DC in hopes of better influencing policy. The magazine fell by the wayside.

Cato remains in Washington, steadily producing public-policy studies, op-eds, and books. As the endnotes to this book testify, its scholars' work provides a wealth of facts and statistics on the federal government's taxation, spending, and other doings. On the other hand, in its policy advocacy, Cato sometimes moves away from libertarian principle and advocates measures that are not libertarian, such as so-called private social security accounts or school vouchers.

Some libertarians see these policies as incremental steps toward liberty, but others, including this author, see them as dangerous steps away from liberty.

Following Cato's move, other libertarian or libertarian-leaning institutions have set up shop in the nation's capital. *Reason*, a widely distributed monthly libertarian magazine based in Los Angeles, now maintains a Washington office. The Institute for Humane Studies (IHS), founded by F.A. Harper in 1961 to promote libertarian scholarship, moved to the Washington, DC area in 1985. Among other things, IHS funds various scholars and holds free seminars for students at various universities around the country. The Institute for Justice, a public-interest libertarian law firm about which we'll say more in Chapters 6, 8, and 9, established its headquarters in Washington in 1991. Many of these Washington-based organizations, including the ones just mentioned, receive significant funding from the Kochs.

Cato's intellectual, strategic, and geographic moves prompted Rothbard to disassociate himself from it in 1981. The next year, he joined with former Ron Paul Congressional Chief of Staff Llewellyn H. Rockwell, Jr. to form the Ludwig von Mises Institute in Auburn, Alabama. (Mises died in 1973, but the project had the blessing of his widow, Margit von Mises, who served as its chair until her death.) The Mises Institute would be what Cato was not: an organization dedicated to advancing the ideas of Austrian economics and libertarianism with no public-policy compromises. As the DC-based organizations have downplayed the issues of monetary freedom and non-interventionist foreign policy, the Mises Institute has deliberately emphasized them. Also, in contrast with some of the Beltway groups, the Mises Institute would not aim its efforts at politicians and policymakers but, like FEE, at scholars and laymen.[12]

Today the Mises Institute is noted especially for its annual Mises University, a one-week intellectual boot camp in which students learn all facets of Austrian economics, and for its website, http://Mises.org, which hosts daily articles, hundreds of hours of audio and video lectures, a blog on economics and liberty, and scanned versions of hundreds of books, old and new, available to download for free. Rockwell also edits his own website, *LewRockwell.com*, which features a fresh slate of articles each day, has a blog, and is the world's best-read libertarian website.

Paul's campaign has taken many of the ideas emphasized by the Mises Institute and *LewRockwell.com* to a much larger audience. His campaign is the most recent major development in the libertarian movement—and that, of course, is where we came in.

THIS BOOK

That summary of libertarianism and libertarian movement history regrettably necessarily leaves out important issues, institutions, and people. But it at least provides some sense of what libertarianism is about and where it has been.

The rest of this book presents libertarian perspectives on a number of today's most important issues. It is an introduction, not a comprehensive guide—but if the reader is interested in learning more about a libertarian topic, there will be plenty of suggestions for further reading (many of which are available online) at the end of each chapter and in the endnotes.

Before we get into the issues, from the economy to drugs to guns and much else, we need to make one more clarification about what libertarianism is, or is not. Libertarianism today is *not* conservatism or liberalism—and that is the subject of the next chapter.

NOTES

1. Milton Friedman, *Capitalism and Freedom* (Chicago: University of Chicago Press, 1982 [1962]), xiv.

2. Leonard E. Read, *Anything That's Peaceful* (Irvington-on-Hudson, NY: Foundation for Economic Education, 1964).

3. Murray N. Rothbard, *For a New Liberty: The Libertarian Manifesto*, rev. ed. (Auburn, AL: Ludwig von Mises Institute, 2006 [1978]), 27.

4. R. J. Rummel, *Death by Government* (New Brunswick, NJ: Transaction Publishers, 1994).

5. Murray N. Rothbard, "Frank S. Meyer: The Fusionist as Libertarian Manqué," *LewRockwell.com*, http://www.lewrockwell.com/rothbard/rothbard48.html (originally published in *Modern Age* in 1981).

6. Thomas J. DiLorenzo, *How Capitalism Saved America* (New York: Crown Forum, 2009), 95–96.

7. Leonard E. Read, "I, Pencil," http://www.thefreemanonline.org/featured/i-pencil/.

8. See DiLonenzo, *How Capitalism Saved America*, 23–27; *Economic Freedom Index of the World Project*, http://www.freetheworld.com.

9. It may be slightly misleading to speak of the "Chicago" School today because Friedman and many others have died, and their approach was largely similar to that of many other mainstream economists. Regardless, the Austria/Chicago distinction still works to distinguish Austrians from mainstream "neoclassical" free-market economists.

10. Richard M. Ebeling, "Milton Friedman and The Chicago School of Economics," *The Freeman* (December 2006), http://www.thefreemanonline.org/from-the-president/milton-friedman-and-the-chicago-school-of-economics/.

11. Ralph Raico provides an overview of the history of liberal thought in a series of essays beginning with "The Rise, Fall, and Renaissance of Classical Liberalism, Part I," *Freedom Daily* (August 1992), http://www.fff.org/freedom/0892c.asp. (This page includes links to the rest of the series.) See also David Boaz, *Libertarianism: A Primer* (New York: Free Press, 1997), 27–58.

12. Full disclosure: I am an adjunct scholar and ardent supporter of the Mises Institute. I have also worked as an intern for the Foundation of Economic Education and the Institute for Justice.

FURTHER READING

DiLorenzo, Thomas J. *How Capitalism Saved America: The Untold Story of Our Country, from the Pilgrims to the Present.* New York: Crown Forum, 2004. DiLorenzo explains how, to the extent we have had them, free-market economic policies created the wealth we enjoy today.

Doherty, Brian. *Radicals for Capitalism: A Freewheeling History of the Modern Libertarian Movement.* New York: PublicAffairs, 2007. Doherty provides a detailed, highly readable history of the libertarian movement.

Read, Leonard E. *Anything That's Peaceful.* Irvington-on-Hudson, NY: Foundation for Economic Education, 1964. The title essay provides a classic statement of the libertarian position; the book also includes "I, Pencil." This book is available online at http://mises.org/books/anything.pdf.

Rothbard, Murray N. *For a New Liberty: The Libertarian Manifesto*, rev. ed. New York: Collier Books, 1978. This remains the most thorough, scholarly introduction to libertarian thought. At nearly 40 years old, it remains accessible and relevant. This book is available online at http://mises.org/books/newliberty.pdf.

2

Libertarians Are Not Conservatives (or Liberals)

I s libertarianism an extreme right-wing political philosophy? Some people think so. After all, Barry Goldwater and Ronald Reagan said they wanted less government, so the thinking goes, libertarians who want *much* less government must be just a bit further down the same path. People who think this often think the Reagan years were great times for libertarians, and even now many people assume that the Republican Party is in the sway of libertarian economic ideology.

The conventional thinking on this is all wrong. Libertarianism is not an extreme form of conservatism or anything like conservatism as that term is commonly used today. Although some libertarians have allied themselves with conservatives in the past, the Bush Administration's policies have driven ever more libertarians to flee from the right.

In 2008, when the Republicans held their convention in St. Paul, Minnesota, Ron Paul drew some 10,000 supporters to his own event, the "Rally for the Republic," across the river in Minneapolis's Target Center. At the rally, Lew Rockwell took the podium to blast Bush's offenses against liberty, and to put an end to any association between conservatism and libertarianism. Rockwell said that Bush's eight years of increasing government did not constitute a betrayal of conservatism, as some had claimed, but rather a fulfillment. Conservatism, he said, had always been about increasing state power, not reducing it. He urged libertarians to reject any connection with the "conservative" label:

> What does conservatism today stand for? It stands for war. It stands for power. It stands for spying, jailing without trial, torture, counterfeiting without limit, and lying from morning to night. There comes a time in the life of every believer in freedom when he must declare, without any hesitation, to have no attachment to the idea of conservatism.[1]

For many or most libertarians today, that time has come.

In this chapter, we will consider the differences between conservatives and libertarians, and why libertarians increasingly reject any identification with the right side of the political spectrum. Also, if people are not mistaking libertarians for conservatives, they are mistaking them for anything-goes liberals—so we will also briefly look at why libertarians are not liberals, either.

WHAT IS A CONSERVATIVE?

To see why libertarians are not conservatives, and not even very similar to conservatives, we will first need to define what a conservative is. Of course, conservatism means different things to different people, including people who call themselves conservative. One might say that conservatives tend to favor economic liberty, but not personal liberty; that conservatives want to preserve the status quo; or that conservatives value tradition and custom. Then there are the neoconservatives, who place the worldwide spread of democracy highest on their list of priorities. Regardless of which common definition one chooses, today's conservatives are not libertarians.

Economic-Liberty Conservatism

Some associate conservatism with laissez-faire capitalism and unfettered, unregulated free markets. The popular perception is that "small-government" conservatives are like libertarians when it comes to the economy. Many people have this impression of Reagan: someone who believes that government has a role to play in imposing certain social values and in maintaining a strong military, but who believes the free market should otherwise be left unhampered. As we will see below, this impression of Reagan and conservatives is not accurate, and even if it were, it would not make conservatives libertarian, or libertarians conservative.

In the early 1970s, political scientist and Libertarian Party founder David Nolan devised a chart (sometimes called the "Nolan Chart") that he believed best depicted the political spectrum. The Nolan Chart defines political philosophies according to how much personal and economic freedom they allow. Here is one version of that chart:

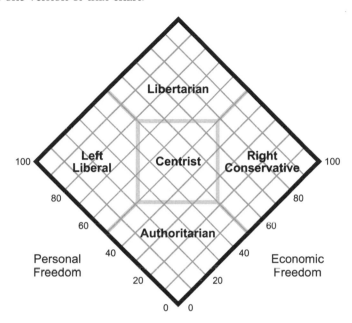

At the far left of the chart are pure liberals. As Nolan defines them, liberals favor maximum "personal" liberty—with respect to sexual and other personal, moral issues—and no economic liberty. On the far right are pure conservatives, favoring maximum economic liberty but no personal liberty. People who favor neither type of freedom, authoritarians, are at the bottom. And people who favor maximum personal and economic freedom, libertarians, are at the top. Most people have a mix of views that would place them somewhere other than the extremes. A libertarian educational organization, The Advocates for Self-Government, has created a 10-question "World's Smallest Political Quiz" (available at its website, http://www.self-gov.org) to help people locate their position on the chart. Libertarians have long used this quiz as an outreach tool because it shows some people that they are more libertarian than they realized.

The Nolan Chart defines libertarians and authoritarians perfectly: Libertarians favor no state controls in any facets of an individual's life, and pure authoritarians see no area that should not be subject to government intrusion.

The chart's definitions of liberal and conservative are questionable. We can perhaps see a tendency of liberals toward more personal freedom in many areas, but not all areas. Many liberals, after all, oppose the personal freedom to carry a firearm; many favor restrictions on free speech through, for example, campus speech codes or the Fairness Doctrine; and many left-wing feminists would abolish pornography. And how many liberals actually call for outright legalization of drugs, prostitution, or other "victimless crimes"? Similarly, conservatives may support more economic freedom than liberals, but their support is far from consistent. Few conservatives call for the repeal of antitrust laws, taxation, or many well-entrenched federal economic interventions. At best—and they are usually not at their best—they may call for relative restraint compared to the leftists' desires. In their responses to the financial crisis that began in 2008, conservatives were all over the map, but generally favored the government "doing something," even if they criticized Democrats' proposals as "big-government" measures.

Another problem with these definitions is that it is difficult to separate economic and personal liberty. Isn't the freedom to sell drugs or sexual services an economic freedom? Isn't the freedom to work under the conditions and for the wages of one's choosing a personal freedom?

These definitions also leave out the critical issue of war. Liberals tend to oppose war (though most supposedly liberal politicians do not do so consistently), while most who identify as conservative have favored the Iraq War and tend to defend U.S. involvement in past wars. This issue is not strictly one of personal or economic freedom—as we will see in Chapter 9, war inevitably impinges on both. It harms personal freedom by depriving its innocent victims of their lives, liberty, and property, and it also harms personal freedom through increased domestic controls that tend to accompany war. War is also antithetical to economic freedom because it requires taxation or inflation for its funding, and it directs resources away from productive uses toward destructive uses. War is so important to many libertarians that it should be entitled to more weight than other issues—yet the chart gives it no weight at all.

But let us say we accept the personal- and economic-liberty definitions as rough approximations of the liberal and conservative positions. This would mean that pure liberals are half-libertarian and pure conservatives are half-libertarian, with neither more libertarian than the other. So under the economic-liberty definition of conservatism, libertarians cannot be called conservatives any more than they can be called liberals.

Status Quo Conservatism

Another definition of conservatism—the most obvious one—is support for maintaining the status quo. In the age of classical liberalism, the "conservatives" supported the statist, mercantilist status quo against the liberals who supported individual rights. The conservatives wanted to ensure that the people who were on top, economically and socially, stayed there, and liberalism presented a threat to the established order.[2]

Status quo conservatives today are much the same. They do not support making government smaller, but may at best want to limit the *rate* of government growth. This seems to be the definition that applies to most politicians who are perceived as conservative. Their Democrat opponents and the media tend to paint them as ruthless cutters of government programs, but the description is almost never accurate.

It should be obvious that libertarians are not at all like status quo conservatives. As Ludwig von Mises put it more than half a century ago, this type of conservatism "is an empty program, it is merely negative, rejecting any change. . . . To conserve what exists is in present-day [1954] America tantamount to preserving those laws and institutions that the New Deal and the Fair Deal have bequeathed to the nation."[3] Libertarianism, in contrast, is radical. Where status quo conservatives seek to conserve, libertarians seek to repeal and abolish. The two groups' goals are not compatible, but antithetical, pulling in opposite directions. That these conservatives might not pull as hard in the direction of bigger government as some others or as leftists scores them no libertarian points.

Traditionalist Conservatism

Another type of conservatism is traditionalist conservatism. Traditionalist conservatives follow in the intellectual footsteps of the British Edmund Burke and the American Russell Kirk. Traditionalist conservatism rejects ideology and rationalism, and instead values virtue, tradition, order, custom, history, religion, hierarchy, and community.[4] Traditionalists view liberty as a worthwhile political goal, but only one among several, and therefore they are not libertarians. Still, the views of many (though far from all) traditionalist conservatives do overlap with those of many libertarians. (A leading traditionalist organization, the Intercollegiate Studies Institute, began in 1953 as the more libertarian Intercollegiate Society of Individualists.)

Some might assume that libertarians and traditionalists would part ways with respect to conservative social values, but this is not necessarily so. Frank Meyer, a founding *National Review* editor, attempted to create a "fusionist" school of thought bridging traditionalist conservatism and libertarianism, and showed that there was no necessary tension between the two because virtue could not be effectively promoted by government—and freedom to choose is essential to true virtue, anyway.[5]

In his 2001 book, *Democracy—The God That Failed*, Hans-Hermann Hoppe argued that a libertarian society would tend to be much more conservative (in the personal, traditional sense) than our present society. He identified ways in which government programs—such as social security, regulation of health

insurance, unemployment insurance, and welfare handouts—break down traditional institutions and discourage conservative personal values:

> These institutions [of compulsory government "insurance" against old
> age, illness, occupational injury, unemployment, indigence, etc.] and
> practices amount to a massive attack on the institution of the family and
> personal responsibility. By relieving individuals of the obligation to pro-
> vide for their own income, health, safety, old age, and children's educa-
> tion, the range and temporal horizon of private provision is reduced, and
> the value of marriage, family, children, and kinship relations is lowered.
> Irresponsibility, shortsightedness, negligence, illness and even destruc-
> tionism (bads) are promoted, and responsibility, farsightedness, diligence,
> health and [personal] conservatism (goods) are punished. The compulsory
> old age insurance system in particular, by which retirees (the old) are sub-
> sidized from taxes imposed on current income earners (the young), has
> systematically weakened the intergenerational bond between parents,
> grandparents, and children. Consequently, not only do people want to
> have fewer children . . . but also the respect which the young traditionally
> accorded to their elders is diminished, and all indicators of family disinte-
> gration and malfunctioning . . . have increased.[6]

The conventional thinking among non-libertarians, including some traditionalist conservatives, is that capitalism and libertarianism promote an
"atomized" individualism where people become detached from their families
and communities. But Hoppe and other libertarians argue that it is government that creates that kind of atomization when it supplants civil society—
families, churches, and other voluntary organizations—with itself.

Some see personal, traditional conservatism as not only a likely result of libertarianism, but also a necessary precondition of a libertarian society. Though
he emphatically rejects "conservative" politics, Lew Rockwell has noted that
no political philosophy exists in a "cultural vacuum." "The family, the free market, the dignity of the individual, private property rights, the very concept of
freedom—all are products of our religious culture. . . . Christianity made possible the development of capital."[7] On the other hand, however, some socially
liberal libertarians take a much different view, arguing that a socially liberal,
tolerant society is a necessary complement to libertarian politics.

Paleoconservatism

Paleoconservatism is a strand of conservative thought that overlaps largely
with traditionalist conservatism.[8] Paleoconservatives reject neoconservatives'

endorsement of the warfare and welfare state, and to this extent find much in common with libertarians. Paleoconservatives want the United States to be a republic, not an empire, and thus have consistently opposed U.S. foreign intervention following the Cold War. They want the decentralized government of the U.S. Constitution as it was originally understood, or perhaps even the Articles of Confederation. In general, they want government to be as local as possible.

To the extent that paleoconservatives (and traditionalists) favor a reduced federal government and greater decentralization, they are closer to being libertarians than other conservatives are. Libertarians just go further—much further—down the decentralization path, to the level of the individual.

Still, paleoconservatives reject the libertarian non-aggression principle. They may favor allowing local or state governments to do much that limits individual liberty. They tend to favor strong federal restrictions on immigration because they see immigrants as disrupting the communities and institutions that would comprise the kind of society they want. Paleoconservatives may also be protectionist, believing trade barriers are necessary, again, to maintain the social order they want to preserve or restore. To the extent paleoconservatives support these things, they are not libertarian, but anti-libertarian.

Outnumbered by mainstream conservatives and liberals who favor an ever-bigger federal government, paleoconservatives and libertarians have emphasized their common ground in recent years, particularly their opposition to neoconservative foreign policy. Ron Paul's presidential campaign attracted supporters from both camps, and his mostly libertarian views won him the endorsement of the paleoconservative-leaning *American Conservative* magazine, which also frequently features articles by libertarians.

The Religious Right

The Religious Right segment of the conservative movement came to prominence in the early 1980s largely as a reaction to *Roe v. Wade*, government attacks on religious schools and broadcasting, and the culture's shift to the left during and after the "free-love" era.[9] Religious Rightism—at least the brand promoted by Rev. Jerry Falwell—seeks to promote, among other things, family values, school prayer, national defense, and the interests of the state of Israel.[10] It opposes abortion, homosexuality, and other perceived assaults on traditional religious values. Religious Rightism is essentially a more populist form of traditionalist conservatism—appealing more to religious fundamentalism than to tradition or history—with special emphasis on certain issues. Many (but not all) Religious Rightists may be more eager than traditionalists to use the federal government to impose their values on the whole of America—for example, through a constitutional ban on homosexual marriage, or a federal ban on abortion, were *Roe v. Wade* to be overturned. They may also favor using state or local governments to do the same. To the extent that evangelical Christians or other religious people want others to voluntarily adopt their values, they have no conflict with libertarianism; indeed, as we have seen above, libertarianism may be highly compatible with their views. To the extent they want government to impose their values on others, they are anti-libertarian.

FROM "OLD RIGHT" LIBERTARIANISM TO NEOCONSERVATISM

There was a brief period in American history when the people called "conservatives" really were libertarians. This was the era of the New Deal and World War II, when most on the left embraced Franklin Roosevelt's policies—but those liberals who did not support Roosevelt suddenly found themselves regarded as the "conservatives" of the day.

The libertarian "conservatives" who opposed Roosevelt's expansion of government at home and abroad were part of a loose coalition known today as the "Old Right." The two most prominent intellectual figures of this movement were journalists H.L. Mencken and Albert Jay Nock, who also happened to be two of its most radical libertarian individualists. The movement's most prominent political figure was Senator Robert Taft, a Republican Senator from Ohio and the son of President William Howard Taft.

In his early-twentieth-century heyday, no one would have called Mencken a conservative. Writing in the *Baltimore Sun* and later the *American Mercury*, Mencken ridiculed all manner of sacred cows in politics, religion, and business. He mocked what he saw as the idiocy of the American mass-man. He attacked excessive patriotism, fundamentalist Christianity, democracy itself, and much else. He was an outspoken opponent of all government censorship and of Prohibition. He was, in sum, an individualist and, in his words, an "extreme libertarian."[11] In his *Notes on Democracy*, Mencken described his libertarian view of government as a criminal enterprise:

> All government, whatever its form, is carried on chiefly by men whose first concern is for their offices, not their obligations. It is, in its essence, a conspiracy of a small group against the masses of men, and especially against the masses of diligent and useful men. Its primary aim is to keep this group [of politicians and bureaucrats] in jobs that are measurably more comfortable than the jobs its members could get in free competition.[12]

Nock, too, was an individualist and hardly a conservative. Nock considered himself a "radical" and an anti-Establishment "anarchist." Nock argued that the U.S. Constitution was enacted to allow business interests to use a powerful central government to enrich themselves at everyone else's expense—not the mainstream conservative line, then or now. Nock elaborated these views in his books, such as *Our Enemy, the State*, in which he referred to the State as a "professional criminal class," and *Memoirs of a Superfluous Man*, which includes his far-from-conservative views on marriage and family.

When Roosevelt's New Deal came along, Mencken, Nock, and other Old Right thinkers saw it as another big-government-and-big-business scam, this time on an unprecedented scale. Nock saw the New Deal as combining the worst aspects of both Prohibition and the economic policy of the 1920s, because the New Deal both limited personal freedom (as Prohibition did) and, despite popular perceptions to the contrary, used government to enrich big business (as past Republican administrations had).

World War II only gave the Old Right more to oppose. Mencken and Nock had opposed America's entry into World War I, and Mencken in particular observed Americans' loss of all their senses when taken in by crude war propaganda. To the Old Right, World War II appeared to be more of the same. The United States had taken actions to prompt Japan to attack and, as evil as Hitler was, Germany posed no imminent threat to the United States.[13] Writing in 1938, Nock articulated a theme that has remained popular among radical anti-war libertarians—that the threat from one's own government is far greater than the threat from any foreign government:

No alien State policy will ever disturb unless our Government puts us in the way of it. We are in no danger from any government except our own, and the danger from that is very great; therefore our own Government is the one to be watched and kept on a short leash.[14]

Unfortunately, these figures found that many on the left who had sided with them or at least tolerated their views in the past were swept up in the causes of the moment. Liberals now saw Roosevelt's program of welfare and warfare as the nation's salvation, and anyone who opposed them as reactionary. Thus—to their shock and disgust—Mencken, Nock, and the others found themselves suddenly branded conservatives after a lifetime of opposing the Establishment's status quo. Radical Old Right libertarian Frank Chodorov, who wrote pamphlets with titles such as "Taxation is Robbery" and published a newsletter called *Analysis*, said that anyone who called him a "conservative" would get a punch in the nose. He clarified: "I am a radical."[15]

After World War II, the Old Right movement dissipated as key figures died off or otherwise faded away. This provided an opportunity for William F. Buckley, Jr. and his magazine, *National Review*, to take the right—that is, the opposition to the leftist mainstream—in a new direction. Buckley identified himself as a conservative, and said he was influenced by such Old Right figures as Nock and Chodorov. He also occasionally invoked free-market thinkers such as Adam Smith and Mises, though it is questionable whether he actually read them.[16] But whatever libertarian sympathies Buckley may have had in his early years, he subordinated them to what he believed to be a more pressing concern: defeat of the Soviet Union in the Cold War. And so in 1952, Buckley declared that the Americans should be willing to accept "Big Government" and a "totalitarian bureaucracy" at home because these were necessary to defeat the Soviets.[17] (Never mind the correct predictions of the Austrian economists, Mises and Friedrich Hayek, that centrally planned economies would fail even without outside help because of planners' inability to engage in economic calculation.) The early *National Review* also took some decidedly illiberal positions—for example, it supported racial segregation, not on grounds of "states' rights," but because whites were the "advanced race."[18]

Libertarian Ronald Hamowy, writing in the conservative-and-libertarian journal the *New Individualist Review* in 1961, characterized the conservatism of *National Review* as "the conservatism not of the heroic band of libertarians who founded the anti-New Deal Right, but the traditional conservatism that has always been the enemy of true liberalism, the conservatism of Pharonic Egypt, of Medieval Europe, of Metternich and the Tsar, of James II, and the Inquisition, and Louis XVI; of the rack, the thumbscrew, the whip, and the firing squad." He added that libertarians should be glad to have the *National Review* crowd, rather than libertarians, labeled as the day's conservatives: "I, for one, do not very much mind that a philosophy which has for centuries dedicated itself to trampling upon the rights of the individual and glorifying the State should have its old name back."[19]

Over the years, Buckley, *National Review*, and the conservative movement became increasingly involved with figures who were ex-socialists who retained a fundamentally statist orientation. These included senior editor James Burnham and, later, "neoconservatives" such as ex-Trotskyite Irving Kristol. These new figures on the right showed minimal interest in the individualist thought of Mencken and Nock, and limited interest in economic freedom at home. Although the magazine published some criticism of the welfare state (its excesses, at least), the anti-war views of the Old Right and of libertarians were entirely unwelcome. A militaristic foreign policy trumped all other considerations.

As mentioned above, one founding editor of *National Review*, Frank Meyer, attempted to create a "fusionism" between conservative and libertarian thought. But Meyer, too, embraced the pro-war foreign policy of his colleagues, which strained his and other conservatives' relations with libertarians during the Vietnam War.[20] After Meyer died in 1972, the libertarian strands of his thought became decreasingly influential, as the neoconservatives and their Wilsonian, utopian vision of a world made safe for democracy under the boot of the U.S. military came to dominate the conservative movement.

When the Soviet Union fell, neither Buckley nor his cohorts turned back to the concerns of the Old Right. Instead, they looked to expand the American empire, and eventually found a new enemy to fight in the Middle East and the global war on terror. In a 2004 interview, Buckley expressed his present disinterest in free-market libertarian thought—among other things. "The trouble with the [past] emphasis in conservatism on the market," said Buckley, "is that it becomes rather boring. You hear it once, you master the idea. The notion of devoting your life to it is horrifying if only because it's so repetitious. It's like sex."[21]

The Republican Party's politicians reflected the intellectual shift on the right. Barry Goldwater is widely perceived as having strong libertarian leanings, but his support for an aggressive Cold War policy, including nuclear war if necessary, was unlibertarian in the extreme. In fairness, Goldwater did introduce some future libertarians to the idea of limited government through his libertarian rhetoric, and sometimes libertarians invoke him as a role model, even if they should know better. Later standard-bearers Richard Nixon and Gerald Ford, however, were irredeemable: they offered a liberal, mainstream brand of big-government Republicanism that was anti-Soviet but not at all libertarian in rhetoric or substance. Nixon was especially bad from the libertarian perspective, not so much for his petty Watergate crimes as for his bombing in Laos and Cambodia; imposition of price controls; inflationary monetary policy (including the end of the gold standard); support for new big-government programs such as the Environmental Protection Agency; and declaration of war on drugs. The economic policies of these administrations were not free-market but a type of Keynesianism. Reagan offered a return to libertarian rhetoric but, as we will see, did not usher in smaller government. Since then, Republicans have occasionally reverted to the free-market talk of Goldwater and Reagan— usually when the Democrats are in the majority and proposing the same kind of spending the Republicans had supported when they were in charge. During the Bush years, though, Republicans in Washington mostly forwent this pretense as they pursued an aggressive foreign policy, created a domestic police state, and grew non-defense spending at a rate far outpacing that of the Clinton Administration.

So it is true that for a fleeting moment in American history, some libertarians found themselves labeled the "conservatives." Even then, however, the label was not accurate, especially with respect to Mencken, Nock, and other radical intellectuals who expressed their disdain for the status quo that existed before the New Deal.

Today, many libertarians look to Old Right figures as their intellectual ancestors. (To the list of important Old Right figures who remain influential we must add, at a minimum, the writers John T. Flynn, Garet Garrett, Rose

Wilder Lane, Felix Morley, and Isabel Paterson.) Ron Paul, for example, invoked the Old Right in urging conservatives to support his policies and his presidential campaign. It seems unlikely, though, that such an appeal will resonate among many of today's conservatives. After all, most of the leading lights of the Old Right were off the scene by 1960, and they really never were part of the right at all. More important, the ideas of the Old Right directly contradict much of what most present-day conservatives believe. Conservatives who have come of age in the past 50 years have only known the pro-war, anti-libertarian conservatism of Buckley and the neoconservatives and the moral policing championed by the Religious Right. The Old Right, despite the "right" label, is not part of their intellectual heritage.

A FAILED ALLIANCE

Despite their differences, some libertarians considered conservatives to be allies until recently. This alliance rested on the false premise that the conservatives were serious about pursuing some libertarian goals.

Several factors may account for this unfortunate alliance's existence. One is opposition to communism: Even if the conservatives were too aggressive in their foreign policy, at least they recognized that communism was evil, unlike so many on the left. Another factor is, again, conservatives' libertarian-sounding rhetoric: Even if the conservatives did not actually reduce government, at least they seemed to recognize that it ideally *ought* to be restrained, unlike liberals who openly advocated bigger government. Sometimes the conservatives could even sound relatively good on foreign policy; after Bill Clinton and the Democrats waged war in the Balkans, George W. Bush, running in 2000, promised not only fiscal restraint, but also a "humble foreign policy" and "no nation-building." Also, some conservative judges seemed more likely to limit government than some liberal judges who saw few limits on Congress's power to regulate all manner of human activities through the Commerce Clause.

These similarities were and are superficial, however, as we have seen from our own brief overview of conservatism's recent history. Some saw through the conservatives' talk and contradictions immediately, but for others it took the strong medicine of a George W. Bush presidency.

Reagan: No Revolution

Rhetoric versus Reality

The popular perception is that Reagan ushered in a "revolution" in government—an essentially libertarian one, in which the federal government was no longer viewed as the solution to problems, but was viewed as itself a problem.

This revolution was even seen as outlasting Reagan, reflected in Bill Clinton's declaration that "the era of big government is over." Only with the election of Barack Obama, pundits opined, did Americans cast off the anti-government ideology that had held sway since Reagan took office.[22]

This popular perception is wrong. Reagan was no libertarian and did nothing to bolster libertarianism. Instead, he grew government and, if anything, stifled the libertarian movement by bringing libertarians and small-government conservatives into his coalition, getting their votes but giving them practically nothing in return.

First, there are the obvious ways in which Reagan was not a libertarian. His religious-right supporters favored much anti-libertarian moral policing, and Reagan paid them back for their support. Reagan drastically escalated the war on drugs, as the percentage of inmates in federal prison for drug offenses increased from 25 percent to 44 percent during his two terms.[23] And he pursued an interventionist foreign policy by, among other things, putting troops in Lebanon, bombing Libya, supporting Saddam Hussein in Iraq, and meddling in Nicaragua in the Iran-Contra matter.

One area in which Reagan did claim to favor personal freedom while running for office was draft registration: he promised to end it on the grounds that it "destroys the very values that our society is committed to defending." By 1982, however, he officially reversed positions because, he said, "we live in a dangerous world."[24] (Of course, it was a world made all the more dangerous by Reagan's own nuclear escalation—another offense against libertarianism.)

Despite all that, Reagan at least favored relatively free-market policies, did he not? Not at all, if one looks at results instead of rhetoric. Although Reagan claimed at times to support free trade, the portion of imports facing restrictions increased 100 percent over the course of his two terms.[25] Reagan railed against government spending and deficits while running for office, but both became far worse under his watch. In 1980, the final year of Jimmy Carter's term in office, government spent $591 billion and ran a $73.8 billion deficit. In 1988, the final Reagan year, government spent over $1 trillion, and ran a $155 billion deficit.[26]

True, those figures are not adjusted for inflation—but the need to adjust only shows that Reagan failed to defeat inflation, too (even if, in fairness, Federal Reserve Chairman Paul Volcker did control it better than his 1970s predecessors). Reagan had promised to restore the gold standard, and on taking office he appointed a commission to study the issue. But that group consisted almost entirely of people who were already known to oppose the gold standard—so its anti-gold findings were a foregone conclusion, no change in monetary policy resulted, and the dollar continued to lose value.[27] (Ron Paul and Lewis Lehrman were on the committee and published a minority report, *The Case for Gold*, which remains in print.) Former Federal Reserve Chairman

Alan Greenspan—a leading culprit in the economic crisis that slammed the American economy about twenty years after Reagan left office—was first appointed by Reagan and is therefore another part of Reagan's anti-libertarian legacy. (More on that in the next chapter.)

One might think that Reagan deserves at least a modicum of libertarian appreciation for being a tax cutter, but this is wrong on two grounds.

First, increasing spending while cutting taxes is not libertarian. If the government spends more than it takes in, it will have to print or borrow the money to make up the difference. If the government prints the money, then taxpayers suffer an "inflation tax" that may be even more destructive than an ordinary tax. If the government borrows the money, then future citizens will have to repay the loans through taxes or inflation (unless the government repudiates the debt). And, of course, all government spending siphons resources from the private sector, which shrinks the amount of private capital available, which, in turn, results in fewer consumer goods produced, which makes society worse off.

Second, Reagan did not effectively cut taxes. Reagan did sign a tax cut in 1981, which went mostly to the wealthy minority, but this cut was immediately offset by an increase in Social Security taxes and by the effects of "bracket creep," as inflation pushed people into higher tax brackets.[28] (Also, rather than take the libertarian step of eliminating mandatory social security, Reagan "saved" it by forcing working people to pay more.) After that, Reagan continued to effectively raise taxes by "closing loopholes" over the course of his presidency. No wonder, then, that government revenues increased from $517 billion in 1981 to $1.031 trillion in 1989[29]—not what one would expect under a libertarian regime committed to cutting government. What about deregulation? The major deregulations for which Reagan is sometimes credited—the oil and gas industry deregulation, airline deregulation, trucking deregulation—were in fact enacted under the Carter Administration, which was perhaps more libertarian than the Reagan Administration, if results count. Carter's deregulation conveniently took effect just in time for Reagan to take credit. But as Murray Rothbard put it, "The Gipper deregulated nothing, abolished nothing. Instead of keeping his pledge to abolish the Departments of Energy and Education, he strengthened them and even wound up his years in office adding a new Cabinet post, the Secretary of Veterans Affairs."[30]

Reagan and the Libertarian Movement

So the Reagan years were bad for liberty—and they were also bad in many respects for the libertarian movement. Anti-government sentiment had grown during the 1970s as a result of various factors, including Vietnam, Watergate, and disastrous economic policies. Reagan tapped into this anti-government sentiment and then used his position not to advance liberty, but to *restore respect for government* and prompt a resurgence of militarism and flag-waving nationalism—a conservative's dream, perhaps, but an anti-state libertarian's nightmare.[31]

Worse, many libertarians were sucked into the administration's orbit early, optimistic because of Reagan's apparent sympathy for libertarian ideas. Some of these libertarians became disillusioned and left Washington, but others adjusted their priorities to fit in and became part of the Establishment. Surveying the damage after eight years, Rothbard charged that "intellectual corruption" among (former or quasi-) libertarians "spread rapidly, in proportion to the height and length of [their] jobs in the Reagan Administration. Lifelong opponents of budget deficits remarkably began to weave sophisticated and absurd apologias, now that the great Reagan was piling them up, claiming, very much like the hated left-wing Keynesians of yore, that 'deficits don't matter.'"[32]

Some libertarians did not join the government, but moved to be closer to it in hopes of gaining influence. Most notably, the Cato Institute moved its headquarters from San Francisco to Washington, DC in 1981. The move did raise the profile of the organization and its people, but Rothbard and other libertarian critics outside Washington have charged that they watered down the message at times to maintain beltway respectability and to appease wealthy benefactors who seek influence, most notably their foremost patrons (to this day), oil billionaires Charles and David Koch. Most significantly, on its move to Washington, Cato promptly deliberately moved away from the pure free-market economics of the Austrian School in favor of more mainstream approaches, and with this also curbed criticism of the Federal Reserve, which at least until recently was the ultimate taboo in Establishment circles. Criticism of aggressive Republican foreign policy became somewhat muted, as well, if not so completely abandoned. And where earlier libertarians had sought radical goals, the new Beltway libertarians increasingly promoted "public policy" compromises such as school vouchers and so-called private social security accounts.[33]

Two decades later, some libertarians' decisions to latch onto Reagan and enter the mainstream Washington "public policy" business do not seem to have borne much fruit. Liberty has not advanced as a result, and it is questionable whether its decline has even been slowed. The enormous growth of government under Reagan and especially under George W. Bush testifies to the failure of this strategy. Lamentably, even after all this, some libertarians who know better continue to invoke Reagan as if he set a good example.[34]

Bush: The Fulfillment

It does not take much sophistication to recognize that George W. Bush was no libertarian—but apparently it takes more sophistication than *Slate* editor-in-chief

Jacob Weisberg has. In October 2008, he published an article in both *Newsweek* and *Slate* called, in its *Slate* version, "The End of Libertarianism: The Financial Collapse Proves that Its Ideology Makes No Sense." The article blamed libertarian policies for the country's economic troubles, relying on the unsupported premises that the country had libertarian economic policies and that certain influential Republicans—he named Alan Greenspan, former Senator Phil Gramm, and Securities and Exchange Commission Chairman Christopher Cox—were in thrall to libertarian ideology and the belief that "markets are always right and governments always wrong to interfere."[35] Running for president, Barack Obama made a similar false assumption when he promised to "restore common-sense regulation," as though there had been no regulation for the past eight years.[36]

How could such confusion have arisen? Certainly not from the facts. Over the Bush years, federal regulations continued to increase. The rate of increase of new federal regulations did decrease from past years, but the Federal Register, in which federal regulations are published, continued to grow: from 64,438 pages in 2001 to 78,090 in 2007.[37]

But the number of regulations does not even tell the whole story because many of Bush's regulations have been especially onerous and economically harmful. In 2002, Bush signed the Sarbanes-Oxley Act, which authorized the creation of new regulations and doubtless will result in the creation of many more over the years ahead. Under Sarbanes-Oxley, corporations with publicly traded stock are forced to prove each year that they are not cooking their books—in other words, they are presumed guilty until they prove themselves innocent. Sarbanes-Oxley was supposed to prevent fraud in the financial services industry in the wake of the Enron and WorldCom scandals, but of course it did nothing to stop the meltdown of the financial industry and the larger economy some five years after it was passed. At the same time, Sarbanes-Oxley discouraged new businesses from becoming listed on the New York Stock Exchange because of the extreme burdens the regulations would impose. As of 2004, companies spent at an average of $4.36 million each to comply with Sarbanes-Oxley.[38] According to Jacob Weisberg, apparently, this is libertarianism—but anyone who has read even this far in this book should know better.[39]

On every other front, Bush is the worst president in many decades from a libertarian perspective, probably one of the worst ever. For example, his Medicare prescription drug bill will cost over $1 trillion over the course of a decade;[40] he signed record-setting farm bills loaded with billions in special-interest spending; and he imposed the No Child Left Behind Act, which greatly increased federal spending on and control over education. When Bush took office, the federal government spent $1.9 trillion per year; his final budget was over $3 trillion.[41] From fiscal years 2001 through 2007, Bush increased spending an average of 4 percent per year, making him the biggest overall spender, in terms of annual increase, since at least Jimmy Carter. He increased military spending an average of 6.7 percent per year, making him the biggest military spender since Franklin Delano Roosevelt.[42] Undoubtedly the hundreds of billions spent on bailouts of Wall Street firms, banks, automakers, and others during Bush's final days in office will make the final Bush figures much worse.

For libertarians or anyone else opposed to war, Bush's record was, of course, atrocious, as he pursued an exceptionally aggressive foreign policy and launched an unjustified war in Iraq that outlasted his presidency. Bush's attacks on civil liberties through the Patriot Act and otherwise are well known (if not well known enough), and his creation of a new Department of Homeland Security bureaucracy made government bigger and more intrusive.

Bush's foreign policy and his creation of a domestic police state, combined with his profligate spending, served as a wake-up call to many who had previously been content to accept the Republicans as the lesser of two evils—and gave rise to Ron Paul's considerable success.

How can we say all of this is the "fulfillment" of conservatism? Because Bush and a Republican Congress diligently advanced the agenda of the two leading groups of conservatives, the neoconservatives and the Religious Right. The neocons support endless war and substantial domestic interventions; the Religious Rightists, as we have defined them, support using government to advance their moral causes; and neither group opposes taxing, spending, or regulation on principle.[43]

So how could the likes of Weisberg confuse Bush's policies with libertarianism? Presumably because so many libertarians had been content to be lumped with conservatives for so long—apparently because they had been duped, because they believed it was the best they could do, or because they believed it would help them get close to power. Whatever their motives, libertarians who attached themselves to the conservative movement and embraced Republican candidates did not advance their cause. It took Ron Paul, someone unafraid to stand apart from the Republican and Washington mainstream for decades, to lead the movement back to independence and respectability, and to provide a clear alternative to both Republicans and Democrats by adhering strictly to principle.

LIBERTARIANS ARE NOT LIBERALS, EITHER

It should not be necessary to cite statistics on government growth under Presidents Clinton and Obama to show that libertarians are not liberals, either. But sometimes people become confused on this, and sometimes libertarians do not help.

As mentioned above, most people who identify as liberal support many policies that would use government coercion against peaceful people, so of course they are not libertarian. Leftists tend to favor government wealth redistribution, compulsory government schooling, and taxing and spending for all manner of things that are important to them. All of this relies on coercion, and therefore violates libertarianism. Leftists also tend to favor gun control, compulsory unionism, regulation of business, antidiscrimination laws, and environmental controls, all of which depend on forcing people to do things leftists want them to do. Modern liberals' *goals*—fairness, alleviation of poverty, a clean environment, less crime—may overlap with those of many libertarians, but their *means* are not libertarian.

Still, "social issues" on which liberals and *some* libertarians may agree tend to create confusion, especially same-sex marriage and abortion.

Same-Sex Marriage

Some libertarians (and non-libertarians) have suggested that libertarianism favors same-sex marriage. It is not obvious that this is so. Libertarianism as we have defined it in this book has nothing to say about same-sex marriage, except that if two people of the same sex want to consider themselves married to one another, the government should not stop them. But there is no libertarian "right" to have the government or anyone else acknowledge a particular type of relationship, and government recognition of same-sex marriage would not, in itself, reduce the power of the government over individuals. If governments currently deny unmarried people (homosexual or otherwise) certain libertarian rights, then libertarians would of course object to that limitation on unmarried people's rights. But this position does not require affirmative support for same-sex marriage; it only requires repeal or revision of existing laws. Some libertarians make the argument that as long as government is in the marriage-recognizing business, it shouldn't discriminate. But this is not a libertarian view per se; it is presumably a view a person holds because of social views that person holds in addition to his or her libertarian views (and those views may be fine, but they are not part of libertarianism per se). The libertarian view is that there is no legitimate reason for government to recognize *any* type of marriage.

Abortion

The other social issue that causes confusion is abortion. Some people believe that libertarianism is pro-choice, but the issue is not so simple.

Libertarians are, of course, opposed to murder. So whether a libertarian is opposed to abortion generally depends on whether a libertarian thinks abortion is murder. That is a question for religion, philosophy, or science; libertarianism itself has no answer to it. So, like everyone else, libertarians are split on this issue. Pro-life libertarians have an organization called Libertarians for Life; pro-choicers have a group called Libertarians for Choice. Notably, and contrary to the stereotype, many prominent libertarians are pro-life, including, for example, Ron Paul and Fox News Channel senior judicial analyst Andrew Napolitano. Regardless of their stance on abortion, however, many libertarians believe that, under our current political system, this issue would be better decided by the states than by the federal government (as it has been under *Roe v. Wade*). And many pro-life libertarians place persuasion above political action as their preferred means of advancing their cause.

We should add that Rothbard argued that libertarianism is pro-choice, even if one believes a fetus is a human life, because a would-be mother is not obligated to let another person live inside her body.[44] Many libertarians, including this author, find that argument problematic, however, because the fetus, if human, is not an invader but (except in cases of rape) someone whom the woman has implicitly invited into her body and caused to be dependent on her.

"Cultural Libertarianism"

Some libertarians argue that libertarianism is not just about property rights and the non-aggression principle, but requires promotion of certain liberal social values.

For example, *Reason* magazine editor Nick Gillespie has suggested that liberty has actually *increased* in important ways in recent years, despite the explosive growth of government and regulation, because certain behaviors have become more socially accepted. For example, Gillespie has observed, you are now "free" to get a hotel room with a member of the opposite sex who is not your spouse—the person at the front desk won't say no and probably won't even give you a dirty look.[45] Libertarian philosopher Roderick Long, writer Charles Johnson, and *Reason* contributing editor Kerry Howley all argue that traditional "gender roles" are oppressive in their own way, and that libertarians should oppose these so that women can have more "freedom" to pursue non-traditional lifestyles.[46]

These thinkers' liberal social views may or may not have merit, but they are not part of libertarianism per se. Again, libertarianism itself is compatible with both liberal and conservative social values. To suggest otherwise is an ideological mistake and probably also a strategic mistake. It redefines libertarianism to mean something that it has never meant to most modern libertarians, and it narrows the audience for libertarianism to only those people who share this liberal worldview. For many people, the beauty of libertarianism is that it lets everyone pursue their values, as long as they do not feel a need to force their views on the rest of the world.

Of course, libertarians are not *only* libertarians. Each person has other values as well. If some libertarians have liberal social values and want to promote those, there is no reason why they cannot or should not do so—just as a libertarian Christian, for example, might try to influence others to adopt both his political philosophy and his religion, or a libertarian Objectivist might urge others to adopt Ayn Rand's philosophy as a whole. It is a mistake, however, for any of these people to insist that libertarianism itself demands their broader philosophy of life.

Similarly, it may be the case that societies with certain social values are more likely to be receptive to libertarian ideas. As we saw above, some people believe that conservative values are more likely to give rise to a free and prosperous society; others, however, believe that liberal values are more conducive to a free society. This debate will continue among libertarians, but all involved should take care to note that this question is separate from the question of *what libertarianism is*.

Common (and Uncommon) Ground

Libertarians do share some common ground with present-day liberals—at least, with consistent, committed liberals. Both are opposed to war. Both are opposed to government handouts to business. Both are open to questioning the Federal Reserve. Both are open to loosening America's drug laws.

Some libertarians, such as the Cato Institute's Brink Lindsey and Will Wilkinson, see enough common ground with liberals to propose a "liberaltarian" (their term) coalition between the two groups.[47] Part of this rests on the assumption, which many libertarians do not share, that libertarians and liberals are on the same page with respect to social issues such as same-sex marriage and abortion. It also assumes that many libertarians and liberals would be willing to make compromises that neither side is likely to make. For example, many libertarians will not get behind the "tax reform" that Lindsey proposes (which does not seem to entail tax *cuts*), and most liberals will not be willing to budge on entitlements or embrace the free market. (Also, Lindsey's personal brand of "pragmatic libertarianism" involves deviations to the *right* on many issues, including war, which presumably would further turn off liberals.)[48] On the other hand, sticking to libertarian principle might at least earn some respect and credibility. Still, to the extent that Lindsey, Wilkinson, and others propose dialogue with liberals to introduce them to libertarian ideas and improve mutual understanding, it makes sense.[49] But to the extent that this strategy would attempt to influence the Democrat Party by becoming part of its coalition of voters (an idea Wilkinson, at least, rejects)—well, the lessons learned from the experience with the Republicans should be enough to discourage such an effort, especially given the Democrats' behavior now that they are in power.

An appealing aspect of the Ron Paul movement was that it attracted self-styled conservatives and liberals who place a higher priority on the issues where they support freedom than they do on other issues where they may be less libertarian. And once in the fold, many of those people have come around on other issues. Although it may not bring electoral success anytime soon, an approach that makes libertarians *out of* conservatives and liberals seems to hold more promise for advancing liberty than an approach that tries to force libertarians into a conservative or liberal mold.

NOTES

1. Llewellyn H. Rockwell, Jr., "The Calamity of Bush's Conservatism," *LewRockwell .com*, September 3, 2008, http://www.lewrockwell.com/rockwell/calamity-of-bush-conservatism .html.

2. See "The Socialism of Conservatism," in Hans-Hermann Hoppe, *A Theory of Socialism and Capitalism* (Boston: Kluwer Academic Publishers, 1989), http://mises.org/ books/Socialismcapitalism.pdf.

3. Ludwig von Mises to John Belding Wirt, letter dated October 23, 1954, quoted in Jörg Guido Hülsmann, *Mises: The Last Knight of Liberalism* (Auburn, AL: Ludwig von Mises Institute, 2007), 992, http://mises.org/books/lastknight.pdf.

4. See generally, Mark C. Henrie, "Traditionalism," in Bruce Frohnen et al., eds., *American Conservatism: An Encyclopedia* (Wilmington, DE: ISI Books, 2006), 870–75.

5. See E.C. Pasour, Jr., "Fusionism," in *American Conservatism: An Encyclopedia*, 338–41.

6. Hans-Hermann Hoppe, *Democracy: The God That Failed* (New Brunswick, NJ: Transaction Publishers, 2001), 195–96.

7. Quoted in Brian Patrick Mitchell, *Eight Ways to Run the Country* (Westport, CT: Praeger, 2007), 77.

8. See Paul Gottfried, "Paleoconservatism," in *American Conservatism: An Encyclopedia*, 651–52.

9. See Daniel McCarthy, "The Authoritarian Movement," *LewRockwell.com*, June 30, 2006, http://www.lewrockwell.com/dmccarthy/dmccarthy60.html.

10. Stephen W. Carson, "Christians in Politics: The Return of the 'Religious Right,'" *LewRockwell.com*, October 30, 2003, http://www.lewrockwell.com/carson/ carson17.html.

11. Quoted in Sheldon Richman, "New Deal Nemesis: The 'Old Right' Jeffersonians," in Robert Higgs and Carl P. Close, eds., *Opposing the Crusader State: Alternatives to Global Interventionism* (Oakland, CA: Independent Institute, 2007), 67.

12. H. L. Mencken, *Notes on Democracy* (New York: Alfred A. Knopf, 1926), 117.

13. Old Right journalist John T. Flynn was among the first to note that Franklin Delano Roosevelt anticipated the Pearl Harbor attack and allowed it to occur, which

other scholars have since documented in more detail. See Justin Raimondo, "The Secret of Pearl Harbor," *Antiwar.com*, May 25, 2001, http://www.antiwar.com/justin/j052501.html.

14. Albert Jay Nock, "The Amazing Liberal Mind," *American Mercury* 44, no. 176 (August 1938): 467–72, quoted in Murray N. Rothbard, *The Betrayal of the American Right* (Auburn, AL: Ludwig von Mises Institute, 2007), 37.

15. Rothbard, *Betrayal of the American Right*, 165.

16. Gary Wills, "Daredevil," *The Atlantic* (July/August 2009): 102–110.

17. Rothbard, *Betrayal of the American Right*, 159.

18. Quoted in Brad DeLong, "From National Review's Archives," *Grasping Reality with Both Hands*, October 2, 2005, http://delong.typepod.com/sdj/3005/10/from_national_r.html.

19. Ronald Hamowy, "National Review: Criticism and Reply," *New Individualist Review* 1, no. 3 (November 1961): 6–7, quoted in Rothbard, *Betrayal of the American Right*, 177.

20. Pasour, "Fusionism," 340.

21. Corey Robin, "Grand Designs," *Washington Post*, May 2, 2004, http://www.washingtonpost.com/ac2/wp-dyn/A58484-2004May1?language=printer.

22. Peter Nicholas, "Obama to Seek Support for Nearly $1-Trillion Recover Plan," *Los Angeles Times*, January 9, 2009, http://www.latimes.com/news/nationworld/nation/la-na-obama-economy9-2009jan09,0,3481662.story.

23. Anthony Gregory, "Government Growth, the Party of Lincoln, and George W. Bush," *LewRockwell.com*, October 29, 2004, http://www.lewrockwell.com/gregory/gregory40.html.

24. Doug Bandow, "Draft Registration: It's Time to Repeal Carter's Final Legacy," Cato Policy Analysis No. 86, May 7, 1987, http://www.cato.org/pub_display.php?pub_id=952.

25. Sheldon Richman, "Ronald Reagan: Protectionist," *The Free Market* (May 1988), http://mises.org/freemarket_detail.aspx?control=489.

26. Doug Casey, "The Life and Death of Reagan: A Sadly Educational Experience," *LewRockwell.com*, July 9, 2004, http://www.lewrockwell.com/orig2/casey7.html.

27. Murray N. Rothbard, "The Reagan Phenomenon," *LewRockwell.com*, http://www.lewrockwell.com/rothbard/rothbard49.html; see also Ron Paul, *End the Fed* (New York: Grand Central Publishing, 2009), 72–77.

28. See Murray N. Rothbard, "Ronald Reagan: An Autopsy," *Liberty* (March 1989): 13–23, http://www.lewrockwell.com/rothbard/rothbard60.html; Sheldon Richman, "The Sad Legacy of Ronald Reagan," *The Free Market* (October 1988), http://mises.org/freemarket_detail.aspx?control=488.

29. William A. Niskanen and Stephen Moore, "Supply Tax Cuts and the Truth About the Reagan Economic Record," Cato Policy Analysis No. 261, October 22, 1996, http://www.cato.org/pub_display.php?pub_id=1120&full=1.

30. Rothbard, "Ronald Reagan: An Autopsy."

31. Ibid.

32. Ibid.

33. See generally David Gordon, "The Kochtopus vs. Murray N. Rothbard," *LewRockwell.com*, April 22, 2008, http://www.lewrockwell.com/gordon/gordon37.html; David Gordon, "The Kochtopus vs. Murray N. Rothbard Part II," *LewRockwell.com*, May 12, 2008, http://www.lewrockwell.com/gordon/gordon39.html.

34. See, e.g., Edward H. Crane, "The GOP Should Dump the Neocons," *Los Angeles Times*, November 4, 2009, http://articles.latimes.com/2009/nov/04/opinion/oe-crane4; "Republican Presidential Candidates Debate," *Cato Dispatch*, May 4, 2007, http://www.cato.org/view_ddispatch.php?viewdate=20070504.

35. Jacob Weisberg, "The End of Libertarianism," *Slate*, Oct. 18, 2008, http://www.slate.com/id/2202489/.

36. Veronique de Rugy, "Bush's Regulatory Kiss-Off," *Reason* (January 2009), http://www.reason.com/news/show/130328.html.

37. Ibid.

38. See Jennifer Haman, "Ron Paul v. SOX," *LewRockwell.com*, July 26, 2007, http://www.lewrockwell.com/orig8/haman2.html.

39. For more refutation of Weisberg, see Anthony Gregory, "Blaming Liberty for the State's Depredations," *LewRockwell.com*, Oct. 20, 2008, http://www.lewrockwell.com/gregory/gregory165.html; D.W. MacKenzie, "Has Libertarianism Ended?" *Mises.org*, Oct. 29, 2008, http://mises.org/story/3162.

40. James Bovard, "The Biggest Medicare Fraud Ever," *LewRockwell.com*, September 1, 2005, http://www.lewrockwell.com/bovard/bovard11.html.

41. Michael D. Tanner, "A Repudiation, But of What?" *Star-Telegram*, November 10, 2008, http://www.cato.org/pub_display.php?pub_id=9781.

42. Chris Edwards, "Presidential Spending," *Cato-at-Liberty*, Sept. 27, 2007, http://www.cato-at-liberty.org/2007/09/27/presidential-spending/.

43. See McCarthy, "The Authoritarian Movement."

44. Murray N. Rothbard, *The Ethics of Liberty* (New York: New York University Press, 1998 [1982]), 98.

45. Daniel McCarthy, "Low-tax Liberalism Redux," *Lewrockwell.com*, March 17, 2005. http:// www.lewrockwell.com/dmccarthy/dmccarthy57.html.

46. Roderick Long and Charles Johnson, "Libertarian Feminism: Can This Marriage Be Saved?" May 1, 2005, http://charleswjohnson.name/essays/libertarian-feminism; Kerry Howley, "We're All Cultural Libertarians," *Reason* (November 2009), available at http://reason.com/archives/2009/10/20/are-property-rights-enough.

47. See, e.g., Brink Lindsey, "Liberaltarians," *The New Republic Online*, Dec. 4, 2006, http://www.cato.org/pub_display.php?pub_id=6800; Will Wilkinson, "Is Rawlsekianism the Future?" *Cato-at-Liberty*, December 4, 2006, http://www.cato-at-liberty.org/2006/12/04/is-rawlsekianism-the-future/.

48. Brink Lindsey, "Am I a Libertarian?" *Liberty* (March 2003), http://libertyunbound.com/archive/2003_03/lindsey-apostasy.html.

49. Lew Rockwell had a remarkable conversation with liberal writer and activist Naomi Wolf on this and other topics, available at http://www.lewrockwell.com/podcast/?p=episode&name=2008-10-30_058_americas_slow_motion_fascist_coup/. One of the

most notable areas of agreement was on the harm caused by the Federal Reserve, an issue in which Lindsey appears to have shown little interest.

FURTHER READING

Carey, George W., ed. *Freedom and Virtue: The Conservative/Libertarian Debate.* Wilmington, DE: Intercollegiate Studies Institute, 1998. This collection of essays looks at the similarities and differences between traditionalist conservatives and libertarians.

Hoppe, Hans-Hermann. *Democracy—The God That Failed: The Economics and Politics of Monarchy, Democracy, and Natural Order.* New Brunswick, NJ: Transaction Publishers, 2000. See especially Chapter 10, "On Conservatism and Libertarianism."

Rockwell, Llewellyn H., Jr. *The Left, the Right, and the State.* Auburn, AL: Ludwig von Mises Institute, 2008. This collection of essays shows how libertarianism stands in opposition to the statism of both the left and the right. This book is available for free online at http://mises.org/books/leftright.pdf.

Rothbard, Murray N. *The Betrayal of the American Right.* Auburn, AL: Ludwig von Mises Institute, 2007. Rothbard shows how the early twentieth century's liberals became labeled conservatives during the New Deal, and how the near-libertarianism of the "Old Right" was overwhelmed by the statist conservatism of *National Review.* This book is available for free online at http://mises.org/books/betrayal.pdf.

3

The Fight for the Economy

Is libertarianism at fault for the economic crisis that began in 2008? Of course not. Libertarians have not been running the show in Washington, and the people in charge have imposed economic policies that are anti-libertarian and anti-free market—both in general and with respect to monetary policy in particular. In fact, before the crisis, libertarians were nearly alone in condemning the main policies that led to it.

In this chapter, we will consider the accusations against libertarianism, why they are false, and what libertarians actually propose to get the country out of its current economic crisis and avoid future crises.

DID LIBERTARIANS CAUSE THE CRISIS?

In the last chapter, we mentioned Jacob Weisberg's article "The End of Libertarianism," in which he blamed libertarianism for the economic crisis. As libertarians speak out, Weisberg suggests they shut up, asking, "Haven't you people done enough harm already?"[1] Weisberg does not get specific regarding what libertarian policies we supposedly had that supposedly caused the crisis, though, and he is not exactly an unbiased source on the subject as the author of a book called *In Defense of Government*.

But Weisberg is not alone. For example, Judge Richard Posner also points the finger at libertarianism in his 2009 book, *A Failure of Capitalism: The Crisis of '08 and the Decline into Depression*. And Posner—unfortunately, from the libertarian's perspective—comes to the issue with a bit more credibility. He is an authority on law and economics and a highly respected jurist, and he has advocated some libertarian ideas in the past, such as the legalized selling of adoption rights (or, as some would have it, "baby selling").[2] Because Posner has perhaps the highest profile and credibility of any of libertarianism's critics, and because he goes into more detail than most, we will consider (and refute) his specific claims about libertarianism.

Posner writes that "the absence of appropriate . . . measures [to prevent a financial crisis] was not the result of too much government but of too little: not of intrusive, heavy-handed regulation of housing and finance, but of hostility to taxation and to government in general, and a general laissez-faire attitude."[3] Later he charges:

> The depression has hit economic libertarians in their solar plexus, because it is largely a consequence not of the government's overregulating the economy and by doing so fettering free enterprise, but rather of innate limitations of the free market—limitations rooted in individuals' incentives, irresponsible monetary policy adopted by conservative officials inspired by conservative economists who thought that easy money was no problem if it did not lead to serious inflation, and in excessive, ideologically motivated deregulation of banking and finance compounded by lax enforcement of the remaining regulations.[4]

> Finally, he says: "Libertarian economists failed to grasp the dangers of deregulating the financial markets and underestimated the risk and depth of the financial crisis. Their influence was a factor in the government's allowing a self-inflicted capitalist wound to infect the economy with its first depression in three quarters of a century."[5]

That is heaping a lot of responsibility on libertarians, many of whom will be surprised to learn that they are not members of a small but growing movement on the fringe of American politics but are in fact part of a group that controls the world's financial markets. So Posner must be applying an idiosyncratic definition of "libertarian" that differs from the definition held by most libertarians (and this book), or he must be confused as to what libertarianism calls for with respect to the financial system, as so many are when they assume that what the capitalism libertarians want is identical to the so-called capitalism that America presently has.

Let's dispose of the low-hanging fruit first. The Bush Administration did not demonstrate "a hostility . . . to government in general," as Posner says, or display a "laissez-faire attitude." Instead, as we noted in the last chapter, President Bush grew government spending more than any U.S. president since at least Jimmy Carter. And that was no accident—the attitude of the Bush Administration and its neoconservative intellectual leaders was anything but laissez-faire. In 2003, Bush supporter and *Weekly Standard* editor Fred Barnes approvingly and correctly called the Bush philosophy "big-government conservatism," and said that Bush was "using what would normally be seen as liberal means—activist government—for conservative ends." And, Barnes noted, the Administration was "willing to spend more and increase the size of government in the process."[6] Notably, Barnes wrote all of this long before Bush took his big-government agenda even further and spent hundreds of billions of dollars to bail out banks and others in response to the financial crisis. So it is hard to say where Posner got the idea that anti-government ideology pervaded the Bush Administration, if Posner looked at anything beyond Bush's occasional free-market campaign rhetoric.

Moving on, Posner identifies "irresponsible monetary policy" as a factor leading to the crisis. Fair enough. But was that monetary policy libertarian, as he implies? Not at all. Let us consider what libertarian monetary policy calls for, and then contrast it with what we have in the United States.

Free-Market Money

In the free market that libertarians advocate, government would not create money. To realize how that is possible, consider how money came into existence in the first place.[7] In primitive societies, people did not have money; instead, they bartered, trading one good for another. Obviously, the barter system is very limiting—you can only trade with someone if you can offer the precise good he or she is looking for. Such a society does not allow people to become very specialized in what they do for a living—you cannot be a full-time music teacher, for example, unless everyone you want to buy something from wants music lessons, and probably most people do not want music lessons. And there is no good way to make "change" (a two-minute music lesson?) when trading such things.

Money comes about when people move beyond this problem. Instead of trying to trade music lessons for everything he needs, our hypothetical teacher could trade lessons for some other thing that is more widely saleable, and then trade *that* for the things that he needs. For example, he might trade his lessons for gold. Gold tends to be widely saleable. It is relatively transportable, and a little bit is worth a lot, so one can carry it around easily. It is durable—people can pass it around without ruining it. It is divisible—one can make change if necessary by breaking the gold down into smaller pieces, and each piece has exactly the same composition as any other piece (it is homogeneous). And it is easy to verify its authenticity. Money does not have to be gold, of course, though historically it often has been, along with silver and other precious metals. Money can be whatever arises by custom as the generally accepted *medium of exchange* through people's voluntary exchanges. An example from modern times: in prison camps, cigarettes have become used as money, presumably because cigarettes were the good on hand that best satisfied the criteria we have just reviewed.[8]

It can be cumbersome to carry metal around; it is easier to carry slips of paper. What we think of as paper money came about when people decided to put their gold and silver money in banks, and received paper certificates back in exchange. These paper certificates were a *money substitute*; people could trade them just as if they were the actual gold and silver. And if someone wanted the gold or silver, he or she could always take the paper to the bank and redeem it.

Government got into the money business only after the private sector had invented it, working its way in slowly until it eventually completely controlled the monetary system. The first step generally was for government to take over the minting business—that is, gold and other metals would still be money as usual, but the government would be in charge of stamping out the coins, generally with the king's face on them. Once they took over the minting business, governments could then start debasing the money—they could shave a little gold or silver off the sides of the coins they issued, or they could mix in a little bit of a less-valuable metal. In this way, a government could use its monopoly over money to enrich itself at everyone else's expense.

When government takes over the paper money business (either directly or through specially privileged banks), debasing the currency becomes even easier. Probably not everyone will try to redeem all of their paper money certificates at the same time, so a government can print more paper certificates than it has in gold or silver to back them up. When governments or banks do this, everyone's money becomes worth less—there is more paper chasing the same amount of goods and services, and, other things being equal, prices go up as a matter of supply and demand. Historically, when economists referred to "inflation," they referred to an increase in the amount of money (or money substitutes) in the economy, such as this. Today, though, people usually use "inflation" to refer to a general increase in prices across the economy. In fact, however, such price inflation is often an *effect* of monetary inflation.

Libertarians view governmental monetary inflation as theft. It is a way that government can print money for itself (or for those whom it favors) to spend, just as a counterfeiter would print and spend fake money. With its new money, the government can outbid others for goods—which amounts to a transfer of wealth to the government from everyone else. The new money drives prices up across the economy; people's money loses value, and people's life savings can be effectively wiped out.

This principle becomes most obvious when government prints *far* too much money and creates a *hyperinflation*. When prices are constantly rising because of government money printing, planning for the future is impossible, as market prices can no longer aid people in making economic decisions, such as what to buy, what to produce, which jobs to take, what lines of production to invest in. The most famous example of hyperinflation comes from Weimar Germany, where people carried piles of their worthless money around in wheelbarrows, and the economic disaster helped pave the way for Hitler to take power.[9] Zimbabwe's recent history provides one of the worst examples ever. In November 2008, that country's annual inflation rate was 89.7 sextillion percent, which meant that prices doubled every 24.7 hours.[10] This plunged Zimbabwe even deeper into chaos than it had already descended. No one, except perhaps President Robert Mugabe and others in Zimbabwe's government, disputes that the Zimbabwe hyperinflation is the result of government printing money to fuel its own spending.

Money and Banking in the United States

The United States is not Zimbabwe (yet), but it has never had a true free market in money. In the eighteenth and nineteenth centuries, governments generally limited which banks could issue banknotes (that is, the paper substitutes for gold or silver), and those privileged banks were allowed to inflate the amount of paper beyond the metal available to a limited extent; that is, their reserve requirement (the portion of deposits they needed to keep on hand) was not 100 percent. Still, banks were necessarily somewhat limited in their ability to inflate because depositors *could* come back and redeem their paper money for gold or silver. "Bank runs" occurred when word got out that a given bank had especially low reserves—and a bank hit by one could be put out of business, as it would not be able to pay off its debts to depositors. So banks had some incentive to behave.

After more than a century of various banking regimes, money and banking became fully, permanently centralized in the United States with the 1913 passage of the Federal Reserve Act.[11] That Act created a central banking system consisting of (1) twelve nominally private (but federally chartered) regional Federal Reserve Banks; (2) a Board of Governors and Chairman appointed by the President of the United States; and (3) a Federal Open Market Committee, which today is composed of the heads of the regional banks plus the members of the Board of Governors. The Federal Reserve System (or "Fed") would thereafter be in charge of the money supply in the United States.

The Fed does not control the amount of money in circulation by simply printing more money or destroying old money in the ordinary sense—at least, not primarily. Instead, the Fed inflates the money supply by buying assets from banks. Traditionally, it has done this through "open-market operations," which entail buying government bonds from a bank that deals in them, such as Goldman Sachs. Since Fall 2008, the Fed has also purchased other types of assets from banks. All banks have checking accounts at their regional Fed bank. When the Fed purchases assets from a bank as we have described, the Fed credits that bank's checking account at the bank's regional Fed bank. When it makes this payment, the Fed essentially creates the money out of thin air—it does not print up the cash, it just electronically adds it to the money in banks' accounts.

When banks receive the Fed's new money, they have more money reserves, which allows them to lend out more to consumers. When the banks have more to lend out, the price of credit—that is, the rate of interest—tends to go down, as a simple matter of supply and demand. So when people talk about the Fed lowering interest rates, they are essentially referring to the Fed inflating the money supply, or, in effect, printing money.[12] Note also that the Fed facilitates government spending through this process. When the federal government borrows money, it does this by selling bonds, which are in turn bought by the Fed with newly created money as we have just described. This is what people mean when they say that government will have to "print the money" to pay for its spending unless it raises taxes.

When the Fed first came into existence, one could still redeem its banknotes for gold or silver, depending on the note. This did not stop the Fed from inflating the money supply, but at least it put the brakes on a little bit. In 1933, however, Franklin Roosevelt criminalized the monetary use of gold through a series of actions authorized by the Emergency Banking Act of 1933.[13] Not only were Americans not allowed to redeem their dollar bills for gold anymore, they also were forced to give up any gold coins or bullion they were holding; the federal government confiscated all of it. After 1933, only certain foreign central banks were allowed to redeem U.S. dollars for gold. The government later ended the ability to redeem notes for silver coins in 1964, and ended the right to redeem notes for silver bullion in 1968. Finally, in 1971, Richard Nixon took the United States off the gold standard entirely and the dollar lost its last remaining link to precious metals.

As a result, today the dollar is simply a fiat currency—paper money backed only by the "full faith and credit" of the U.S. government. Legal tender laws force people to accept the dollar, as the bills say right on them, for "all debts public and private."

From this brief summary, we can see that money provision in the United States today has nothing to do with libertarianism or laissez-faire. Money is not created, like most other goods, from the voluntary actions of countless individuals interacting on the market, but by an organization created and given monopoly powers by the federal government, including a Chairman and Board of Governors appointed by the President of the United States.

Booms and Busts

Government monopoly over money is bad, but for libertarians who subscribe to the Austrian School of economics, as many or most do, it gets even worse. Under the Austrian theory of the business cycle—for which Friedrich Hayek won the 1974 Nobel Prize in economics—the central bank's interference with interest rates through money creation sets the business cycle into motion. This creates booms, like the dot-com bubble or the housing bubble, and busts, like the dot-com collapse and the recession (or depression) that began in 2008. This is not an economics textbook, and we cannot do the theory full justice in this space—but we will cover it concisely to continue to show how libertarians' view of the Fed is anything but friendly, and the Fed is anything but free market.

To illustrate the theory, we will return to the example of a hypothetical pure free market. On the free market—where money and banks would be fully private—banks could only lend out money that people actually saved; that is, they could not print extra notes or make extra electronic deposits in people's checking accounts to lend out an amount of money that exceeds the bank's cash (gold or silver) reserves because to do so would be inflationary and fraudulent.[14] The more money people saved, the more money banks would have available to lend out, and the lower the price of borrowing (the interest rate) would be. The less money people saved, the less banks would have available to lend out, and the higher the interest rate would be. The rate of interest would be the result of nothing but voluntary actions by savers and borrowers—or, to put it in economists' terms, it would be the result of the supply of and demand for loanable funds. The amount of investment that occurred in the economy would be determined by the amount of people's savings.

In this hypothetical free market, a low rate of interest (and the corresponding high rate of saving) would prompt businesses to take out loans to fund new projects because it would be more affordable for them to do so. These projects would especially include long-term projects to produce goods higher in the "structure of production" than consumer goods—for example, minerals that go into other products, or machines that make other machines that make other machines that make consumer products. Businesses could be confident that consumers would later have money to spend on the products that ultimately result from this long-term investment because it was consumer saving that allowed the businesses to borrow the money in the first place.

As we have noted above, the interest rate under our current real-world banking system is *not* driven only by what people save; it is manipulated by the Fed. So when the Fed artificially lowers interest rates by essentially printing money, this prompts businesses to borrow and begin long-term projects—even though there are no consumer savings to match. In fact, because of the low interest rates, consumers have saved less than they otherwise would have. Businesses then go forward with these projects just as they would in the hypothetical free market. But many of these projects will prove to be *malinvestments*—when they are complete, businesses will discover that consumers do not have the money to buy the final products, as the low interest rate had falsely signaled they would, because consumers had not actually been saving money. As a result, there will be a bust, as businesses across the country have created a structure of production that does not match what consumers actually demand and can afford. Many long-term projects will be only partly completed, and will have to be scrapped, which will create temporary unemployment. The chain reaction in the economy can be severely disruptive until the errors of the boom are corrected.

In his book on the 2008 crisis, Thomas E. Woods, Jr., borrows an example from Ludwig von Mises to compare the errors of the boom phase (based on incorrect signals from interest rates) to the construction of a house based on inaccurate plans:

> Imagine a home builder who believes he has 20 percent more bricks than he actually has. He will build a different kind of house than he would if he had an accurate count of his brick supply. (Assume he can't buy any more.) The dimensions will be different. The style may even be different. And the longer he goes without realizing his error, the worse the eventual reckoning will be. If he finds out his error only at the very end, he'll have to tear down the whole (incomplete) house, and all those resources and labor time will have been squandered. Society will be that much poorer.[15]

A Failure of Capitalism?

So, back to Richard Posner, who, along with many others, blames libertarianism and "limitations of the free market" for the recent bust. To recap, he alleged that those "limitations" are rooted in "individuals' incentives, irresponsible monetary policy adopted by conservative officials inspired by conservative economists who thought that easy money was no problem if it did not lead to serious inflation, and in excessive, ideologically motivated deregulation of banking and finance compounded by lax enforcement of the remaining regulations."[16]

There is some truth in what Posner says here: he is just wrong to implicate libertarianism in any of it.

It is true that there was "irresponsible monetary policy." From the start of 2002 to the start of 2006, the Fed injected $200 billion into the banking system through open-market operations—which, because banks only have a 10 percent reserve requirement, means that banks could lend out ten times as much as that, or $2 trillion, all of it new money.[17] This inflation of the money supply made interest rates exceptionally low. The low interest rates caused people and businesses to take out loans, which they used to invest in houses, stocks, and other things. Lower interest rates meant lower monthly mortgage payments, which drew more people in to take out mortgages in particular. As banks extended credit to more and more people, the people receiving it were less and less creditworthy. More people getting into the market drove prices up; people began buying houses not to live in them, but just to "flip" them for a profit.

This increase in prices for houses and stocks did not reflect an increase in real underlying value—it was just a speculative bubble. For example, housing prices went up, but the rents those houses could earn did not because there were not that many people actually wanting to live in them. Stock prices went up, but the dividends the stocks could pay did not. That is, the stocks went up not because the companies were performing exceptionally well, but because people could afford to speculate in them because of the cheap money the Fed was making available, and the speculation itself drove prices up—for a while. Consumers went deep into debt, too, as low interest rates on home equity loans enabled them to use their houses as high-limit credit cards, and they spent the money on consumer goods. This created a boom in expensive consumer goods, such as HUMMER SUVs, luxury cars, and designer clothes (which, incidentally, demonstrates that the consumerist culture that liberals so often decry is not entirely the product of the free market).

As every American knows—and as the Austrian business-cycle theory would predict—the bubble eventually burst. Investors began to realize that the housing boom was just a bubble, and that the securities derived from very risky mortgages were not as valuable as they believed. They began to sell, and then the entire structure of high prices in the housing sector collapsed. As the banks ended their loose lending practices, people did not have the money to buy all the houses that were being built, and people with adjustable-rate mortgages or interest-only mortgages could not afford to keep them. Many of those people had never intended to live in the houses they had bought long-term, if at all, but instead planned to flip them, so they had not worried about being able to afford them past the first few years of (what they expected to be) low payments. But when the market collapsed, there was no more flipping to be done. So these people were stuck with houses mortgaged for much more than their value—and many people, of course, just walked away. As of this writing, housing prices are still falling. The speculative boom made it appear that people valued houses, and would have money to pay for the houses they were buying. But countless houses, including many new or nearly new houses, sit empty. It should be obvious that the economy wasted resources that it could have spent elsewhere by building these houses—and that with a free market in money, they never would have been built.[18]

So, sure, the Fed is culpable, just as Posner says. But what does the Fed have to do with libertarianism or the free market? As we have seen, it is a fundamentally governmental institution that centrally plans the production of money, which libertarians believe the market alone should supply. A free market in money and banking would mean no Fed, no bubble, and no current crisis.

Posner also blames "individuals' incentives" for the crisis. What he means here is that it arguably made sense for individuals to take out low-interest loans in the hopes of making money flipping houses or investing in other risky things because the potential profit was large, but the potential loss, particularly on a mortgage that one could walk away from with relative impunity, was low. The same was arguably true for individual banks: they knew they were making ever-riskier loans, urged by the Fed and other federal policies, but it made sense for them to do so to compete against the other banks that were doing it and because the likelihood of the bank going bankrupt still appeared to be low. The same applies to Wall Street firms that invested in risky financial instruments.

It is true that individuals all took these actions in pursuit of their own self-interest, and that this precipitated a crisis. But what prompted and allowed individuals to do all of this? Only the Fed's loose monetary policy, which, we have seen, is essentially action by the government, not by the market. As economic commentator Peter Schiff has noted: "President Bush said, in one of his speeches, 'Wall Street got drunk.' And he was right, they were drunk. So was Main Street. The whole country was drunk. But what he doesn't point out is: where did they get the alcohol?"[19] They got it from the Fed.

Posner also points to "deregulation" as a culprit and specifically to regulations that allowed various financial institutions to compete with ordinary banks, which encouraged banks to make riskier loans. Posner observes that "before deregulation, banks would get into serious trouble with their regulators if they made . . . enough risky loans to create a nontrivial risk of bankruptcy."[20] But as we have seen, the reason why banks can be undisciplined in the first place in lending out depositors' money is because the Fed provides them with reserves that allow them to extend loans to ever-riskier borrowers. Federal regulators could control lending standards, but nothing would constrain the banks as much as a genuine free market.

Banks were given even more incentive to engage in risky behavior by the Federal Deposit Insurance Corporation, which insures depositors' money up to $100,000 (though at the time of this writing, that amount has been bumped up to $250,000, supposedly temporarily). Where the federal government promises a bailout, as it does with deposit insurance, it creates a "moral hazard," as economists call it, that banks will take risks with depositors' money. Again: *an anti-libertarian government policy.*

Then there are Fannie Mae and Freddie Mac. Posner calls these entities "private," but of course they are not private in the usual sense. They are "Government-Sponsored Enterprises" (GSEs) with a variety of special privileges from the government—for example, a $2.25 billion line of credit with the U.S. Treasury. Fannie and Freddie are in the business of buying mortgages on the secondary market—that is, they pay banks to take mortgages off their hands. Fannie and Freddie, under pressure from the Clinton Administration, pushed banks to make ever-riskier loans by lowering the standards for the loans that they would buy. Fannie and Freddie could take on these risky loans because of their special line of government credit and because everyone knew that in the worst-case scenario the federal government would bail them out. Another moral hazard created by the government, not the free market.[21] As Posner notes,[22] the federal government also helped drive housing prices up through "ownership society" policies designed to encourage people to buy houses.[23] These included special tax breaks for people making mortgage payments. Libertarians favor tax breaks, of course, but targeting tax breaks to achieve specific policy goals, instead of simply lowering taxes across the board, can distort the market. The Community Reinvestment Act also helped pump up the bubble by forcing banks to give mortgages to people who otherwise would not have qualified. Again, *not* libertarian.

So when Posner and others claim that libertarianism, laissez-faire, or deregulation caused the economic crisis, they overlook that the Federal Reserve pulls the strings in the world of money and banking, and that government creates moral hazards that prompt banks and individuals to take risks they wouldn't otherwise take. The crisis may be a failure of "American capitalism," but it is not a failure of the laissez-faire capitalism that libertarians advocate because that has not existed. Of course, Posner and other critics could (and no doubt would) claim that we would have *other* economic problems if we did not have a Federal Reserve and instead had free-market money. (There are rebuttals to those arguments, too, for which we do not have space here.)[24] But regardless of what they think of libertarian economics, they cannot blame libertarianism for *this* crisis.

How could such confusion have arisen? Primarily because many people assume that laissez-faire capitalism is the system that we have now, when in fact it is not. Why do people make that assumption? Because politicians, especially Republicans, tend to say that we do, regardless of their actual philosophy or practices when they are in power. Also, people remember the Cold War, in which we were supposedly the capitalists (and *relative to the Soviet Union*, we were). With respect to the Federal Reserve's role in capitalism, some libertarians are at fault because they have deliberately consistently failed to criticize central banking or to argue for free-market money. As mentioned in the previous chapter, this was a strategy the Cato Institute took beginning in the early 1980s. Even now, some of its scholars publish articles arguing that the meltdown was not former Fed chairman Alan Greenspan's fault and declare that Ben Bernanke has performed well, and they often argue for policies they believe the Fed should adopt to keep prices stable, rather than just argue for monetary freedom and an *end* to the Fed.[25]

(Probably these are the putative libertarians to whom Judge Posner has had the most exposure, but he still should have done his homework, so that is no excuse.) Alan Greenspan is at fault for the capitalism confusion, too—in the 1950s, he was a close associate of Ayn Rand (and took far different positions on money and banking), so he remains falsely associated with hardcore laissez-faire ideology in many people's minds.

As we will see below, while many Washington-based libertarians ignored this issue, others kept the monetary freedom idea alive, and today it is one of the movement's hottest issues.

LIBERTARIANS PREDICTED THE MELTDOWN

Libertarians not only did not cause the crisis, they also warned against it when everyone else assumed the housing boom was nothing to worry about and did not want to hear any naysaying about the Fed or its policies. Now the same libertarians who predicted the crisis suggest a way out—and Washington still mostly ignores them.

Austro-libertarian economists (that is, libertarians who subscribe to the Austrian School of economics) writing for the Ludwig von Mises Institute began warning of the housing bubble soon after the Federal Reserve began to lower interest rates in the early 2000s. Robert Blumen may have been the first when, in 2002, he warned that Fannie Mae's policies were creating a "nightmare of resource misallocation and massive systemic risk."[26] In March 2003, Frank Shostak observed that housing prices were going up as a result of lower interest rates since the beginning of the decade, and that this bubble was likely to burst.[27] In August 2003, Christopher Mayer noted the same phenomenon.[28] In June 2004, Mises Institute Senior Fellow Mark Thornton said that the rise in housing prices was "too good to be true." He wrote: "The Federal Reserve and the Mac-Mae family (Freddie, Fannie, Sallie, etc.) have conspired to create a housing bubble in the US and as the old saying goes, 'what goes up must come down.'" He concluded: "Given the government's encouragement of lax lending practices, home prices could crash, bankruptcies would increase, and financial companies, including the government-sponsored mortgage companies, might require a taxpayer bailout."[29] In November 2004, economist Stefan Karlsson noted that "the sector that poses the greatest threat to the economy is the household sector, which is spending and borrowing at an unsustainable level."[30]

Today, in hindsight, it may seem obvious to everyone that there was a housing bubble and that it was bound to burst. But at the time most people did not see it, or did not want to. Said Alan Greenspan, then-Chairman of the Fed in 2004 ("with rather garbled grammar"): "The notion of a bubble bursting and the whole price level [for housing] coming down seems to me, as far as a nationwide phenomenon . . . is really quite unlikely."[31] In 2005, pro-Fed "supply-side" economist Alan Reynolds scoffed: "'Housing bubble' worry-warts have long been hopelessly confused. It would have been financially fool-hardy to listen to them in 2002 and it still is."[32] These optimists were far from alone—essentially all of government and Wall Street took the same view, which is how the bubble continued to grow and why many investors had no reservations about becoming involved in mortgage-backed securities and related financial products.

The libertarian-leaning Austrian who perhaps received the most ridicule—and who has since received the most credit—for predicting the crash may be Peter Schiff, an economic commentator who heads his own brokerage firm, Euro Pacific Capital, specializing in foreign stocks. A YouTube video called "Peter Schiff Was Right," which has been viewed over 1.5 million times, shows Schiff in a series of TV news appearances from 2006 and 2007, in which other pundits ridicule and literally laugh at him for suggesting that the housing market would collapse.[33] (Other compilations of Schiff's predictions go back as far as 2002.)[34] On the first clip in the video, from an August 2006 CNBC appearance, Schiff explains that "the problem with the U.S. economy is that we have too much consumption and borrowing and not enough production and saving, and what's going to happen is the consumer is going to stop consuming and start rebuilding his savings, especially when he sees his home equity evaporate." Supply-side economist Art Laffer, debating Schiff, replies by saying, "I don't believe any of it. . . . The United States economy has never been in better shape. . . . Monetary policy is spectacular." Laffer argues that the country's wealth has increased, but Schiff points out that "all that's increased are the paper values of stocks and real estate. But that's not real wealth. When you see the stock market come down and the real estate bubble burst, all that phony wealth is going to evaporate, and all that's going to be left is the debt that we accumulated." The clips that follow show similar scenes: Schiff claims that houses and/or stocks are greatly overvalued, and co-panelists call his ideas ridiculous. In another video, Schiff again suggests that the United States has not increased its productive capacity, but rather simply created the appearance of wealth with a speculative boom, to which another pundit replies, "Excuse me—I'm from Detroit. Have you been in an auto plant lately?"[35] Of course, the cheap credit available to consumers through home equity loans and other means fueled purchases of cars—many of which were later repossessed or abandoned when their owners could no longer make the payments. And the fate of the Detroit automakers less than three years after this exchange is now well known.

Ron Paul also sounded the alarm, long before he began his 2008 presidential campaign. In 2003, on the floor of the House of Representatives, he predicted the harm Fannie and Freddie's loosening of lending standards would cause:

> Ironically, by transferring the risk of a widespread mortgage default, the government increases the likelihood of a painful crash in the housing market. This is because special privileges to Fannie and Freddie have distorted the housing market by allowing them to attract capital they could not attract under pure market conditions. . . .
>
> Like all artificially created bubbles, the boom in housing prices cannot last forever. When housing prices fall, homeowners will experience difficulty as their equity is wiped out. Furthermore, the holders of the mortgage debt will also have a loss. These losses will be greater than they would have otherwise been had government policy not actively encouraged over-investment in housing. . . .
>
> Congress should act to remove taxpayer support from the housing GSEs before the bubble bursts and taxpayers are once again forced to bail out investors who were misled by foolish government interference in the market[36]

During his tenure in Congress, Paul has taken full advantage of opportunities to grill Alan Greenspan and his successor Ben Bernanke at hearings of the House Financial Services Committee. Each time, Paul asks the Chairman questions about the harmful effects of government-controlled fiat money, including inflation and economic bubbles, and each time he receives little in the way of substantive answers; the Fed chairmen just express confidence in their own abilities to centrally plan the economy.[37]

When he launched his campaign for the 2008 Republican presidential nomination, Paul chose to make the Federal Reserve a central issue (as he had in his 1988 run), together with U.S. foreign policy. At first, even some libertarians who shared his views were skeptical of this approach because monetary issues might go over the heads of ordinary Americans. Instead, though, monetary policy turned out to be a major rallying point for Paul's supporters as the economy got worse and even many mainstream pundits began to acknowledge the Fed's role in the crisis. When Paul made an appearance at the University of Michigan, even he was surprised to find students chanting "End the Fed!" as they held Federal Reserve Notes (dollar bills) in the air and burned them. Historian and author Thomas Woods was surprised when he gave a speech at Ron Paul's Rally for the Republic and found that he had to pause for cheers to subside after he mentioned the Austrian theory of the business cycle, a phenomenon heretofore known only to some economics geeks and studious libertarians. Monetary policy may remain a mystery to most Americans, but Paul's campaign made many more people aware of how the Fed works—and made them angry about it.

Paul began talking about the 2008 economic crisis while his Republican primary opponents continued to deny that it was even happening. In a January 2008 debate, Paul said, "I believe we're in a recession. I think it's going to get a lot worse if we continue to do the things we've done in the past. You have to understand that over-stimulation in an economy by artificially low interest rates by the Federal Reserve is the source of the recession."[38] His opponents disagreed; none would admit that the United States was in a recession. Former Senator Fred Thompson said he saw "no reason to believe we're headed for an economic downturn," and Senator John McCain said, "I don't believe we're headed into a recession. I believe the fundamentals of this economy are strong, and I believe they will remain strong," a view he would maintain well into the election season, to his political detriment.[39] In December 2008, the National Bureau of Economic Research would release figures that showed that the United States was indeed in a recession—and had been since December 2007, one month before that debate where the other Republicans denied the recession's existence or possibility.[40]

LIBERTARIANS RESPOND TO THE CRISIS

Against the Fed

Paul and other libertarians have taken advantage of the anti-Fed momentum built during the campaign and the economic crisis. In February 2009, Regnery published Woods's book *Meltdown: A Free-Market Look at Why the Stock Market Collapsed, the Economy Tanked, and Government Bailouts Will*

Make Things Worse. Written for a popular audience, it presents the Austro-libertarian view of the causes and cures of the economic crisis in detail. The book entered the *New York Times* best-seller list immediately upon publication—surely the first libertarian book on monetary policy to appear there—and remained on the list for eleven weeks. In September 2009, Paul published his own book on monetary policy, with the blunt title of *End the Fed*, which entered the *New York Times* non-fiction best-seller list at number 6 upon its release.

Paul advanced the cause in Congress, too, with far more success among his colleagues than in the past. In February 2009, he introduced House Bill 1207, "The Federal Reserve Transparency Act," which would allow the first meaningful audit of the Federal Reserve, and a majority of his fellow Congressman soon signed on as co-sponsors of the legislation. Such an audit would reveal who receives the Fed's money, and how much, and, Paul hopes, would make people recognize that the Fed should not be attempting to centrally plan the economy at all. The long-term goal, of course, remains to allow people to use free-market money of their choosing, to end the Federal Reserve, and to take away the government's ability to inflate, spend without limit, and create artificial booms and busts.

Against Bailouts and "Stimulus"

Libertarians also spoke out against the billions of dollars spent to keep struggling banks, automakers, and others afloat. A key component of the Austrian business cycle theory is that a recession is *necessary* for the economy to correct the errors that were committed during the boom. That is, the malinvestments that have built up during the boom must be liquidated. For example, housing prices must fall until the houses can be sold. Businesses that have invested in the wrong types of products must be allowed to fail, so that others can buy up their assets and use them more efficiently. Bailouts to prop up prices or firms only delay the inevitable, and encourage the economy to go further in the wrong direction. The longer the recession is delayed (or prolonged) through government bailouts, the more errors will pile up, and the worse the inevitable correction will be. Economist Dominick Armentano explains:

> Economic booms "malinvest" labor and capital and recessions are necessary to "Clean out" these malinvestments. Declining prices allow consumers to more easily purchase products (homes, autos) in excess supply; inventories are reduced and supply and demand are brought into balance. And declining profits weed out business organizations and their

managers that have invested poorly during the boom; bankruptcy allows resources to flow to more profitable areas of the economy. A sustainable recovery is now possible.

It should be obvious that random bailouts can short-circuit the recovery process by propping up poorly performing companies and slowing resource reallocation. With tens of billions in lost profits, General Motors and Chrysler have demonstrated vast inefficiency; yet taxpayer bailouts will preserve their poor management and high-cost union jobs. Worse, other more efficient automobile suppliers will lose their sales to these Detroit dinosaurs and may, themselves, require subsidies. It just never ends.[41]

Or, as economist Benjamin Powell has put it, bailouts "don't work because they strive to maintain the status quo. But the status quo is the problem and exactly what needs to be corrected."[42]

Government ownership stakes in bailed-out firms also greatly disturb libertarians. As self-described (but non-Austrian) libertarian Harvard economist Jeffrey Miron observed in a CNN commentary:

Government ownership means that political forces will determine who wins and who loses in the banking sector. The government, for example, will push banks to aid borrowers with poor credit histories, to subsidize politically connected industries, and to lend in the districts of powerful members of Congress.[43]

The same objections apply to government "stimulus" spending—it is just more direction of resources away from things that consumers actually want and more spending of money that hasn't been saved (instead, the government must get the money through taxes, debt, or inflation). It is substituting the political means, the force of government, for the economic means, free exchange among individuals, and making politically unfavored ordinary people worse off as a result.

Republicans advocate lower taxes as a "stimulus" for the economy, and libertarians agree that lower taxes are good. The problem with Republican proposals, however, is that they do not include comparable reductions in spending. If the government keeps spending while lowering taxes, this may stimulate some economic activity, but the government will still have to get the money for its spending from somewhere—and increasingly, it may need to turn to the Fed's printing press to do so, as foreign governments become less inclined to lend the United States money. More money printing can only lead to greater disaster for the reasons covered throughout this chapter.

MONETARY FREEDOM

We have said a lot about economics in this chapter, and about the economic ideas to which many libertarians subscribe. But even if the Austrian theory of the business cycle did not explain everything—if, say, it could be shown that other factors cause booms and busts—libertarians would still favor monetary freedom and an end to the Federal Reserve. First, as a matter of libertarian principle, people should be free to accept or not accept whatever they want for payment—the government should not force people to accept its paper as legal tender. Second, the Federal Reserve essentially allows the government to print money, which no one denies puts it in a position to impoverish everyone through inflation. Third, the Federal Reserve allows the government to spend more than it takes in, subtly passing on the costs of that spending to the economy as a whole rather than making those costs obvious through taxes. It spends much of that money to carry out policies that infringe upon liberty, and in any event all government spending reduces the amount of capital available to produce goods in the private sector.

In fact, events do appear to be validating libertarians' economic ideas. As the United States remains mired in a depressed economy, the issue of monetary freedom is likely to remain high on the libertarian agenda—and maybe, thanks to libertarians, on the national agenda, too.

NOTES

1. Jacob Weisberg, "The End of Libertarianism," *Slate*, Oct. 18, 2008, http// www.slate.com/id/2202489/.

2. For details, see Donald J. Boudreaux, "A Modest Proposal to Deregulate Infant Adoptions," *Cato Journal* 15 (1995): 117–135, http://www.cato.org/pubs/journal/cj15n1-7 .html.

3. Richard A. Posner, *A Failure of Capitalism: The Crisis of '08 and the Descent Into Depression* (Cambridge, MA: Harvard University Press, 2009), 113.

4. Ibid., 306.

5. Ibid., 311.

6. Fred Barnes, "A 'Big Government Conservatism,'" *Opinion Journal*, August 15, 2003, http://www.opinionjournal.com/extra/?id=110003895.

7. This description of the origin of money is adapted from Carl Menger, *Principles of Economics* (Auburn, AL: Ludwig von Mises Institute, 2007 [1871]), 257–262, http:// mises.org/books/Mengerprinciples.pdf.

8. R.A. Radford, "The Economic Organization of a P.O.W. Camp," *Economica* 12 (1945): 189–201, http://facstaff.uww.edu/kashianr/POWCampRadford.pdf.

9. See William L. Shirer, *The Rise and Fall of the Third Reich* (New York: Simon & Schuster, Inc., 1960): 61–62.

10. Steve H. Hanke, "R.I.P. Zimbabwe Dollar," *Cato.org*, February 9, 2009, http:// www.cato.org/zimbabwe.

11. On the various banking systems in U.S. history, see Murray N. Rothbard, *A History of Money and Banking in the United States: The Colonial Era to World War II* (Auburn, AL: The Ludwig von Mises Institute, 2002), http://mises.org/books/historyof money.pdf.

12. For a more detailed, but still concise, summary, see Robert P. Murphy, "The Worst Recession in 24 Years?" *Mises.org*, October 1, 2007, http://mises.org/story/ 2728.

13. For a more detailed discussion of the gold confiscation from a libertarian perspective, see Thomas E. Woods, Jr. and Kevin R.C. Gutzmann, *Who Killed the Constitution? The Fate of American Liberty from World War I to George W. Bush* (New York: Crown Forum, 2008), 82–101.

14. Austrian economists endlessly debate whether under "free banking" banks could issue paper money in excess of their gold (or silver or whatever) on hand, as long as depositors were informed up front that the bank would do it, or whether this practice is inherently fraudulent and harmful to the economy. We will resist the temptation to jump into that fray and just say that, under free banking, banks would at least be severely constrained in their ability to do this by competition and fear of bank runs, which is surely better than the government-monopoly fiat-money status quo. For some of the debate on this issue, see, for example, Hans-Hermann Hoppe, Jörg-Guido Hülsmann, and Walter Block, "Against Fiduciary Media," *Quarterly Journal of Austrian Economics* 1 (1998): 19–50 (taking the 100 percent reserve view) and George A. Selgin and Lawrence H. White, "In Defense of Fiduciary Media—or, We Are Not Devo(lutionists), We Are Misesians!" *Review of Austrian Economics* 9, no. 2 (1996): 83–107.

15. Thomas E. Woods, Jr., *Meltdown: A Free-Market Look at Why the Stock Market Collapsed, the Economy Tanked, and Government Bailouts Will Make Things Worse* (Washington, DC: Regnery Publishing, Inc., 2009), 75.

16. Posner, *A Failure of Capitalism*, 306.

17. Robert P. Murphy, "Evidence That the Fed Caused the Housing Boom," *Mises.org*, December 15, 2008, http://mises.org/story/3252.

18. See George Reisman, "The Housing Bubble and the Credit Crunch," August 10, 2007, http://www.georgereisman.com/blog/2007/08/housing-bubble-and-credit-crunch .html.

19. Peter Schiff, "Why the Meltdown Should Have Surprised No One" [video], http://www.youtube.com/watch?v=EgMclXX5msc.

20. Posner, *A Failure of Capitalism*, 22.

21. For a more detailed discussion, see Woods, *Meltdown*, 13–17 and Christopher Westley, "How Fannie and Freddie Made Me a Grumpy Economist," *Mises.org*, July 21, 2008, http://mises.org/story/3053.

22. Posner, *A Failure of Capitalism*, 113.

23. Apparently thinking that it would become a popular catchphrase, the Cato Institute used the "ownership society" label to promote other ideas, such as so-called private social security accounts. See *Ownership Society*, http://www.cato.org/special/ownership_ society. Other libertarians attacked the "ownership society" concept from the outset.

See, e.g., Llewellyn H. Rockwell, Jr., "The Ownership Society," *Mises.org*, September 3, 2004, http://mises.org/story/1601.

24. One argument is that free-market money would cause deflation, which many mainstream economists consider to be disastrous. For a rebuttal of this argument, see, for example, Robert P. Murphy, "Defend the Gold Standard," *Mises.org,* March 16, 2009, http://mises.org/story/3368.

25. David R. Henderson and Jeffrey Hummel, "Greenspan's Monetary Policy in Retrospect," Cato Institute Briefing Paper No. 109, Nov. 3, 2008, http://www.cato.org/pub_display.php?pub_id=9756.

26. Robert Blumen, "Fannie Mae Distorts Markets," *Mises.org*, June 17, 2002, http://mises.org/story/986.

27. Frank Shostak, "Housing Bubble: Myth or Reality?" *Mises.org*, March 4, 2003, http://mises.org/story/1177.

28. Christopher Mayer, "The Housing Bubble," *The Free Market* (August 2003), http://mises.org/freemarket_detail.aspx?control=450.

29. Mark Thornton, "Housing: Too Good to Be True," *Mises.org*, June 4, 2004, http://mises.org/story/1533.

30. Stefan Karlsson, "America's Unsustainable Boom," *Mises.org*, November 8, 2004, http://mises.org/story/1670.

31. Shostak, "Housing Bubble."

32. Alan Reynolds, "No Housing Bubble Trouble," *Washington Times*, January 9, 2005, http://www.cato.org/pub_display.php?pub_id=4243.

33. "Peter Schiff Was Right 2006–2007 (2nd Edition)" [video], http://www.youtube.com/watch?v=2I0QN-FYkpw.

34. See, for example, "Peter Schiff's Predictions (2002–2009)" [video] http://www.youtube.com/watch?v=VCv32qaINIQ.

35. "Peter Schiff Was Right 2006–2007 – CNBC edition" [video], http://www.youtube.com/watch?v=Z0YTY5TWtmU.

36. Ron Paul, "Fannie Mae and Freddie Mac Subsidies Distort the Housing Market," September 10, 2003, http://www.house.gov/paul/congrec/congrec2003/cr091003.htm.

37. Transcripts of some of these exchanges are in Ron Paul, *End the Fed* (New York: Grand Central Publishing, 2009).

38. "Republican Debate Transcript, Myrtle Beach, SC," *CFR.org*, Jan. 10, 2008, http://www.cfr.org/publication/15249.

39. Ibid.

40. Rex Nutting, "U.S. Recession Began in December 2007, NBER Says," *MarketWatch*, December 1, 2008, http://www.marketwatch.com/story/us-recession-began-in-december-2007-nber-says.

41. Dominick Armentano, "The Obama Stimulus Plan Won't Work," *LewRockwell.com*, January 21, 2009, http://www.lewrockwell.com/armentano-d/armentano16.html.

42. Benjamin Powell, "Avoid Japan's Mistakes," *The Washington Times*, March 8, 2009, http://www.washingtontimes.com/news/2009/mar/08/avoid-japans-mistakes/.

43. Jeffrey Miron, "Why This Bailout Is As Bad As the Last One," *CNN.com*, October 14, 2008, http://www.cnn.com/2008/POLITICS/10/14/miron.banks/index.html.

FURTHER READING

Hazlitt, Henry. *Economics in One Lesson*. Auburn, AL: Ludwig von Mises Institute, 2008 [1946]. This short classic is still relevant and is still the best place to start to learn about free-market economics. This book is available online at http://www.fee.org/pdf/books/Economics_in_one_lesson.pdf.

Paul, Ron. *End the Fed*. New York: Grand Central Publishing, 2009. Paul argues that the Fed "should be abolished because it is immoral, unconstitutional, impractical, promotes bad economics, and undermines liberty."

Rothbard, Murray N. *What Has Government Done to Our Money?* Auburn, AL: Ludwig von Mises Institute, 2008 [1991]. Rothbard explains the origin, history, and economics of money and the effects of government money meddling. This book is available online at http://mises.org/books/whathasgovernmentdone.pdf.

Woods, Thomas E., Jr. *Meltdown: A Free-Market Look at Why the Stock Market Collapsed, the Economy Tanked, and Government Bailouts Will Make Things Worse*. Washington, DC: Regnery Publishing, Inc., 2009. Woods analyzes the causes and cures of the current crisis in detail from an Austrian, free-market perspective.

4

The Fight for Marijuana
(and Other Drugs)

A s we have seen, sometimes libertarians are mistaken for the men in suits who control the American financial system and who caused its collapse. Other times, though, libertarians are mistaken for hippies who just want the government to let them smoke pot.

It is true that libertarians want to legalize drugs, but not necessarily because libertarians have a personal interest in drug use. Libertarians support legalization because they believe peaceful people should be free to do as they please, which includes ingesting the substances of their choosing. Libertarians also see the drug war as one of government's most destructive programs because it not only interferes with drug users' rights, it also harms and kills innocent people caught in the crossfire and turns police into "soldiers." Plus, the law does not just restrain recreational drug users; it also literally kills sick people who could use marijuana to ease their pain and prolong their lives. The war on drugs also earns libertarians' special hatred because, like so many other wars, it came about not in response to a serious threat, but mostly because of dishonest government officials, fraudulent propaganda, and the desires of powerful special interests.

Libertarians propose an immediate end to the drug war. This would be a dramatic course change for the United States but, as we will see, it is really not so radical—it would just return us to the successful libertarian drug policy

America had for most of its history. And although the war on drugs is unlikely to end soon, libertarians have enjoyed some successes, and more may be on the horizon. Some states have decriminalized marijuana, legalized medical marijuana, or both, and others are moving to join them despite federal law to the contrary. The mainstream media also is paying unprecedented attention to the prospect of marijuana legalization. If the tide does turn in favor of freedom, it will be because of persistent efforts by libertarians and their allies.

OUR LIBERTARIAN PAST

For most of U.S. history, all drugs were legal. How legal? As libertarian writer Harry Browne put it, "Few people are aware that before World War I, a 9-year-old girl could walk into a drug store and buy heroin."[1] In fact, before Bayer sold aspirin, it sold Heroin™ as a "sedative for coughs."[2] (As a German company, Bayer was forced to give up the trademark after World War I under the Treaty of Versailles.) One heroin-laced cough syrup promised in its mail-order catalog: "It will suit the palate of the most exacting adult or the most capricious child."[3] Cocaine, first manufactured by Merck, was popular, too.[4] Parke-Davis (which is now a subsidiary of Pfizer) advertised a "cocaine kit" that it promised could "supply the place of food, make the coward brave, the silent eloquent and . . . render the sufferer insensitive to pain."[5] Late-nineteenth-century advertisements for "Cocaine Toothache Drops" promised users (including children such as those depicted in the ads) an "instantaneous cure."[6] Another popular product, "Mrs. Winslow's Soothing Syrup," contained one grain (65 mg) of morphine per ounce, and was marketed to mothers to quiet restless infants and children.[7] McCormick (the spice company) and others sold "paregoric," a mixture of highly concentrated alcohol with opium, as a treatment for diarrhea, coughs, and pain, with instructions on the bottle for infants, children, and adults.[8] Another medication called laudanum was similar, but with 25 times the opium. Heroin and opium were both marketed as asthma treatments, too.[9] And, of course, cocaine was an ingredient in Coca-Cola from 1886 until 1900.[10]

All these products were available "over the counter." A doctor, pharmacist, or anyone else could advertise them and sell them with no prescription or other special permission. Drugs were like any other good on the market.

Marketing heroin to children? Putting coke in Coke? Many people would take all this as evidence that *of course* the government needed to step in and do something. But the widespread availability of these products did not cause the disaster one might expect.

In hindsight, it may not seem right that people casually took narcotics or routinely gave them to their children. On the other hand, in the years before acetaminophen, ibuprofen, or even aspirin (which was not introduced until 1898), people had few alternatives to treat pain. So as easy as it might be for us to criticize nineteenth-century Americans for using them, these drugs often really did help people and may have been their best alternative.[11] And they were not just used by ignorant people taken in by snake-oil salesman; for example, Benjamin Franklin took laudanum to control pain from kidney stones late in his life.[12]

Life under legalization was not perfect, of course. There were addicts. But most opium addicts became addicted because someone in the medical profession got them started on it, just as doctors today inadvertently hook people on legal drugs.[13] Some people became addicted through patent medicines they took on their own—but addicts were just a small portion of the market for these products.[14] Many people became opium addicts essentially because of government. During the Civil War, the United States fed opium addiction as it issued some 10,000,000 opium pills and 2,841,000 ounces of opium powder to the army.[15] As a result, drug addiction became known as the "soldier's disease."[16] Other factors that drove people to addiction were state and local alcohol prohibition and increasing social disapproval of alcohol, which prompted people to substitute opium for liquor. In states where alcohol was prohibited, opiate use rose by 150 percent.[17] An 1872 study by the Massachusetts State Board of Health found that the temperance movement had caused an upswing in opiate use and noted that opium could be "procured and taken without endangering the reputation for sobriety," and was seen as "more genteel" than alcohol.[18]

Opium addiction rose in the decades after the Civil War, but soon so did education and understanding about drugs and their addictive, dangerous nature among both physicians and the public. The rise of mass media helped; for example, the *Ladies' Home Journal* published numerous exposés on narcotic-laced patent medications.[19] Meanwhile, the market produced safer medicines, such as aspirin. As a result of these factors, addiction peaked near the end of the nineteenth century and then began a long decline without any need for a government "war."[20]

And although America did have addicts in the nineteenth century, perhaps as much as 0.5 percent of the population,[21] there are some things it notably did not have. Most important, there was virtually none of the violence, death, and crime we associate with the present-day drug problem. Most drug users were not street criminals; instead, the typical addict was, as author Mike Gray put it, "a middle-aged southern white woman strung out on laudanum."[22] Many or most opium addicts led more or less normal lives and managed to keep their addiction hidden.[23] Things were not perfect—as they never will or can be—but there was no real crisis when all drugs were legal.

THE WAR ON DRUGS

Libertarians often point out that the federal government is not good at much that it tries to do, but even they will agree that government is good at one thing: exploiting small problems by portraying them as "crises" that only the federal government can solve and exploiting them to permanently expand government power. The government is also good at pleasing big business and other special interests while appearing to act in the public interest. The war on drugs is an example of both phenomena; as we will see, it was originally justified on flimsy grounds that practically no one would accept today.

Dubious Foundations

Narcotics and Cocaine

An obvious factor leading to drug prohibition was the temperance movement. It succeeded in getting alcohol banned in numerous states and, of course, ultimately banned nationwide from 1919 until 1933. If temperance activists could succeed in banning wine, which had played an important role in the history of civilization itself, it is not too surprising that they would have some success in prohibiting other substances that were less well understood or accepted. But temperance activists focused first and foremost on alcohol, and likely would not have achieved federal drug prohibition without help from other powerful interests.

One early factor was U.S. foreign policy, driven by the interests of big business. The Chinese had long sold tea and silk to the British East India Company in exchange for opium. As a result, opium use became widespread in China, which troubled its rulers. The Theodore Roosevelt Administration decided to take advantage of this by expressing concern over the opium problem and pressing for an international ban on the opium trade. This would curry favor with the Chinese and encourage them to open their markets to the United States. (We should note here that libertarians *do* favor open markets, but do not approve of governments using citizens' rights as a bargaining chip in this way.) To have credibility in pressing for international agreements restraining the opium trade, the United States took quick action to ban imports of smoking (as opposed to medicinal) opium.[24]

Bigotry and xenophobia were another major factor leading to drug prohibition. Chinese immigrants were partly responsible for spreading opium use in America, so prohibitionists found a receptive audience among whites who feared the prospect of their daughters being lured into the Chinaman's opium den.[25] Early anti-opium laws in western states explicitly discriminated against Chinese immigrants.[26]

Absurd fears about cocaine-crazed blacks fueled support for cocaine prohibition. Dr. Hamilton Wright, the leading anti-drug crusader during the Theodore Roosevelt Administration, told Congress that cocaine "is often the direct incentive to the crime of rape by the Negroes," despite a lack of evidence for this or even for the proposition that blacks used cocaine more than whites.[27] Still, Southern Senators especially bought into the widespread myth that black men on cocaine essentially became crazed zombies who were—yes, some people believed this—invulnerable to .32 caliber bullets.[28]

Professional and industry groups, most notably the American Pharmacological Association, also helped enact drug prohibition. Big pharmaceutical companies did not like competition from patent medications, and pharmacists did not like it that people other than themselves could sell drugs. Regulation of drug distribution, even if it imposed costs on pharmaceutical companies and pharmacists to some extent, could be worthwhile to them if they could bear the costs while their smaller, less diversified competitors could not.[29]

Before the federal government attacked drugs, various states did. A number of states banned opium, morphine, and heroin around the turn of the century with little success. Many patent-medicine manufacturers received exemptions from the law and then distributed their medicines without indicating the prohibited substances' presence on their product labels, which caused more people to unwittingly become addicted to drugs. Increased addiction only bolstered the case for the federal government to step in. The first major federal action was the Pure Food and Drug Act of 1906, which required patent-medicine producers to list their products' ingredients on their labels. Although this may seem relatively inoffensive from a libertarian perspective—after all, libertarians oppose fraud—this gave professional and industry groups such as the American Medical Association and American Pharmacological Association some protection from competition, and it encouraged them to take further political action.

Congress passed further-reaching legislation in 1914 with the Harrison Narcotics Tax Act. The Harrison Act did not prohibit any drugs outright, in part because Congress was not certain that it had the authority to do so under the Commerce Clause. (Today's Congressmen would no doubt find this uncertainty quaint.) Instead, the Act banned distribution of narcotics and cocaine for non-medicinal purposes and limited who could sell the drugs for medicinal purposes. It required all involved in the distribution of narcotics to register with the federal government and to pay a tax of one dollar per year, and it required distributors to keep records. The Act also exempted sellers of certain medicines that contained the drugs in very small amounts.[30]

Pharmacists and pharmaceutical companies accepted the Harrison Act because they could better afford its recordkeeping costs than their competitors. The next step came when Congress amended the Act in 1919 to allow the

Bureau of Internal Revenue to prohibit "addict maintenance" (that is, giving drugs in regulated doses to addicts) by physicians.[31] The result was that thousands of physicians were imprisoned for prescribing narcotics that had always been legal.[32] By this time, the American public was even more receptive to prohibitionist efforts. World War I propaganda led people to view sobriety as a patriotic duty and drugs as a plot by the Germans. A not-so-sober 1918 *New York Times* editorial claimed that the Germans were deliberately addicting the rest of the world to drugs and alcohol to create a "world of 'cokeys' and 'hop fiends,' which would have been absolutely helpless when a German embargo shut off the supply of its pet poison."[33]

Marijuana, the Killer Weed

Cocaine and narcotics prohibition came about for dubious reasons—pleasing China, the pharmaceutical industry's desire to eliminate competition, bigotry, World War I, and fanatical temperance activists—but the decision to prohibit marijuana was even less justifiable.

In 1930, the government established the Federal Bureau of Narcotics, led by Commissioner Harry Anslinger. In his position, Anslinger essentially decided who could legally manufacture narcotics for medical purposes in the United States, and he granted that privilege to just a handful of companies. In exchange for favorable treatment, these companies would otherwise do Anslinger's bidding; specifically, they would provide Congressional testimony as needed, including, when Anslinger wanted it, testimony as to the great potential harm of marijuana.[34]

It is odd that anyone would have pursued marijuana prohibition in the 1930s, if only because so few people used it, but Anslinger targeted it anyway. No one is sure why, but one suggested reason is because, like any bureaucracy, the Federal Bureau of Narcotics had to justify its budget, particularly during the Great Depression.[35] Plus, some suggest, Anslinger and the bureau wanted publicity.[36]

During the 1930s, Anslinger and the Federal Bureau of Narcotics launched a propaganda campaign against pot. In speeches, Anslinger declared: "Take all the good in Dr. Jekyll and the worst in Mr. Hyde—the result is opium. Marihuana may be considered more harmful. . . . It is Mr. Hyde alone."[37] The bureau was eager to provide "information" on the putative dangers of marijuana to journalists; marijuana horror stories began to appear in newspapers and periodicals, virtually all of them acknowledging Anslinger's bureau or its publications for their "facts."[38] A 1934 *St. Louis Post-Dispatch* article described the effects of marijuana:

[T]he physical attack of marijuana upon the body is rapid and devastating. In the initial stages, the skin turns a peculiar yellow color, the lips become discolored, dried and cracked. Soon the mouth is affected, the gums are inflamed and softened. Then the teeth are loosened and eventually, if the habit is persisted in, they fall out. . . .

[People in traveling jazz bands] take a few puffs off a marijuana cigarette if they are tired. . . . It gives them a lift and they can go on playing even though they may be virtually paralyzed from the waist down, which is one of the effects marijuana can have.[39]

Anslinger himself published an article in *American Magazine* called "Marijuana: Assassin of Youth," in which he told of a young "marijuana addict" who, while "pitifully crazed," slaughtered his family of five with an ax.[40]

Another likely factor leading to prohibition was, once again, bigotry, this time mostly against Mexicans. Mexicans brought marijuana smoking to the United States when about one million of them migrated here after their country's 1910 revolution.[41] Some people resented Mexicans anyway, in part for their willingness to work for low wages during the Depression, and marijuana provided another excuse to attack them.[42] Anslinger also testified before Congress that marijuana "causes white women to seek sexual relations with Negroes."[43]

Powerful interests lined up in support of marijuana prohibition. Big pharmaceutical companies did so because they were beholden to Anslinger and because they did not want competition from marijuana, which they could not profit from themselves because it was a common plant. Chemical company DuPont supported the legislation because it would treat hemp (a form of cannabis that cannot be used to get high, but which serves numerous industrial purposes very well) just like other marijuana, which would eliminate competition for DuPont's synthetic products.[44]

Still, despite the propaganda and prejudice, there was not much public demand for marijuana prohibition when Congress nonetheless passed the Marihuana Tax Act of 1937.[45] There was not much evidence or debate, either. As legal scholars Charles H. Whitebread II and Richard J. Bonnie put it, the hearings "are near comic examples of dereliction of legislative responsibility."[46] Anslinger was the primary witness at the Congressional hearings, and he presented stories of the boy with the ax, another man who decapitated his best friend while under the influence,[47] a 15-year-old who "went insane," and other anecdotes derived from newspaper clippings.[48]

The American Medical Association provided a witness, a Dr. William C. Woodward, who pointed out that Anslinger had little more than hearsay evidence from newspapers to back up his claims. Although marijuana use in prisons and by children were supposed justifications for the law, Woodward pointed out that there was no evidence as to how many prisoners actually used marijuana, or how many children used it. For refusing to endorse the legislation, Congressmen accused Woodward of "obstruction."[49]

When the bill made it to the House floor, it received less than two minutes of debate. A Republican Congressman asked whether the American Medical Association supported the bill, and a committee member, Fred M. Vinson—who had been present and asked questions at length during the committee hearings, and who would later become Chief Justice of the U.S. Supreme Court—responded with a bald-faced lie: "Their Doctor Wentworth (sic) came down here. They support this bill 100 percent."[50] It was late at night, so they passed the bill without further substantive discussion, and soon the president signed it.

The Marihuana Tax Act was like the Harrison Act in that it just imposed a tax on marijuana transactions and limited who could conduct them. Over time, though, because so few were licensed to distribute marijuana, it essentially became a criminal law that prohibited possession and sale of marijuana.

Escalation

The 1951 Boggs Act increased penalties for unauthorized sale and possession of both narcotics and marijuana, lumping the two together, in part on the theory put forth by Anslinger that marijuana use was a gateway to narcotics use. (The "gateway drug" idea has since been well discredited.)[51] The 1956 Narcotics Control Act further increased penalties.[52]

Still, the "war on drugs" as we know it did not really start until Richard Nixon became president. As president-elect, Nixon was looking for an issue that could tap into people's anxieties about domestic unrest and make himself look tough on crime. Because the federal government had no authority to go after common street crime, his advisors suggested drugs.[53] Government statistics about heroin use—if not the actual facts—helped Nixon's strategy. In 1969, the Bureau of Narcotics reported that there were 68,088 heroin addicts in the country; two years later, the number leaped to 559,000. That seems like quite a crisis, so Nixon vowed to "take every step necessary" to address the "national emergency."[54] Never mind, of course, that the numbers were all made up. The Bureau of Narcotics had arrived at the 1969 number by looking at the number of addicts who had gotten in trouble with the law. In 1971, the Bureau decided (arbitrarily) that this method likely understated the number of addicts by 800 percent—so it started multiplying its total by eight. So the change in the official number of heroin users had nothing to do with any actual increase in heroin use, but just reflected a change in methodology. In 1972, the next election year, Nixon decided he did not like the appearance of a huge increase in drug addiction under his watch, so he asked the Bureau to change its methods again. The Bureau obliged, and arbitrarily cut the number of addicts to 150,000 in its next report.[55]

Nixon signed the Comprehensive Drug Abuse Prevention and Control Act of 1970 into law; this law included the Controlled Substances Act, which set up the anti-drug regime we still have today. Nixon also appointed a presidential commission to consider the effects of marijuana and, to his embarrassment, it found that marijuana had no causal connection with crime and recommended legalization. So, of course, Nixon rejected the recommendation, and the drug war marched on.[56]

The Carter Administration was fairer-minded and seriously considered legalization. The President told Congress: "Penalties against possession of a drug should not be more damaging to the individual than the use of the drug itself."[57] But that idea never advanced. One problem was that Carter faced opposition from law-enforcement groups who expected their annual drug-war budget increases. As one former Arizona appellate judge has noted, this is an example of how the drug war advances based on "institutional empire-related goals wholly separate from pot's evils."[58] The proposal further derailed when the press discovered that Carter's head of drug policy, Peter Bourne, had given an otherwise-legal prescription to a White House staffer in a false name to protect her privacy, and had recently attended a party where cocaine and marijuana were present.[59] Bourne resigned and his successor promised to *increase* marijuana penalties.[60]

To return to a theme from Chapter 2, the Reagan years were a step back for liberty and a step forward for big government. In June 1982, Reagan announced: "We're taking down the surrender flag that has flown over so many drug efforts. We're running up a battle flag."[61]

The Reagan Administration took full advantage of the Prohibition-era tactic of forfeiture: seizing without notice any assets the government *alleged* were involved in a crime before charges had been filed or an individual had been convicted. As Reagan Associate Attorney General Stephen Trott put it, this meant accused drug offenders could be "forfeiting everything they own—their land, their cars, their boats, everything."[62] It also means that innocent family members whose property allegedly was used in an offense could lose their homes and personal possessions. The proceeds of such forfeitures are shared among law-enforcement agencies, giving police a strong incentive to go after people's private property to enrich their departments. Today, law enforcement agencies continue to use this tactic to take property without due process of law. One study found that 80 percent of people suffering asset forfeiture were never even charged with a crime, and most of them were not drug kingpins losing luxury items but ordinary people losing things like their cars and homes.[63]

The Omnibus Crime Bill of 1984 that Reagan pushed for and won also increased prison terms, including mandatory life sentences for people who were found to be "principals" in a continuing criminal enterprise. The Anti-Drug Act of 1988 piled on still more, as did the Crime Bill of 1994, signed by Bill Clinton, which even imposed the death penalty for some drug dealers.

The War on Drugs Today

The government continues to wage the drug war as fiercely as ever. Harvard economist Jeffrey Miron conservatively estimates that, based on government figures, the federal government spends at least $13 billion per year enforcing drug laws, and state and local governments spend at least $30 billion enforcing them.[64] But that is just the obvious monetary cost in the form of government spending specifically on drug laws: There are other costs that libertarians point out.

Crime

The drug war imposes costs on people who do not use drugs by creating violent crime. Because drugs are illegal, prices are much higher than they otherwise would be. Coca leaves, for example, are extremely cheap to grow and process into cocaine; the high cost of cocaine comes instead from the expense and risk of sneaking it into the United States and selling it. Some drug addicts have trouble affording their habit because of the artificial expense the drug war creates and they turn to violent crime to get money. If drugs were legal, they would also be cheap—which means that, yes, perhaps more people would use them, but the streets would have fewer violent criminals. And if drugs were legalized, the product would no longer be sold by criminal gangs at war with each other, so the streets would become safer. The product would also be purer and safer, not "cut" with potentially harmful substances. Law enforcement could also direct its resources away from drug enforcement to real crimes such as murder, theft, and rape.

The drug war has also created a huge prison population. Thanks to the drug war, the United States has the largest prison population of any country in the world, and the highest rate of prisoners per capita in the world.[65] As Ethan Nadelmann of the pro-legalization Drug Policy Alliance has observed: "The United States has five percent of the world's population and 25 percent of the world's incarcerated population. . . . We now imprison more people for drug law violations than all of western Europe, with a much larger population, incarcerates for all offenses."[66] Because prisons depend on drug offenders for so much of their "business," the prison guards' union strongly opposes any efforts at drug legalization; it spent almost $2 million to defeat a recent California initiative that would have diverted some marijuana offenders from prison into treatment and saved taxpayers nearly $2 billion. Incidentally, that measure also would have made possession of small amounts of marijuana a non-criminal infraction (comparable to a speeding ticket)—so the alcoholic beverage industry opposed it, too.[67]

More Innocent Victims

Another cost of the war on drugs is that it is often carried out like a war, with paramilitary police acting as soldiers and innocent bystanders becoming collateral damage. Historically, the police and the military have served very different functions. The police (supposedly) have existed to "serve and protect" the people in their community, and in doing so they (theoretically) have been required to follow strict procedures and obey strict limitations prescribed by the courts and the Constitution. On the other hand, the military basically exists to, as a common phrase has it, kill people and break things. Soldiers search and destroy, read nobody any rights, and consider the incidental killing of innocent people to be a necessary part of their job. Thanks especially to Reagan-era laws and directives allowing the military to provide training and equipment to federal, state, and local civilian law enforcement, the war on drugs has blurred the lines between police and the military—and innocent people are being killed as a result.

In 1981, Congress passed the Military Cooperation with Law Enforcement Act, which authorized the military to become involved in the drug war, and to give local police departments access to military resources, including equipment, for drug enforcement. A 1986 directive from President Reagan allowed yet more cooperation between civilian law enforcement and the military. In 1988, Congress ordered the National Guard to assist law enforcement, so it now flies armed helicopter missions in search of marijuana crops. In 1989, President George Bush created six regional task forces within the Department of Defense, which coordinate military and civilian drug war activities, including joint training of military units and police. As of 1994, the Department of Justice and Department of Defense have a memorandum of understanding under which the military can transfer to state and local police departments items that were previously reserved for use by the military during wartime.[68] From 1997 through 2005, for example, the federal Law Enforcement Support Program handled millions of orders to transfer military equipment from the Pentagon to civilian law enforcement, including 235 aircraft; 7,856 M-16 machine guns; and 181 grenade launchers.[69]

Along with the increased availability of military equipment has come a vastly increased used of SWAT (Special Weapons and Tactics) teams. In the

late 1960s, SWAT teams came into existence to handle rare difficult circumstances such as hostage negotiations, hijackings, or barricaded suspects.[70] Since
the Reagan administration, though, SWAT teams have increasingly been used
in the drug war. As of 1996, 65 percent of towns of 25,000 to 50,000 residents
had a SWAT team, with another 8 percent planning to form one.[71] Given
the trendline and the tendency toward even more police militarization since
September 11, 2001, it is safe to assume those numbers have only increased. In
addition, even some *very* small towns are getting SWAT teams—two examples
are Middleburg, Pennsylvania (pop. 1,363) and Mt. Orab, Ohio (pop. 2,701).[72]

As a result of all this militarization, one can read endless tragic stories of
SWAT teams that invaded the wrong house looking for drugs and killed or at
least brutalized, abused, and otherwise terrorized the innocent people inside. A
typical "no-knock" raid by a SWAT team involves either breaking down the
suspect's door with a battering ram or blowing it open with explosives. Once
inside, the team members deploy a "flash grenade" to disorient the house's
occupants; then all the occupants of the house are quickly ordered to lie on
the ground and are handcuffed. Sometimes they use tear gas, too. One can
imagine how innocent people respond to men in black invading their homes
in the middle of the night. The SWAT invaders typically do not look like
policemen, so many people assume that their houses are being robbed and nat-
urally reach for any firearms they may have on hand for self-defense—and
then they are shot on sight by the police. Or, maybe the homeowner succeeds
in shooting the invader—and finds himself on trial as a cop killer.

The police do not always go to the wrong house, of course. Sometimes they
go to the "correct" house—the one a paid informant told them was involved
in drug-dealing—and then go through their shock-and-awe-and-humiliation-
and-mayhem routine only to find that their tip was no good. The use of paid
informants creates more deadly hazards for innocents in the war on drugs.

In case all this sounds a bit hard to believe, some libertarian journalists have
diligently chronicled the abuses of paramilitary police in general, and in the drug
war in particular. *Reason* magazine senior editor Radley Balko provides facts and
figures on police militarization and details dozens of specific incidents in his
2006 study, *Overkill: The Rise of Paramilitary Police Raids in America*. Libertarian
writer William Norman Grigg does so extensively as well in articles published
on *LewRockwell.com* and elsewhere, and on his blog, *Pro Libertate*.[73]

The Bad Neighbor

The U.S. drug war also creates suffering for people in other countries, especially in Latin America. Historically, people in countries such as Peru, Ecua-
dor, Bolivia, and Colombia used coca leaves as a natural remedy. Chewed or

made into tea, coca leaves have health benefits, including protection against altitude sickness which affects many in the Andes. When it is not processed into cocaine, coca is something of a miracle plant, with lots of health benefits and no drawbacks. So for the people of the Andes, coca has been a way of life for thousands of years.

Then the U.S. drug war disrupted all of that. Under Reagan (again), the United States began pressuring Latin American governments to outlaw substances that were prohibited in the United States—or else. The United States began a system under which it certifies various drug-producing or drug-transiting "source" countries as compliant or non-compliant with U.S. drug-fighting efforts. Under this system, the United States threatens to take away disobedient governments' foreign aid and impose trade sanctions (among others) against them.[74] So Latin American leaders, even though they may resent U.S. influence, have had little choice but to play ball.

Because the war on drugs makes the price of drugs go up, it also makes drugs highly profitable for the people who deal in them. This has made Latin American drug cartels extremely wealthy and powerful, and has created widespread corruption. Colombia's drug problem provides an example, and Manuel Noriega—a one-time drug-war ally who later was the impetus for a U.S. invasion of Panama—is another.

In the past decade, one especially egregious drug-related offense against foreigners has been the U.S.-funded "Plan Colombia" (originally championed by then-Senator Joseph Biden) under which the government has attempted to eradicate South American coca crops by spraying defoliant from planes. This has of course destroyed some coca crops (owned by poor peasant farmers), but it has not stopped or significantly reduced cocaine production. At the same time, Plan Colombia has inadvertently destroyed other crops in the process (more collateral damage inflicted on innocent poor people) and exposed people to toxic defoliants. Needless to say, none of this has prevented anyone in the United States who wants to use cocaine from doing so.

Today some of the drug war's worst effects are felt in Mexico, where the death toll is rising as drug cartels battle each other—and battle *even more* after drug-war efforts take one cartel out and rivals move in to take over its turf. As libertarian foreign policy scholar Ted Galen Carpenter has documented, from January through mid-November 2008 alone, some 4,500 people were killed in drug-related violence in Mexico.[75] The violence is worst near the U.S. border, and has made the area unsafe for U.S. tourists. Since 2005, Tijuana tourism has dropped by about 90 percent, and half of Tijuana's downtown businesses have closed.[76] And the Mexican violence is now spilling over into America itself, as drug cartel hit men target people (often, family members of people in the drug trade) in the United States for murder and kidnapping.[77]

Libertarians would be the first to point out that drug gangs that kill, kidnap, and commit other violent crimes should be stopped. But libertarians would also point out that pursuing these particular criminals will not stop the drug trade or the violence. Only the repeal of drug prohibition will take the drug business out of criminals' hands, just as the end of Prohibition took the alcoholic-beverage business out of gangsters' hands.

MEDICAL MARIJUANA

Probably the hottest topic for drug-war opponents today is medical marijuana. But it is important to note that libertarians support legalization of *all* drugs and view *all* drug prohibition as destructive and immoral. And libertarians do not believe that an individual should need a doctor's permission to use marijuana or any other drugs. In fact, libertarian psychiatrist Thomas Szasz opposes the "medical marijuana" movement inasmuch as it accepts the premise that the state should have any say at all over what a person may choose to consume as medicine.[78] Writer Sheldon Richman agrees, arguing that the medical marijuana cause "does not advance liberty" because it "empowers doctors, not the rest of us."[79]

Still, probably most libertarians view the medical marijuana movement's successes as steps in the right direction. If marijuana is legalized for medical use, something that was once totally forbidden will at least be available to some people without fear of state sanctions, and to that limited extent, liberty will increase. Plus, legalization of marijuana for one purpose could make it more likely that marijuana will be legalized for any purpose, as some of the drug's mystique will be stripped away and more people will come to realize that it is nothing like the "killer weed" Anslinger once portrayed it as.

In addition, some of the biggest heroes, and most tragic martyrs, of the medical marijuana fight have been libertarians.

Marijuana as Medicine

Does marijuana have medical benefits that other legal drugs do not offer? Again, the libertarian's first response is: Who cares? People should be free to pursue whatever treatments they believe are best for their health; it is not for government to decide what the most appropriate remedy is.

That said, the evidence strongly shows that marijuana *does* have ample benefits that, for many, cannot be matched by legal prescription drugs. Studies have shown that marijuana is useful to reduce nausea and vomiting, to stimulate appetite, and to promote weight gain. For cancer and AIDS patients, this can mean the difference between life and death, as it can allow them to keep their medicines down without vomiting. Smoked marijuana has also been shown to reduce muscle spasticity from spinal-cord injuries and multiple sclerosis (MS), and it diminishes tremors in MS patients. And it has been shown through the experiences of doctors and patients to help with migraines, depression, seizures, insomnia, and chronic pain.[80] Recent scientific research suggests that the cannabinoids in marijuana may even fight cancerous tumors.[81]

Despite all this, the federal government continues to classify marijuana as a Schedule I drug, which means that (1) it has a high potential for abuse; (2) it has no currently accepted medical use in treatment in the United States; and (3) there is a lack of accepted safety for its use under medical supervision.[82]

In 1986, the federal government did approve the medical use of Marinol, a marijuana-derived pill, with a doctor's prescription for use as anti-nauseant and appetite stimulant. The trouble is, marijuana provides its best benefits when smoked (or inhaled through an even safer method, vaporization). An obvious problem with taking a pill as an anti-nauseant is that the extremely nauseated people may not keep it down. Also, smoking or vaporization quickly delivers marijuana's active ingredient, THC, but Marinol must go through the stomach and small intestine before being absorbed, and it passes through the liver, which transforms it into other things. As a result, the body does not even absorb 90 percent of the THC in Marinol. Two hours after swallowing a 10 to 15 milligram Marinol pill, 84 percent of subjects in a study had *no* measurable THC in their blood; after six hours, 57% still had none. On the other hand, a person who smokes 2 to 5 milligrams of THC feels effects within minutes, and once they start feeling effects, they can regulate their intake by smoking more or less as needed. Some may view medical marijuana users' smoking as an excuse to get high, but Marinol pills are more likely to have intense psychoactive effects.[83] Then there is the cost. While a Marinol regimen costs $1,000 per month, smoked or vaporized marijuana would only require a plant that a person can grow themselves for little or nothing.[84]

Libertarian Heroes of the Medical Marijuana Movement

In 1996, medical marijuana activists—some thoroughgoing libertarians, some not—succeeded in passing a California ballot initiative, Proposition 215, which removed state-law prohibitions on marijuana for medical purposes, with a doctor's recommendation. In the years since, medical marijuana dispensaries have opened across the state, and countless patients have found much-needed relief. But the battle is not over, even in California, let alone in the rest of the country. Marijuana is still illegal for *any* purpose under federal law, so the federal government continued its war on California pot smokers—even those dying of cancer or AIDS—as though Proposition 215 had never happened. For more than a decade, California medical marijuana dispensaries have been operating in constant fear of federal raids. To its credit, the Obama Administration has at last backed off on these raids—for now.

Two libertarian activists stand out among the government's most notable victims in the years following Proposition 215.

One of them, Peter McWilliams, was the author of 35 nonfiction books, including numerous *New York Times* best-sellers and *Ain't Nobody's Business If You Do*, a popular book on the libertarian position that "victimless crimes" should not be crimes at all. In the 1990s, McWilliams suffered from both cancer and AIDS. No anti-nausea drug on the market would allow him to keep his vital medications down except the last one he tried, marijuana. After he began smoking pot, his nausea subsided and he was able to keep his medication down. His cancer soon went into remission and his AIDS viral count dropped from 12,500 to an undetectable level.

In July 1998, McWilliams was arrested on federal drug charges for growing marijuana for himself and other patients. He was freed on $250,000 bail, on the condition that he not use marijuana—a condition he accepted for fear his mother would lose her house. At his trial, McWilliams was forbidden to mention that he was terminally ill, that he used marijuana to treat his symptoms, or that medical marijuana use was legal under California law. He vomited throughout the court proceedings, but was forbidden from explaining the reason for the vomiting. Ultimately he pled guilty in hopes of receiving leniency in his sentence, but he choked to death on his own vomit while awaiting sentencing in 2000 at age 50.[85] His story remains a powerful educational tool for libertarians illustrating the injustice of the drug war.

Steven Kubby's unpleasant experience with the criminal justice system ended more happily. Kubby has suffered from adrenal cancer since 1968, and in 1976 his cancer spread to his liver and other parts of his body. He underwent surgeries, radiation, and chemotherapy, but eventually he decided to self-medicate with marijuana. Kubby's doctor was amazed to find him alive years later. (Although it cannot be proven that marijuana cured Kubby, recent studies do suggest that marijuana can indeed fight cancer itself in addition to fighting various symptoms of cancer and cancer treatments.)[86] In 1996, Kubby played a pivotal role in drafting and promoting Proposition 215.

In 1998, acting on an anonymous tip, the Pacer County, California sheriff began investigating Kubby and eventually raided his home with twelve armed officers. Kubby and his wife were then prosecuted for growing and possessing the marijuana, Proposition 215 notwithstanding. Held in a cold prison cell for three days after his arrest, Kubby became ill as his blood pressure went up rapidly and he vomited frequently. His long-time physician wrote to the Superior Court warning of the potential consequences if he remained untreated, including possible death by arrhythmia, heart attack, cerebral hemorrhage, or cerebral vascular occlusion.[87]

Kubby got out of prison and survived until trial. His wife was acquitted on all charges; he received a mistrial on his marijuana charges but was found guilty of possessing a small amount of two other hallucinogens, psilocybin and peyote. He appealed, and while on appeal received permission from the court to move with his family to Canada. Once in Canada, the terms of his appeal were changed and he was classified as a "fugitive." After an unsuccessful five-year battle in the Canadian legal system, he returned to California in January 2006 and was immediately arrested, removed by police from the Alaska Airlines jet he had flown in on, and taken to prison to serve out his sentence. In prison, he was allowed to take Marinol, which mitigated his symptoms to an extent but did not stop him from experiencing constant nausea, severe pain, high blood pressure, and blood in his urine. Fortunately, he was released for good behavior in less than two months. In 2008—when patients' right to be free from state-level prosecution under Proposition 215 was beyond any legal doubt—a California judge dismissed all the charges against Kubby and he no longer has any criminal record.

Kubby has been active in libertarian politics. He ran for California governor as a Libertarian in 1998 (shortly before his arrest), and sought the Libertarian Party's presidential nomination in 2008 with the backing of party founder David Nolan. In addition to his all-around libertarian activism, he remains a leader of the medical marijuana movement.

Fighting the Feds

Because federal drug laws remain a threat to California users—the Obama Administration could resume raids at any time—libertarians have taken the fight to the federal government, including the U.S. Supreme Court.

In 2004, libertarian law professor Randy Barnett represented two California medical marijuana patients before the federal courts and ultimately the United States Supreme Court in *Gonzales v. Raich*.[88] His clients were Diane Monson, a businesswoman whose severe back spasms and pain were only relieved by marijuana; and Angel Raich, who suffers from various illnesses that require her to use medical marijuana to keep food down and survive. Monson grew her own marijuana to treat herself, and Raich received her marijuana for free from two caregivers.[89]

Barnett and two other lawyers sued the federal government on behalf of Monson and Raich. They argued that the federal government lacked authority to prosecute Monson, Raich, and others like them because Congress's power under the Commerce Clause extends only (at best) to regulation of interstate commercial activity, and growing and using marijuana within the state of California is neither interstate nor commercial in nature. They also argued that the law violated Fifth Amendment Due Process rights.

The U.S. District Court for the Northern District of California rejected these arguments, but the U.S. Court of Appeals for the Ninth Circuit agreed with the Commerce Clause argument. The matter then went before the U.S. Supreme Court, where Barnett and the marijuana users lost, 6 to 3. One might have expected the court's liberal members to side with libertarians on this issue, just as many liberals supported Proposition 215. Instead, however, the liberal members' devotion to federal power over the states trumped any compassionate concerns, and each of them sided with the government. Justice Antonin Scalia, who in the past had taken a relatively narrow view of Congress's Commerce Clause power, sided with the majority as well, on the ground that Congress should be allowed to decide for itself what means are necessary and proper to fight its interstate war on drugs, even if that includes some activities that are in themselves purely intrastate. That left Chief Justice William Rehnquist, Justice Sandra Day O'Connor, and Justice Clarence Thomas to dissent. Writing separately, Justice Thomas expressed the view of many libertarians: "If Congress can regulate this under the Commerce Clause, then it can regulate virtually anything—and the Federal Government is no longer one of limited and enumerated powers."

After the Supreme Court's decision, the case went back to the Ninth Circuit for consideration of the Due Process claim, which the court had passed over in its previous decision. The Ninth Circuit then rejected the argument because, it held, the right to smoke medical marijuana has not been recognized as a "fundamental right" worthy of constitutional protection. Libertarians, of course, would consider ownership of one's body and the right to do what is necessary to preserve one's life by any peaceful means necessary to be "fundamental."

Raich maintained the status quo. California will not prosecute marijuana users, but the federal government could resume doing so at any time. As recently as June 2009, the feds sentenced medical marijuana dispensary owner Charlie Lynch to prison for a year and a day simply for operating his business, which is lawful under California law.[90] That is why some libertarians and their allies on this issue are seeking to change federal law rather than count on federal prosecutors to exercise their discretion appropriately.

As of this writing, legislation is pending in Congress—introduced by liberal Democrat Barney Frank and co-sponsored by Ron Paul and Dana Rohrabacher, a California Republican who was formerly a radical libertarian—to decriminalize possession of up to 3.5 ounces of marijuana and non-profit transfer of marijuana up to 1.0 ounces, for any use, medical or otherwise. Frank,

Paul, and Rohrabacher also co-sponsored another bill that would move marijuana from Schedule I to Schedule II, allowing doctors to prescribe it for medical use. The legislation seems unlikely to pass, as we will discuss below, but at least it puts the issue before the public and adds to its perceived legitimacy as an alternative.

FIGHTING THE PROPAGANDA

Another means by which libertarians have fought the drug war is by exposing the dishonesty and exaggerations of government anti-drug propaganda. We have done so to some extent in this chapter, simply by quoting the government's propaganda against marijuana, which, like the movie *Reefer Madness*, is self-refuting and comical to anyone who has the slightest familiarity with the plant's actual effects.

Libertarian journalist Jacob Sullum, a senior editor at *Reason* magazine, has gone further in his book, *Saying Yes: In Defense of Drug Use*. Sullum attacks "voodoo pharmacology," the idea that certain substances make a person go crazy or literally lose control of themselves and commit terrible acts or become desperate addicts. Of course, voodoo pharmacology is precisely what Anslinger invoked in seeking marijuana prohibition, and propaganda today still insists that drugs such as cocaine and Ecstacy can have these effects. Sullum points out that while recreational drugs occasionally have negative effects, they do not "make" people do terrible things and usually do not turn people into instant addicts.

Sullum also notes that alcohol, which has virtually universal acceptance among politicians and everyone else outside of certain religious groups, would seem at least as bad if described in the manner we describe other recreational drugs. After all, it is a "toxin that causes dizziness, headache, vomiting, and blackouts; impairs speech, judgment, coordination, cognition, and memory; and depresses respiration, which can lead to death after a single drinking session."[91] The double standard makes little sense, and Sullum offers ample evidence that there are many casual users of illegal drugs ranging from marijuana to heroin who manage to live normal lives and not become addicts, just as there are many casual drinkers whose lives have not been ruined by "demon rum." A recent book, *Marijuana Is Safer* (in the "Further Reading" below), also emphasizes how much safer marijuana is in every respect than alcohol.

Here of course we run into the danger of conflating libertarianism and libertinism, and of making it sound as though libertarians actually advocate recreational drug use rather than the mere elimination of drug prohibition. But the point for libertarians is not whether a person should or should not take drugs; the point is that drugs, whatever their harms or benefits otherwise, do not in fact turn people into violent zombies. That means that no government policies premised on such supposed effects are justified, even if one assumes (contrary to libertarianism) that such effects would justify drug prohibition. It means that it makes sense to treat these drugs at least as liberally as we treat already-legal drugs such as alcohol, and let individuals choose whether to use them, for what purpose, and in what quantities.

VICTORY IN SIGHT?

Although the drug war has only escalated over the decades, there is a slim possibility that the tide will turn in favor of liberty in the relatively near future.

Paul Armentano, a libertarian who is the deputy director for the National Organization for the Reform of Marijuana Laws (NORML), says that he sees three factors coming together that are leading more people to question the drug war.[92]

One is the depressed economy, as people see the expense of the drug war, but they do not necessarily perceive any benefits. Ethan A. Nadelmann of the Drug Policy Network expressed a similar idea in a December 2008 *Wall Street Journal* op-ed, in which he stated that "there's nothing like a depression . . . to make taxpayers question the price of their prejudices. That's what ultimately hastened [alcohol] prohibition's repeal, and it's why we're sure to see a more vigorous debate than ever before about ending marijuana prohibition, rolling back other drug war excesses, and even contemplating far-reaching alternatives to drug prohibition."[93] Some California legislators have recently considered marijuana legalization, if only as a source of tax revenue to help mitigate the state government's budget crisis.[94]

Another factor Armentano identifies is the violence along the Mexican border. People notice that similar violence does not arise over, say, the alcohol trade, and some people notice that it is the *illegality*, not anything inherent in the product, that gives rise to the violence.

A final factor is Americans' knowledge that drugs, especially marijuana, are not nearly as dangerous as government propaganda would have them believe. The government's own survey figures show that 40.4 percent of Americans admit to using marijuana, and about half of all Americans under 50 have done so.[95] Undoubtedly, many of the rest have observed others using marijuana and know that the drug tends to make a person *less* of a threat to others, not more of one, and is not especially addictive.

Poll numbers on marijuana legalization also increasingly give cause for encouragement. A 2009 Zogby poll commissioned by NORML found that 44 percent of Americans agreed that marijuana should be "taxed and legally regulated like alcohol and cigarettes," and a majority, 58 percent, of respondents on the west coast agreed with the same statement.[96] Another 2009 Zogby poll found that 52 percent of adults agreed that it "makes sense to tax and regulate" marijuana.[97] A 2009 CBS/*New York Times* poll reached a similar result, finding that 41 percent of Americans support legalizing marijuana—up from just 27 percent in a 1979 poll.[98] Other polls have found substantial majorities of Americans agreeing that people should be allowed to use medical marijuana under some circumstances.[99]

Even the mainstream media—which in the past has been happy to help fuel anti-drug hysteria—seems to be getting more sympathetic to relaxed drug laws. CNN, *Time*, and the *New York Times* have all run pieces respectfully recognizing legalization or at least liberalization as an alternative. Virginia Senator Jim Webb published an article in *Parade* magazine calling for an end to draconian prison sentences for non-violent offenders—that is, drug offenders—though he did call for increased fines.[100] A 2009 editorial in *The Economist* says of the drug war that "[b]y any sensible measure, this 100-year struggle has been illiberal, murderous, and pointless."[101] The *Wall Street Journal* published Ethan Nadelmann's op-ed, "Let's End Drug Prohibition" in late 2008, and in 2009 Arianna Huffington, editor of the popular liberal *Huffington Post* website, criticized the Obama Administration for not seeking substantial reform of drug laws and called for "a full-scale war on the war on drugs."[102] Shortly after Barack Obama's election, *Esquire* approvingly reported that the new president might push for substantial drug reform or even marijuana legalization in a second term.[103] (Obama's words and actions in office refute this, however; his "drug czar" Gil Kerlikowske has stated that, with respect to marijuana, "'legalization' is not in the president's vocabulary.")[104]

Despite all the factors showing increasing public skepticism of the war on drugs and support for marijuana legalization, Armentano and other long-time anti-prohibitionists remain skeptical that libertarians will see much progress anytime soon. The law-enforcement lobby, which includes the prison industry lobby, is strong and can be counted on to oppose any measures that loosen drug laws at all. According to Armentano, politicians who see the poll numbers may privately admit that decriminalization makes sense and that many people support it—but, for reasons unknown, they do not believe the people in *their* district support it. And many liberals who theoretically support relaxed drug laws do not actually want Democrats in office to expend political capital fighting for this cause because they place a higher priority on issues such as socialized medicine, "climate change," or winning the next election.

That means that if the issue is going to stay alive and gain ground, it will be up to libertarians to keep leading the fight against government lies and violence and in support of individual rights and personal liberty.

NOTES

1. Harry Browne, "The Drug Crisis," *LewRockwell.com*, February 3, 2005, http://www.lewrockwell.com/browne/browne32.html.

2. "Before Prohibition: Images from the Preprohibition Era When Many Psychotropic Substances Were Legally Available in America and Europe," *University at Buffalo Department of Psychology Addiction Research Unit*, 2001, http://wings.buffalo.edu/aru/preprohibition.htm.

3. Mike Gray, *Drug Crazy: How We Got Into This Mess & How We Can Get Out* (New York: Random House, 1998), 43.

4. Ryan Grim, *This Is Your Country On Drugs: The Secret History of Getting High in America* (Hoboken, NJ: John Wiley & Sons, 2009), 31.

5. David F. Musto, "Opium, Cocaine, and Marijuana in American History," *Scientific American* (July 1991): 20–27, http://www.drugtext.org/library/articles/musto01.htm. You can see a color photo of the kit at http://cocaine.org/parkedavis-works.htm.

6. "Before Prohibition."

7. Ibid.

8. Ibid.

9. Ibid.

10. Ibid.

11. Ibid.

12. Musto, "Opium, Cocaine, and Marijuana."

13. Mark Thornton, *The Economics of Prohibition* (Salt Lake City: University of Utah Press, 1991), 57.

14. Ibid., 61.

15. Ibid., 57.

16. James P. Gray, *Why Our Drug Laws Have Failed and What We Can Do About It* (Philadelphia: Temple University Press, 2001), 21. Some have questioned the extent to which the Civil War contributed to widespread opium addiction. See Grim, *This Is Your Country*, 26.

17. Thornton, *The Economics of Prohibition*, 61.

18. Grim, *This Is Your Country*, 28–29.

19. Ibid., 37.

20. Musto, "Opium, Cocaine, and Marijuana."

21. Thornton, *The Economics of Prohibition*, 60.

22. Mike Gray, *Drug Crazy*, 43.

23. Ethan A. Nadelmann, "Should We Legalize Drugs? History Answers," *American Heritage Magazine* 44 (February/March 1993): 42–48, http://www.americanheritage.com/articles/magazine/ah/1993/1/1993_1_41_print.shtml.

24. Thornton, *The Economics of Prohibition*, 62; see also Mike Gray, *Drug Crazy*, 41–50.

25. Mike Gray, *Drug Crazy*, 47.

26. Thornton, *The Economics of Prohibition*, 60.

27. Mike Gray, *Drug Crazy*, 46.

28. Ibid., 46; Thornton, *The Economics of Prohibition*, 60.

29. Thornton, *The Economics of Prohibition*, 59–61; Grim, *This Is Your Country*, 41.

30. Grim, *This Is Your Country*, 42–43.

31. Thornton, *The Economics of Prohibition*, 64.

32. "History of Federal Regulation: 1902–Present," *FDAReview.org*, http://www .fdareview.org/history.shtml.

33. Grim, *This Is Your Country*, 43.

34. Mike Gray, *Drug Crazy*, 73.

35. Thornton, *The Economics of Prohibition*, 66.

36. Ibid.

37. Mike Gray, *Drug Crazy*, 77.

38. Thornton, *The Economics of Prohibition*, 65.

39. M.W. Childs, "A Drug Menace at the University of Kansas—How a Number of Students Became Addicts of the Strangely Intoxicating Marijuana Weed," *St. Louis Post-Dispatch* (Sunday Magazine) (April 8, 1934): 272–73, quoted in James P. Gray, *Why Our Drug Laws Have Failed*, 24 n.17.

40. Harry Anslinger, "Marijuana: Assassin of Youth," *American Magazine* (July 1937): 150, quoted in James P. Gray, *Why Our Drug Laws Have Failed*, 24.

41. Grim, *This Is Your Country*, 45.

42. Thornton, *The Economics of Prohibition*, 66.

43. Rudolph J. Gerber, *Legalizing Marijuana. Drug Policy Reform and Prohibition Politics* (Westport, CT: Praeger, 2004), 9.

44. Grim, *This Is Your Country*, 45.

45. Thornton, *The Economics of Prohibition*, 66.

46. Charles H. Whitebread II and Richard J. Bonnie, "The Forbidden Fruit and the Tree of Knowledge: An Inquiry into the Legal History of American Marijuana Prohibition," *Virginia Law Review*, 56 (1970): 971, 1053.

47. U.S. House of Representatives, *Additional Statement of H. J. Anslinger, Commissioner of Narcotics*, April 27, 1938, http://www.druglibrary.org/schaffer/hemp/taxact/ marihuanalarmingmenace.htm.

48. Mike Gray, *Drug Crazy*, 79; Whitebread and Bonnie, "The Forbidden Fruit," 1056–57.

49. Whitebread and Bonnie, "The Forbidden Fruit," 1058.

50. Mike Gray, *Drug Crazy*, 81.

51. Lynn Zimmer and John P. Morgan, *Marijuana Myths, Marijuana Facts* (New York: Lindesmith Center, 1997), 33–38.

52. Whitebread and Bonnie "The Forbidden Fruit."

53. Dan Baum, *Smoke and Mirrors: The War on Drugs and the Politics of Failure* (Boston: Little, Brown, and Company, 1996), 13–15.

54. Mike Gray, *Drug Crazy*, 95.

55. Ibid.

56. Gerber, *Legalizing Marijuana*, 17–26.

57. Mike Gray, *Drug Crazy*, 98.

58. Gerber, *Legalizing Marijuana*, 28.

59. Mike Gray, *Drug Crazy*, 98.

60. Gerber, *Legalizing Marijuana*, 30.

61. Mike Gray, *Drug Crazy*, 100.

62. Gerber, *Legalizing Marijuana*, 41.

63. Leonard W. Levy, *License to Steal: The Forfeiture of Property* (Chapel Hill, NC: University of North Carolina Press, 1995), 127.

64. Jeffrey A. Miron, "The Budgetary Implications of Drug Prohibition," December 2008, http://leap.cc/dia/miron-economic-report.pdf.

65. Adam Liptak, "U.S. Prison Population Dwarfs That of Other Nations," *New York Times*, April 23, 2008, http://www.nytimes.com/2008/04/23/world/americas/23iht-23prison.12253738.html?_r=1&pagewanted=print.

66. James Vinici, "US Has the Most Prisoners in the World," *CommonDreams.org*, December 6, 2006, http://www.commondreams.org/headlines06/1209-01.htm.

67. Paul Armentano, "Who's Getting Rich Off Prohibition? Just Look Who Opposes CA's Prop. 5," *Alternet.org*, November 1, 2008, http://www.alternet.org/blogs/rights/105685/.

68. This paragraph's summary is based on a list in Diane Cecilia Weber, *Warrior Cops: The Ominous Growth of Paramilitarism in American Police Departments*, Cato Institute Briefing Papers No. 50, August 26, 1999, 5, http://www.cato.org/pubs/briefs/bp50.pdf.

69. Radley Balko, *Overkill: The Rise of Paramilitary Police Raids in America* (Washington, DC: Cato Institute, 2006), 8, http://www.cato.org/pubs/wtpapers/balko_whitepaper_2006.pdf.

70. Weber, *Warrior Cops*.

71. Balko, *Overkill*, 9.

72. Ibid.

73. http://freedominourtime.blogspot.com/.

74. Ted Galen Carpenter, *Bad Neighbor Policy* (New York: Palgrave Macmillan, 2003), 124–34.

75. Ted Galen Carpenter, *Troubled Neighbor: Mexico's Drug Violence Poses a Threat to the United States*, Cato Institute Police Analysis No. 631, February 2, 2009, http://www.cato.org/pub_display.php?pub_id=9932.

76. Ibid., 3.

77. Ibid.

78. Thomas Szasz, "Benjamin Rush and 'Medical Marijuana,'" *The Freeman* (March 2005): 22–23, http://www.fee.org/pdf/the-freeman/szasz0305.pdf.

79. Sheldon Richman, "Medical Marijuana is Not a Libertarian Cause," *Freedom Daily*, June 15, 2005, http://www.fff.org/freedom/fd0503b.asp.

80. Zimmer and Morgan, *Marijuana Myths*, 17.

81. Paul Armentano, "Unlocking a Cure for Cancer—With Pot," *LewRockwell.com*, August 17, 2004, http://www.lewrockwell.com/orig5/armentano-p1.html.

82. Gerber, *Legalizing Marijuana*, 14; 21 U.S.C. Sec. 812(b)(1).

83. The facts up to this point in this paragraph are derived from Zimmer and Morgan, *Marijuana Myths*, 18–19.

84. Gerber, *Legalizing Marijuana*, 82.

85. William F. Buckley, Jr., "Peter McWilliams, R.I.P.," *Uexpress.com*, June 20, 2000, http://www.uexpress.com/ontheright/index.html?uc_full_date=20000620.

86. See Paul Armentano, "Unlocking a Cure for Cancer—With Pot," *LewRockwell*
.com, August 17, 2004, http://www.lewrockwell.com/orig5/armentano-p1.html.

87. Brian Doherty, "The Crimes of Pot Justice," *Reason.com*, February 6, 2006,
http://www.reason.com/news/printer/34165.html.

88. *Gonzales v. Raich*, 545 U.S. 1 (2005).

89. Randy E. Barnett, "The Presumption of Liberty and the Public Interest: Medical
Marijuana and Fundamental Rights," *Washington University Journal of Law and Public Policy*
22 (2006): 33, http://law.wustl.edu/Journal/22/p29Barnett.pdf.

90. "New at Reason.tv: 'This Is an Injustice and I Think Everyone Has Gotten the
Message'—Is Charlie Lynch's Year-and-a-Day Sentence the End of Medical Marijuana
Prosecution?" *Reason.com*, June 12, 2009, http://www.reason.com/blog/printer/134090.html.

91. Jacob Sullum, *Saying Yes: In Defense of Drug Use* (New York: Jeremy P. Tarcher/
Putnam, 2003), 54.

92. All items referencing Mr. Armentano in this section are derived from an interview the author conducted with him on June 30, 2009.

93. Ethan A. Nadelmann, "Let's End Drug Prohibition," *Wall Street Journal*, December
5, 2008, http://online.wsj.com/article/SB122843683581681375.html.

94. Alison Stateman, "Can Marijuana Help Rescue California's Economy?" *Time*,
March 13, 2009, http://www.time.com/time/nation/article/0,8599,1884956,00.html.

95. These figures can be found at the Substance Abuse & Mental Health Data
Archive, http://www.icpsr.umich.edu/quicktables/quicksetoptions.do?reportKey=23782-
0001_du%3A7. The relevant results are summarized by Russ Belville, "Who Are You?
US Government Statistics on Adult Marijuana Users," *NORML's Daily Audio Stash*,
April 13, 2009, http://stash.norml.org/who-are-you-us-government-statistics-on-adult-
marijuana-users/.

96. "Zogby Poll: Nearly Six Out of Ten West Coast Voters Support Taxing and
Regulating Marijuana Like Alcohol," *NORML.org*, February 19, 2009, http://norml.org/
index.cfm?Group_ID=7806.

97. Ryan Grim, "Majority of Americans Want Pot Legalized: Zogby Poll," *The Huffington Post*, May 6, 2009, http://www.huffingtonpost.com/2009/05/06/majority-of-americans-
wan_n_198196.html.

98. "Zogby Poll."

99. "Favorable Medical Marijuana Polls," *NORML.org*, http://norml.org/index
.cfm?Group_ID=3392.

100. Jim Webb, "Why We Must Fix Our Prisons," *Parade*, March 29, 2009, http://
www.parade.com/news/2009/03/why-we-must-fix-our-prisons.html.

101. "How to Stop the Drug Wars," *The Economist*, March 5, 2009, http://www
.economist.com/PrinterFriendly.cfm?story_id=13237193.

102. Arianna Huffington, "Ending the War on Drugs: The Moment is Now," *Huffington Post*, May 14, 2009, http://www.huffingtonpost.com/arianna-huffington/ending-
the-war-on-drugs-t_b_203768.html.

103. John H. Richardson, "Obama on Marijuana Legalization," *Esquire.com*, December
23, 2008, http://www.esquire.com/the-side/richardson-report/obama-marijuana-legalization-
122308.

104. Marc Benjamin, "Drug Czar: Feds Won't Support Legalized Pot," *The Fresno Bee*, July 22, 2009, http://www.fresnobee.com/local/story/1553061.html.

FURTHER READING

Carpenter, Ted Galen. *Bad Neighbor Policy: Washington's Futile War on Drugs in Latin America*. New York: Palgrave Macmillan, 2003. Libertarian foreign policy scholar Carpenter shows the effects and futility of the drug war in Latin America.

Fox, Steve, Paul Armentano, and Mason Tvert. *Marijuana Is Safer: So Why Are We Driving People to Drink?* White River Junction, VT: Chelsea Green Publishing, 2009. This book shows how marijuana is much less dangerous than alcohol and how its legalization would make us all safer.

Gray, Mike. *Drug Crazy: How We Got Into This Mess & How We Can Get Out*. New York: Random House, 1998. Gray provides a detailed, compelling history of the drug war and its consequences.

Sullum, Jacob. *Saying Yes: In Defense of Drug Use*. New York: Jeremy P. Tarcher/Putnam, 2003. Sullum, a libertarian journalist, challenges the government's propaganda on the dangers of illegal drugs.

Thornton, Mark. *The Economics of Prohibition*. Salt Lake City: University of Utah Press, 1991. Austro-libertarian economist Thornton details the history and consequences of alcohol and drug prohibition and proposes a free-market solution. Available for free online at http://mises.org/books/prohibition.pdf.

5

The Fight for Health Freedom

Despite all their differences, here is something guaranteed to bring conservatives and libertarians together: a Democrat president who is threatening a government takeover of the healthcare industry. In 2009, many libertarians were delighted to see thousands of Americans show up at "town hall" meetings held by their senators and representatives to protest so-called healthcare reform.

But while they share conservatives' desire to stop Democrats' plans; libertarians do not defend the status quo. Conservatives like to call it "the greatest healthcare system in the world," but libertarians see problems in the current U.S. system—problems that not only make the cost of care much higher than it needs to be, but also cause thousands of unnecessary deaths each year. This is because the current healthcare system is not a free-market system at all. It is a system that has been severely distorted by government, and that libertarians say can only be fixed by repealing existing government interventions, not by adding new ones.

DEREGULATE INSURANCE

Make no mistake: Libertarians agree that liberals identify a real problem when they lament the "rising cost of health care." But to fix this problem, libertarians suggest looking at *why* healthcare became so expensive and addressing that root cause, rather than just layering more government on top of our current system.

A Distorted Market

For example, instead of calling for more regulation or government funding with respect to insurance, one might first ask why insurance companies play such a central role in our healthcare system. It was not always so. For most of America's history, people simply paid doctors directly for the services they used, and those services did not cost all that much. Some people still alive can recall the days of the two-dollar house call. This leads to another question: Why does the cost of care keep going up? Contrary to what some critics might suggest, it is not because of capitalism, but because of government.

Because of government, insurance began playing a major role in American healthcare during World War II. During the war, the federal government limited the amount of money businesses could pay their employees—instead of a minimum wage, there were *maximum* wages. Employers still needed to compete to attract the best employees, and they could do this by offering health benefits, which did not count as wages. After the war, employer-provided health insurance continued because the federal government exempted employer-provided health benefits from income taxation, making it desirable for workers.

Libertarians favor tax breaks, of course, but as we saw in Chapter 3 with tax breaks for people paying mortgages, selective tax breaks (rather than across-the-board tax cuts) can distort the market. In the healthcare market, people were driven to use insurance rather than pay for healthcare directly as they mostly otherwise would have. Today, thanks to these policies (and programs such as Medicare and Medicaid), third parties—either insurance companies or the government—pay for almost all healthcare in America. For every dollar spent on healthcare in the United States, either the government or insurance companies pays 86 cents.[1]

What is wrong with that? For one thing, it makes us spend more on healthcare than we would if the money came directly from our own pockets. To illustrate this point, economist Arnold Kling suggests we imagine what would happen if we had "eating insurance," which let us pass on all of our restaurant bills to an insurance company for payment.[2] If someone else were footing all or most of the bill, would we eat at McDonald's or Morton's Steakhouse? Would we eat just enough to satisfy our hunger, or would we eat as much as we could? For most people, to ask the question is to answer it—when someone else is paying, we consume more.

In the healthcare context, having an insurance company cover costs prompts people to receive non-essential care and procedures they would not get if they were spending their own money. That is, they spend beyond what the services are really worth to them. Michael F. Cannon and Michael D. Tanner explain: "Since patients pay an average of only 14 cents for each dollar of care, they tend to demand medical care that costs $1,000 even if it only provides $140 of value."[3] Also, when people spend their own money, they tend to be cost-conscious—they shop around, which forces sellers to compete on price. With insurance companies footing the bill, people have no incentive to do this—their co-payment (if any) is probably the same in any event, so why bother? By causing people to demand more services and lose any concern for cost, our insurance-based system drives prices far higher than they would otherwise be. For procedures that insurance typically does not cover, such as cosmetic surgery, there is price competition, and we do not see this problem. For example, people shop for LASIK eye surgery, which insurance typically doesn't cover, and the cost of that *fell* from about $2,100 per eye in 1996 to about $1,600 in 2005, while the quality of the service improved.[4]

To control the rising costs that result from our insurance-based system, many employers started putting their employees in "managed care" organizations such as health maintenance organizations (HMOs). Under managed care, bureaucrats decide where people may go for care and what services will be covered. The managed-care organization keeps its costs down by attempting to mimic, to some extent, what patients would do if they were spending their own money. People who are covered by such a plan become frustrated because it seems like someone else is making decisions about their health. Some of these people then come to believe that government needs to "reform" healthcare, without understanding how government caused their problem in the first place.

The libertarian solution to all of this is to take away the special tax-exempt status for employer-provided health benefits. (And, libertarians would add, cut taxes at the same time, so workers' tax burden does not increase.) This would likely prompt people to buy relatively inexpensive "catastrophic" insurance to cover emergencies and to just pay outright for more routine services. The result would be more informed healthcare consumers and much lower prices.

Insurance, True and False

There is another major factor—created by the government—that contributes to rising insurance costs in America: to a large extent, health insurance as we know it is not really insurance.

With true insurance, people who face approximately the same risk of suffering some particular harm get together and pool their risk, so that when the harm inevitably befalls some members of the group, those people will be compensated. It is important that everyone in the group face approximately the same level of risk—otherwise, high-risk people will benefit at the expense of low-risk people. For example, if Nevadans were to pool their risk of suffering a flood with Louisianans, everyone would pay the same premium, but the Nevadans would receive almost no payouts. In other words, the Nevadans would systematically subsidize the Louisianans. No Nevadans in their right minds would want to do this (except as an act of charity), so they do not pool their risk in this way.[5]

With health insurance, the government forces people with very different levels of risk into the same pool by prohibiting insurers from charging people who face higher risks more and people who face lower risks less. In states that mandate "community rating," insurers must put *everyone* in a particular geographical area in a single pool and charge them all the same rate, regardless of their age or medical condition. As a result, people who are at low risk are forced to subsidize those who are at high risk. Of course, if you subsidize something, basic economics predicts that you will get more of it. And because this system subsidizes people who engage in unhealthy risk behaviors, it *encourages* those behaviors, which means that more people engage in them, and everyone's premiums go up. (This suggests one reason, among many, why America's "obesity epidemic" is mostly caused by government, not fast-food purveyors.)[6]

The law also forces insurance companies to cover things that are not really "risks" at all. For example, with the rare exception of rape, it is completely under a woman's control whether she will take actions that may cause her to become pregnant. Indeed, becoming pregnant is something many people do deliberately, so it is not an insurable "risk" at all. Yet under federal law, employer-provided insurance must cover pregnancy-related expenses. As a result, people who do not face the "risk" of pregnancy—because they are incapable of becoming pregnant or choose not to do things that could get them pregnant—are forced to subsidize people who have children.

The libertarian way out of this problem is true insurance deregulation. Economist Hans-Hermann Hoppe explains:

> To deregulate the industry means to restore it to unrestricted freedom of contract: to allow a health insurer to offer any contract whatsoever, to include or exclude any risk, and to discriminate among any groups of individuals. Uninsurable risks would lose coverage, the variety of insurance policies for the remaining coverage would increase, and price differentials would reflect genuine insurance risks. On average, prices would drastically fall. And the reform would restore individual responsibility in health care.[7]

Who Benefits?

So libertarians favor insurance deregulation. The insurance companies, however, aren't clamoring to be deregulated in this way. Instead, they (and the pharmaceutical companies) strongly supported the healthcare scheme proposed by Democrats in 2009. Why? Because they stood to profit from it. In the absence of any legal requirement that they do so, many young people choose not buy health insurance; they believe (not unreasonably) that they do not need it because they are unlikely to get sick. The Democrats' health plan, however, would force these people to have insurance—which would mean more business for the insurance companies. Libertarian journalist John Stossel has observed that Democrats' claims that people who protest healthcare reform are tools of "corporate interests" don't ring true because "big business supports government control."[8]

Ignorant critics sometimes accuse libertarians of wanting to let big businesses run everything, but big business's support for so-called healthcare reform gives just one more example of why that is not so. As we will see, that is especially true in the drug business, where powerful interests like the big-government status quo.

END THE FDA

As conservatives worry about "death panels" deciding who lives and who dies under Democrats' healthcare plans, they fail to notice that the government already operates a "death panel"—namely, the Food and Drug Administration (FDA), which kills tens of thousands of people every year by denying them the freedom to choose potentially life-saving treatments.[9] If libertarians could enact just one healthcare reform, it would almost certainly be to abolish the FDA.

Some people will find the idea that the FDA "kills people" shocking. They reasonably assume that the FDA exists to protect consumers from unscrupulous pharmaceutical companies that would otherwise put harmful products on the market. Libertarians see thing differently: They see the FDA mostly *benefiting* pharmaceutical companies and harming consumers by restricting their freedom to pursue treatments that could save their lives. Libertarians also see what the FDA does—telling people what medicines they may and may not take—as a gross violation of the fundamental right to make decisions about one's own body and health.

History

There was not always an FDA in the United States, and many countries today lack an equivalent to the FDA. In the pre-FDA days, drug makers did not regularly poison their customers or cause other serious widespread harm. A few tragic isolated incidents, however, allowed government to ratchet up its power over medicine and, by extension, people's bodies and lives.

In 1938, a product called Sulfanilamide Elixir poisoned 107 people because its maker had not conducted sufficient testing. If testing had been done, the maker would have discovered that one of the ingredients, diethylene glycol (otherwise known as antifreeze), was deadly because it ruined people's kidneys. Congress responded quickly, passing the 1938 Food, Drug, and Cosmetic Act. This required manufacturers to submit an application to the FDA before putting a drug on the market. The application had to include, for example, the product's ingredients and the results of safety testing.

Even after the 1938 Act, almost all drugs were available "over the counter" unless the manufacturer said otherwise; with few exceptions, governments still mostly respected people's right to choose what medicines to buy and take. In fact, in passing the 1938 Act, a House committee mentioned that the law was "not intended to restrict in any way the availability of drugs for self medication."[10] That changed in 1951, when Congress established the divide between prescription and non-prescription drugs that exists to this day, and which gives doctors unprecedented power over their patients' lives and freedom.

In 1962, another drug, thalidomide, caused severe birth defects after pregnant women in Europe took it for morning sickness. Public concern over this gave Congress an opportunity to pass legislation it was already considering: the 1962 Kefauver-Harris Amendments to the earlier Act. These added, among other things, a requirement that drug makers show that proposed drugs are not only safe, but also *effective*. (Never mind that thalidomide, which prompted the legislation's passage, *was* effective.) A 1976 law added similar rules for medical devices. Other laws and regulations have piled on additional restrictions over the years.

Effects

To most people, this sketch of FDA history may look like progress, with government taking incremental steps to make sure certain tragedies are not repeated. Libertarians, however, would argue that the FDA causes far more deaths—tens of thousands each year—than it prevents.

One way the FDA kills people is by keeping beneficial drugs off the market. Why would it do this? Because FDA bureaucrats face a strong incentive to err on the side of caution in the extreme. Suppose the FDA approves a drug that turns out to be unsafe for some people who take it. Dead bodies, deformed babies, or other graphic horror stories will be all over the TV news—and the FDA will be blamed. Now suppose the FDA decides not to approve a drug that would actually save people's lives. Who will ever know? More people will die of heart disease, cancer, or whatever the drug would have treated, but in most cases no one will trace the cause to the FDA's failure to approve this particular drug. Or, if they do, they will not be able to get much attention because the harm is too indirect to make for an exciting headline. So of course the FDA would rather make this second kind of mistake than the first—and the way to do that is to not approve drugs.

Another way the FDA kills people is by waiting a long time to approve drugs. Just as it has an incentive to err grossly on the side of caution in deciding whether to approve a drug, the FDA also has an incentive to approve a drug later rather than sooner—even if that means that sick people will suffer or die in the meantime. Former FDA official Henry Miller has described how the bureaucrats he worked with deliberately dragged their feet to avoid blame:

> With quintessentially bureaucratic logic, my supervisor refused to sign off on [a new drug] approval—even though he agreed that the data provided compelling evidence of the drug's safety and effectiveness. 'If anything goes wrong,' he remonstrated, 'think how bad it will look that we approved the drug so quickly.' Characteristically, the supervisor was more concerned with 'cover,' in the case of an unforeseen mishap, than with getting an important new product to patients who needed it.[11]

How many lives do such delays cost? It is hard to say precisely, but estimates range from 21,000 to 120,000 per decade. For example, it likely cost tens of thousands of lives when the FDA kept some beta-blocker drugs, which treat hypertension and help prevent heart attacks, off the market for years after they had been available in other countries.[12]

Yet another way the FDA kills people is by depriving consumers of information. Despite the First Amendment, the FDA has the power of prior restraint over drug makers' speech. Manufacturers cannot tell customers about the all the ways their products might improve their health or save their lives without the FDA's permission—and the FDA is very stingy with its permission. For example, when clinical studies showed that one aspirin per day could reduce the risk of a first heart attack in men by nearly 50 percent, FDA commissioner Frank Young called representatives of companies that make aspirin to his office and warned them that they must not include this information in their marketing or packaging. The likely result? Tens of thousands of deaths per year of people who would have taken aspirin if the aspirin manufacturers had been allowed to tell them about these studies.[13] How could the FDA justify this? On the ground that aspirin could increase risk for a certain type of stroke in a tiny minority of men. But those men are far outnumbered by those who would benefit.[14] Again, the FDA bureaucrats erred on the side of caution—that is, they erred on the side of protecting *themselves*.

The process of getting a drug approved by the FDA is extremely expensive, and this too hurts people in a way that no one ever sees. From 1987 to 2005, the cost of bringing a drug to market doubled, putting the current figure at over $800 million and rising.[15] There are many drugs that would be profitable to create and bring to market if the makers did not have to spend the extra hundreds of millions of dollars to jump through the FDA's hoops. But because of these added costs, it is not worthwhile for companies to pursue these projects—and numerous potentially beneficial products are never created at all.

How many deaths does the FDA cause in total? Economist Daniel Klein estimates that the FDA kills at least 50,000 people each year.[16] And it is safe to say that the number of lives the FDA takes is far greater than the number of lives that it saves. After all, before the FDA regulated the drug market as it does now, there were some isolated tragedies, but not many mass deaths. Even the infamous Sulfanilamide Elixir incident killed just 107 people. Libertarians would not downplay the loss of those lives—but they would point out that this number is almost nothing compared to the numbers who die at the FDA's hands.

One reason why FDA regulation does not save all that many lives is because drug sellers have strong incentives not to harm or kill their customers even in the absence of regulation. Manufacturers that mislabel drugs or sell unsafe products will face lawsuits and large jury verdicts. In addition, killing customers is bad for business. And in the absence of regulation, independent agencies and publications such as *Consumer Reports* (or *Good Housekeeping* or a medical equivalent of Underwriters Laboratories) could inform people about the safety and effectiveness of various drugs, as they do even now. In the age of the Internet, word about problems with drugs would be likely to get out fast.

Who Benefits?

If the system is so harmful, why does it exist? Who benefits from it and wants to keep it alive? Many well-meaning people support it because they sincerely believe that the FDA is necessary to protect people from predatory big businesses. In fact, though, the FDA is itself a tool of big business—and the pharmaceutical companies benefit from it as much as anyone. They may clash with the FDA over particular issues, but "Big Pharma" would not want the FDA to just go away; the major drug companies benefit too much from the system to let it go. Because the cost of seeking FDA approval is so high, mostly only existing big companies can afford to go through it. Start-up competitors cannot. So as long as the FDA serves as a gatekeeper in this way, the dominant players in the industry are unlikely to face a major challenge from outsiders—and that arrangement suits them just fine.

There is also the "revolving door" problem. FDA officials want high-paying private-sector jobs after they leave government. The obvious industry in which they would get such jobs is the pharmaceutical industry—so FDA officials have a strong incentive to not upset the drug companies too much. As a result, the system serves the needs of drug companies more than it serves the needs of consumers.

Who Decides?

For libertarians, opposing the FDA is not just about adding up the number of lives a policy saves or kills. It is fundamentally a question of liberty: Who should make decisions about what a person can do to protect his or her health, the government or the individual?

The FDA presumes to decide on behalf of *everyone* whether a drug is safe or effective. But what does it mean to say that a drug is "safe" or "effective"? No drug is truly "safe." All drugs can have adverse side effects in some people. About 106,000 people die each year from adverse reactions to legal prescription drugs, which makes legal prescription drugs one of the leading causes of death in the United States.[17] And why should "safety" matter to a person who is terminally ill and who will die anyway if he or she cannot find a cure? As Richard Epstein has pointed out, it makes sense to take a drug that kills 90 percent of the people who take it, but cures the other 10 percent, if there is a 91 percent chance you will die if you *don't* take it.[18] Yet the FDA would never allow someone to take such an "unsafe" drug under any circumstances.

No drug is categorically "effective," either. Whether a drug will work depends on an individual's specific circumstances. In testing effectiveness, the FDA looks at whether the *average* person who takes a drug sees better results than the *average* person who takes a placebo. But why should the average matter? If a drug helps *some* people, then why shouldn't some people be allowed to take it if they want to?

To aggregate risks as the FDA does and then make one decision for everyone in the country is senseless. So is asking whether a drug is safe and effective in the abstract. The real question is whether a drug is *safe enough* and *likely enough to be effective in your case* that it is *worth taking*. And that is a judgment call. For a libertarian, it makes no moral or practical sense to give this decision to a bureaucrat in Washington instead of the person whose health and life are at stake.

The War on Supplements

The FDA does not just limit people's freedom to take ordinary drugs; it also interferes with people's ability to learn about and take natural supplements that may promote health and protect against disease.

In the 1980s and early 1990s, the FDA cracked down—hard—on providers of vitamins and natural remedies. For example, in 1992, FDA agents burst into a Kent, Washington clinic run by Jonathan Wright, M.D., brandishing rifles and yelling, "Raid! Raid! Raid!" As agents held doctors, staff, and patients at gunpoint, other agents ransacked the office, went through patient files, and made off with medical equipment and supplies of Vitamin B-12 and B-Complex. Dr. Wright's crime? He still does not know. He was never charged with anything. But the FDA's view was that doctors should not treat people with natural remedies such as vitamins, as Dr. Wright did, and apparently it decided that an armed raid would be an effective way to make that view clear. A year later, the FDA raided nearly 40 health food stores, in many cases with SWAT teams carrying assault rifles and wearing flak jackets.[19]

As it happened, many of the physicians threatened by the FDA's crackdown were libertarians. They decided to do something about the assault on their liberty by forming the American Association for Health Freedom to promote freedom for physicians and patients who want to pursue alternative methods of healing. The new group helped lead the charge for passage of the Dietary Supplement and Education Act of 1994, which required the FDA to treat natural supplements as foods, not medicines, and allowed supplement providers to make "statements of nutritional support" about their products, as long as they did not claim that their products could help treat any particular condition. It also allowed health food stores to sell books on the benefits of supplements—which the FDA had previously tried to stop them from doing, despite the First Amendment.

Despite these provisions, the 1994 Act did not put an end to the FDA's attacks on supplement providers and their free-speech rights. Durk Pearson and Sandy Shaw—libertarian scientists who specialize in health and "life extension"—have had to continue fighting this battle for more than a decade and a half. And they have had some success.

In 1994, Pearson and Shaw sued the FDA because it prohibited supplement providers from telling consumers about the possible health benefits of various products. For example, the FDA barred providers of fish-oil supplements from telling customers that coldwater fish oils with omega-3 fatty acids could reduce the risk of cardiovascular disease, even though, as of 1994, there were 174 scientific papers showing this to be true. The FDA also barred sellers from making the well-supported claim that folic acid supplements for pregnant women were a more effective source for reducing the risk of neural-tube defects in their babies than food sources of folic acid. Five years later, the U.S. Court of Appeals for the District of Columbia finally decided in favor of Pearson, Shaw, and supplement providers, holding that the FDA violated their First Amendment rights.[20] The FDA responded to this decision by ignoring it. The FDA continued to prohibit sellers from making the claims about the products—a rare occasion in American history where the executive branch has brazenly defied a federal court decision. Pearson and Shaw returned to court to get an order that the FDA comply, and got their final victory in 2001 after seven years of litigation. In terms of human health, the cost of the FDA's fight was huge. Pearson and Shaw estimate that if sellers could have informed consumers about the benefits of fish oil, half of the three hundred thousand deaths each year from sudden heart attacks would have been prevented.[21] If sellers had been allowed to advertise the benefits of folic acid supplements, thousands of babies might have been spared crippling birth defects.[22]

Pearson and Shaw have continued the fight through more First Amendment lawsuits against the FDA over other supplements. In 2009, they filed a suit to vindicate their right to promote selenium's well-documented ability to reduce the risk of various cancers and to produce anti-carcinogenic effects in the body.

While Pearson, Shaw, and others have worked on the judicial side, Ron Paul has promoted the cause in Congress by introducing bills to increase health freedom. One, the Health Freedom Act, would remove the FDA's power of prior restraint on speech; the FDA could only stop supplement providers from making a claim if it could show that the claim was false by clear and convincing evidence—putting the burden on government instead of citizens. The Health Information Protection Act would impose a similar restriction on the Federal Trade Commission (FTC). Current law allows the FTC to force advertisers to prove that their claims are true; the proposed Act would reverse that burden by preventing the FTC from taking action against a supplement provider unless it could show that the provider's claims are false by clear and convincing evidence—again, putting the burden where one would expect it to be under the Constitution: on government, not the people.

END MEDICAL LICENSING

Another way to reduce healthcare costs and increase freedom is to end licensure for medical professionals. Libertarians believe that anyone should be allowed to provide any medical service without a government-mandated license and without jumping through any other government-imposed hoops.

Probably this suggestion will cause some people to envision people being butchered by quacks in the mold of Dr. Nick Riviera from *The Simpsons* TV show, but this fear is not warranted. Without government licensing, consumers would become more informed about who they're receiving their care from. As with drugs, private agencies (and possibly medical schools or groups such as the American Medical Association) could certify a doctor's level of training and quality. Doctors would pay for this certification, but the certifying agencies would have to remain honest—if they did not, consumers would not trust their seal of approval as a sign of quality, and it would not be worth anything. Consumers could also receive information on doctors from consumer reporting services and from other patients posting their experiences online.

It is true that not every doctor would be of top quality under this system. But that is also true now. As it is, half of all doctors finished in the bottom half of their med-school class, but unless you grill your doctor about this (which almost no one does) or go to a top hospital such as the Mayo Clinic, there is little way to know if *your* doctor finished at the bottom of the class. A system of private certification would likely provide better information.

Of course, without licensing, some people would *want* a doctor with less training, or of "lower quality," if it could save them money. As Milton Friedman observed, not all consumers want or need "Cadillac" quality medical care for their every medical need; many would be happy to pay less and settle for a "Chevrolet," especially for routine matters.[23] Under the present regime, people are forced to go to medical doctors for many services that someone with less training could perform. Eliminating licensure would allow people to specialize in these simpler services and charge less for them than a medical doctor (M.D.) would.

Of course, if anyone seriously proposed to eliminate medical licensure, doctors would strongly oppose it. In doing so, they would claim that they were only concerned with the public's health and safety, and undoubtedly many of them would mean that sincerely. But, in fact, they would be primarily advancing their own selfish economic interests. Doctors profit from the current system because it keeps out competition. That is why their predecessors set up the state's licensing scheme in the first place. It is, in effect, a medical cartel, and it lets them keep the prices they charge high. (The legal cartel, of which this author is a member, works the same way.)

Probably the public will not be ready to repeal medical licensure anytime soon. The strong economic arguments in its favor are perhaps too subtle for a mass audience, and it would be easy enough for politicians and the medical lobby to conjure scary images of unlicensed doctors mangling helpless patients. But if libertarians cannot have it all now, there are intermediate steps that would help, such as allowing nurses or, better, people without any license to perform more routine procedures that do not require an M.D.'s extensive training. To the extent that licensing requirements are loosened, freedom will increase, costs will go down, and everyone—except the medical cartel—will benefit.

LEGALIZE ORGAN SALES

No discussion of the government and healthcare would be complete, from a libertarian perspective, without discussing the current shortage of organs for transplant. Libertarians point out that this shortage is the government's fault because the government has banned the sale of human organs under the 1984 National Organ Transplant Act.

How the Government's Organ Ban Kills People

Economics 101 predicts the result of a government ban on organ sales. Where the government sets an upper limit on the price of a good or service that is lower than the market price, there will be a shortage of that good or service. Americans above a certain age have had first hand experience with this phenomenon because they waited in long lines for gasoline after the government imposed price controls in the 1970s. Because of this disastrous experience, even most politicians today know better than to suggest price controls for gasoline and most other goods.

Yet we do have a price control on organs—a maximum price of zero dollars. So you can give a kidney away for free, but you cannot sell it. Because most people understandably are not willing to give away a kidney to anyone but a close friend or family member, there is a shortage, and 6,000 people die each year waiting for an organ. The average wait time to receive a kidney is five years (and rising), and more than 40 percent of the people who need a kidney may die during that period.[24]

We would not have this shortage, and most of those people would not die waiting, if organ sales were legalized. If you could pay someone for a kidney, instead of just asking them to give one away for free, more kidneys would become available—and, as with every other product on the market where buyers and sellers may freely set the price, there would be no shortage.

Many people object to freedom in organ sales, but libertarians have responses. Some people object because they think it would be unfair: they fear that poor people wouldn't be able to afford organs and rich people could. But of course organs are not unusual in this respect. Wealthy people can buy more of everything than poor people, including other things that are essential to life, such as food and medical care in general. So why should we ban sales of organs in particular because rich people can more easily afford them? Besides, it is not obvious that poor people would be deprived of transplants if there were a free market in organs. Charities would be able to raise money to buy organs for people who need them—something they cannot do now. As it stands, there is *nothing* any charity can do to help a poor person who is on the waiting list get an organ. Organ sales would give those people a chance they do not have now.

A libertarian would not advocate that the government pay for organs for the poor because libertarians do not believe that government should pay for anything. But if government did pay for organs on the market, instead of just paying for kidney patients' dialysis as it does now, this would not only save lives, it could also save taxpayers money. No one can know how much kidneys would cost on the market, but buying someone a kidney would almost certainly be cheaper than paying for years of dialysis. One study puts the likely savings to the government (and thus to taxpayers) at $270,000 per transplant.[25]

Some object that legalized organ sales would allow people to "exploit" the poor by pushing people who are desperate for money to part with their organs. This paternalistic objection assumes that the "exploited" person is not capable of deciding what is best for himself or herself. But there is no reason to believe that people would be "exploited." Fraud—false promises about benefits or risks—would still be illegal, of course, and as with any voluntary exchange, people would only sell an organ if they believed that doing so would be more beneficial to them than not doing so. This objection also downplays the tremendous potential benefit for people with low incomes to have this opportunity to make a substantial amount of extra money.

Other objections to organ sales are even less well-founded. Some people find it immoral, degrading, or otherwise distasteful for people to sell organs rather than give them away. Libertarians would say that it is fine for them to think that, but it is hardly a justification for telling people what they can and cannot do with their own bodies, or for condemning 6,000 people each year to death. Why should one person's desire not to have his or her moral sensibilities offended outweigh someone else's right to life itself? Richard Epstein suggests we look at organ sales much as we look at free speech: If you are offended by someone else exercising his or her rights, *too bad*. As he puts it, "My outrage at your sale of your organ is no reason to ban it any more than my pleasure at your organ sale is reason to compel it. Too many forms of conduct offend too many people for any legal system to respond to them all."[26] People who find organ sales offensive could refuse to participate in the organ market or, better, could give their organs away for free in protest.

LifeSharers Responds to the Crisis

As the organ shortage has become worse, people have pursued innovative ways of reducing the harm it causes. One way is to set up "paired donations" of kidneys—where one recipient who has a willing donor of the wrong blood type "trades donors" with another patient in the same situation, so each has a donor who is a match. Another way is to allow exceptionally altruistic people to make a "non-directed donation" of a kidney to any person who might need it.[27]

One libertarian has taken an innovative approach to encourage more people to donate and mitigate the shortage. David Undis, a retired insurance executive, founded an organization called LifeSharers in 2002. Anyone can join LifeSharers for free,[28] on one condition: The person must agree to be an organ donor, and must agree that, if the member dies, his or her organs will go first to any fellow LifeSharers members who need them. Then, whatever is left may go to the broader waiting list of people who need organs, whether they are LifeSharers members or not.

LifeSharers helps fight the organ shortage because it provides a "payment" for agreeing to be an organ donor: If another member dies and you are in need of one of his or her organs, you are at the head of the line to receive it. Undis emphasizes that this adds some fairness to the system—people who have expressed their willingness to be organ donors (by joining LifeSharers) get priority over people who have not. Undis's view is: Why should you be first in line to receive an organ if you are not willing to donate your own? If you would rather have your own organs burned or buried on your death, why should you have the first chance at someone else's organs when they die? As Undis sees it, it is only fair that those who are willing to give should take priority if they need to receive. (This fairness angle is not a libertarian view per se, but it is compatible with libertarianism.)

LifeSharers is admirable from the libertarian perspective because it is a purely voluntary, non-political means of fighting government-created harm. The project remains in its infancy, with about 15,000 members at this writing, but it has steadily grown. Still, LifeSharers will never fix the organ shortage by itself because the "payment" members receive is surely less than the monetary amount they could receive on the market. Plus, LifeSharers only affects donations of organs after people die, not donations of kidneys from living people. (Donations from living people are essential because kidney patients need to receive a kidney as early as possible to maximize their chances for survival—they cannot afford to wait for the right person to die.)[29] Until the government lifts the ban on organ sales, there will still be a shortage, and government will still have the blood on its hands of the people who die each year waiting for an organ.

TOO RADICAL?

Some people will read this chapter and think the proposals here are too radical to be politically practical or helpful in our present situation. But libertarians say that radical change is needed. The left proposes radical changes and is taken seriously; in fact, we have already seen radical change, as government over the course of the twentieth century increasingly interfered with people's health freedom in ways unprecedented in human history. So why shouldn't libertarians be radical? The conservative agenda will not do. The conservative program is essentially a *negative* one—the conservatives are against "ObamaCare," but what are they for? Managed care, ever-increasing costs, and ever-increasing revenue for the medical cartel and Big Pharma? Mass deaths while people wait for drugs to be approved or organs to be donated? Theirs is not a cause that should inspire anyone.

Libertarians have a positive vision—a country where people are free to pursue the treatments they deem best, doctors and others are able to provide information and services that patients want at more affordable prices, and many more lives are saved. That is radical, but not impossible, and libertarians consider it worth fighting for.

NOTES

1. Michael F. Cannon and Michael D. Tanner, *Healthy Competition: What's Holding Back Healthcare and How to Free It* (Washington, DC: Cato Institute, 2005), 47.

2. Arnold Kling, *Crisis of Abundance: Rethinking How We Pay for Health Care* (Washington, DC: Cato Institute, 2006), 51–52.

3. Cannon and Tanner, *Healthy Competition*, 51.

4. Devon M. Herrick and John C. Goodman, "The Market for Medical Care: Why You Don't Know the Price; Why You Don't Know about Quality; And What Can Be Done about It," *National Center for Policy Analysis*, March 12, 2007, http://www.ncpa.org/pub/st296?pg=5.

5. See Hans-Hermann Hoppe, "A Four-Step Healthcare Solution," *Mises.org*, August 14, 2009, http://mises.org/story/3643.

6. See Anthony Gregory, "The War on Obesity and Social Conflict," *LewRockwell.com*, August 20, 2009, http://www.lewrockwell.com/gregory/gregory191.html.

7. Hoppe, "A Four-Step Healthcare Solution,"

8. John Stossel, "Big Business Goes Big for Health Care Reform," *ABC News*, August 13, 2009, http://abcnews.go.com/print?id=8323583.

9. On the FDA and death panels, see Jim Fedako, "Yes, Virginia, There Will Be Death Panels," *Mises Economics Blog*, September 10, 2009, http://blog.mises.org/archives/010642.asp.

10. Daniel B. Klein and Alexander Tabarrok, "History of Federal Regulation: 1902–Present," *FDAReview.org*, http://www.fdareview.org/history.shtml.

11. Henry I. Miller, "How Government Stunted an Industry," *Hoover Digest* (2002), http://www.hoover.org/publications/digest/4495981.html.

12. Daniel B. Klein and Alexander Tabarrok, "Theory, Evidence and Examples of FDA Harm," *FDAReview.org*, http://www.fdareview.org/harm.shtml.

13. Paul H. Rubin, "FDA Advertising Restrictions: Ignorance Is Death," in Robert Higgs, ed., *Hazardous to Our Health? FDA Regulation of Health Care Products* (Oakland, CA: Independent Institute, 1995), 29–30.

14. Ibid., 32.

15. Cannon and Tanner, *Healthy Competition*, 118.

16. Daniel B. Klein, "Economists Against the FDA," *Ideas on Liberty* (September 2000), http://www.independent.org/printer.asp?page=/publications/article.asp?id=279.

17. Jason Lazarou, Bruce H. Pomeranz, and Paul N. Corey, "Incidence of Adverse Drug Reactions in Hospitalized Patients: A Meta-analysis of Prospective Studies," *Journal of the American Medical Association*, 297 (1998): 1200–05, available at http://jama.ama-assn.org/cgi/content/full/279/15/1200.

18. Richard A. Epstein, *Overdose: How Excessive Government Regulation Stifles Pharmaceutical Innovation* (New Haven, CT: Yale University Press, 2006), 116.

19. Mike Adams, "Tyranny in the USA: The True History of FDA Raids on Healers, Vitamin Shops, and Supplement Companies," *NaturalNews*, April 12, 2007, http://www.naturalnews.com/021791.html.

20. Larry Van Heerden, "Abolishing the FDA," *The Freeman* (March 2007): 27–31, http://www.fee.org/pdf/the-freeman/0703heerden.pdf.

21. David Jay Brown, "Truth, Freedom, and the FDA," *SmartPublications*, http://www.smart-publications.com/articles/MOM-pearson-shaw.php.

22. Heerden, "Abolishing the FDA."

23. Milton Friedman, *Capitalism and Freedom* (Chicago: University of Chicago Press, 1982 [1962]), 153.

24. Arthur J. Matas, "A Gift of Life Deserves Compensation," *Cato Policy Analysis* No. 604, November 7, 2007, http://www.cato.org/pub_display.php?pub_id=8780.

25. Ibid., 6–7.

26. Richard A. Epstein, *Mortal Peril: Our Inalienable Right to Health Care?* (Cambridge, MA: Perseus Books, 1999), 227–28.

27. Matas, "A Gift of Life," 3.

28. To join LifeSharers, see http://www.lifesharers.org.

29. Matas, "A Gift of Life," 2.

FURTHER READING

Cannon, Michael F. and Michael D. Tanner. *Healthy Competition: What's Holding Back Health Care and How to Free It*. Washington, DC: Cato Institute, 2005. The authors describe how government has distorted the healthcare market and propose reforms (including some more incremental ones than we have discussed here) to increase freedom and choices.

Higgs, Robert, ed. *Hazardous to Our Health? FDA Regulation of Health Care Products.* Oakland, CA: Independent Institute, 1995. This collection of essays shows in detail how the FDA is responsible for thousands of deaths.

Klein, Daniel B. and Alexander Tabarrok. *FDAReview.org,* http://www.fdareview.org. This website, a project of the libertarian Independent Institute, examines the evidence and finds that the costs of the FDA far outweigh the benefits.

6

The Fight for Educational Freedom

Most people assume we need government schools to have an educated, prosperous society, but libertarians see things differently. Libertarians see compulsory government education as both unnecessary and as a major, unjustified restriction on freedom.

For libertarians, the first problem with America's system of government schools is compulsory funding: Tax laws force everyone to pay for the schools regardless of whether they use, want, or like them. The second problem is compulsory attendance: Truancy laws force children to attend government schools or government-approved alternatives. The third problem is the compulsory curriculum: Schools deny parents control over what their children are taught. Worse, the government uses its schools to propagandize and portray itself in the most favorable light possible. Then there is the quality of those schools children are forced to attend, which tends to be low. Through their one-size-fits-all approach, government schools encourage conformity and mediocrity rather than individual excellence and real learning.

So just as most people favor separation of church and state, libertarians favor separation of school and state. According to libertarians, parents should be free to educate their children in any manner they see fit, whether that means sending them to a private school, sending them to private tutors, homeschooling them, or pursuing some other alternative. Libertarians believe that under this free-market system, there would be more and better education.

OUR LIBERTARIAN PAST

In a September 2009 speech broadcast to classrooms across the country, President Barack Obama told America's schoolchildren:

> The story of America isn't about people who quit when things got tough. It's about people who kept going, who tried harder, who loved their country too much to do anything less than their best. It's the story of students who sat where you sit 250 years ago, and went on to wage a revolution and found this nation.[1]

Obama's history lesson was false. In fact, America's founders did not sit where American schoolchildren sit. Many of them did not sit in school much at all, let alone in the sort of compulsory government schools we have today.

President Obama's statement implies that we have always depended on government to cultivate the best and brightest minds, and that without this system we would be impoverished and ignorant. Libertarians would point out that the reality is much different: We have had a private educational system in the past, and it educated people very well.

For example, contrary to Obama's suggestion, many of America's founders had little to no formal schooling, but they were hardly ignorant. George Washington, for example, dropped out of school at age twelve. Benjamin Franklin dropped out at ten, and then proceeded to give himself an extremely rigorous education, as he documented in his *Autobiography*. As education scholar Samuel Blumenfeld has noted, "Of the 117 men who signed the Declaration of Independence, the Articles of Confederation, and the Constitution, one out of three had only a few weeks of formal schooling, and only one in four had gone to college." Yet, he notes, anyone "who reads the debates and essential documents of that period must conclude that colonial education was of a very high order and that the freedom from government control was conducive to the sprit of independence the colonists had."[2]

In fact, early Americans were exceptionally well educated for their time and even, in many respects, by present standards, with no compulsory government schooling and little, if any, government funding for schools. Once again, then, libertarians' proposals are not as radical as they may at first seem, but instead call for a return to successful policies of the past.

In early America, the educational system was essentially libertarian. Although there were some tax-funded schools, especially in Massachusetts and

Connecticut, there was no compulsory schooling as we know it, and parents and students were free to pursue whatever methods of teaching and learning suited them best. As a result, private schools thrived. In populated areas, teachers would "hang out a shingle" and advertise. Different schools offered different services: some taught the basic "three Rs," while others taught specialized subjects such as applied mathematics and accounting.[3] Historian Robert Seybolt reports on the real-world effects of a free market in colonial times:

> In the hands of private schoolmasters the curriculum expanded rapidly. Their schools were commercial ventures, and, consequently, competition was keen. . . . Popular demands, and the element of competition, forced them not only to add more courses of instruction, but constantly to improve their methods and technique of instruction.[4]

Education scholar Joel Spring notes that by the 1790s, the majority of children in many states attended private schools.[5] Those without money were not left out—large cities had "free-school" societies, funded by philanthropists or religious groups (and sometimes partly by government), which built and operated schools for the poor.[6]

In those days, people recognized that school classrooms were not the only way to learn, and not necessarily even the best way. In the South, poor children often learned through apprenticeship programs, and wealthier people, such as Thomas Jefferson, learned from private tutors.[7] Home education was common, even for children who eventually went to school, as mothers would teach children to read before they reached school age.[8] People learned from their churches, too. Sunday schools didn't just teach religion; they also taught basic skills such as reading and writing, especially to the poor.[9] Then there were libraries, which were rarely government-supported, but instead received funding from member fees and, later, charity.[10]

The result of all of these educational opportunities was exceptional literacy among the general public. It is difficult to imagine a visitor from Europe being much impressed by Americans' literacy today, but in 1812 French immigrant Pierre Du Pont de Nemours remarked:

> The United States are more advanced in their educational facilities than most countries. They have a large number of primary schools; and as their paternal affection protects children from working in the fields, it is possible to send them to the schoolmaster—a condition which does not prevail in Europe. Most young Americans, therefore, can read, write and cipher. Not more than four in a thousand are unable to write legibly—even neatly . . .[11]

Alexis De Tocqueville made similar observations, noting, for example, that even though the pioneers on the Western frontier did not have formal schools, their huts generally contained at least a few volumes of Shakespeare.[12] Jacob Duche, Chaplain of Congress, described in 1772 the culture of ideas that colonial American education had created: "The poorest laborer upon the shore of Delaware thinks himself entitled to deliver his sentiments in matters of religion or politics with as much freedom as the gentleman or scholar. . . . Such is the prevailing taste for books of every kind, that almost every man is a reader. . . ."[13]

Statistics support these observations. Professor Lawrence Cremin has estimated that male literacy in the colonies ranged from 70 to 100 percent.[14] Other research shows that from 1650 to 1795, male literacy rose from 60 percent to 90 percent, and female literacy rose from 30 percent to 45 percent. From 1800 to 1840, literacy in the North rose from 75 percent to somewhere between 91 and 97 percent. In the South during that same time period, it went from 50 to 60 percent to 81 percent.[15] Writer and educator John Taylor Gatto notes that "by 1840 the incidence of complex literacy in the United States was between 93 and 100 percent wherever such a thing mattered."[16] In 1850, just before Massachusetts imposed compulsory schooling, literacy in that state was at 98 percent.[17]

More proof of early Americans' literacy can be found in the books that they bought and read. Estimates vary on how many copies of Thomas Paine's *Common Sense* sold when it was published in 1776, but they range from 120,000 to 500,000 copies—impressive in any event for a colonial population of about two and half million.[18] From its publication in 1783 through 1818, when the United States had a population of less than 20 million, Noah Webster's *Spelling Book* sold five million copies.[19] James Fenimore Cooper's *Last of the Mohicans* sold millions, as did the novels of Walter Scott.[20]

THE MOVE TO COMPULSION

If Americans were so literate without compulsory government schools, why do we have them? Not because there was a shortage of education. And even if some people were unable afford to go to school in the past, governments would not have had to form their own school systems to fix this; they could have just given people money to attend private schools. As libertarian writer Sheldon Richman has noted, "When the government decided to help poor people buy food, it didn't build state grocery stores. It issued food stamps that are used at private stores."[21] So why did it set up state schools? Because certain groups wanted to mold society into a particular "unified" image and saw government schools as the way to achieve this.

America's first compulsory schooling laws were imposed by the Puritans—the theocrats of witch-trial fame who dominated colonial Massachusetts. As a colony, Massachusetts had compulsory education laws (eventually including government-funded schools) for about half of the seventeenth century, from 1642 until King James's Declaration of Indulgence granted religious freedom in 1692. The Puritans made no secret of their purpose in operating their schools: to enforce "purity of doctrine" in people's religious beliefs.[22]

After the American Revolution, educational freedom existed in most of the country, as it had before, but because of their Puritan heritage, Massachusetts and Connecticut began leading the way toward compulsion; the Massachusetts State Constitution even gave the legislature authority to enforce compulsory school attendance. Through the first half of the nineteenth century, Massachusetts had both fully private schools and town schools that were funded partly by government and partly by student tuition. Finally, in 1852, the state imposed the first statewide compulsory schooling system along the lines that we know today. Others then followed.

Several groups pushed for compulsory schooling over the course of the nineteenth century. Foremost among them was a new Unitarian intellectual elite, which rejected the Calvinist Puritans' doctrine of original sin and believed in man's supposed goodness and perfectibility—and wanted to use the schools to help create the perfect society they thought was possible.[23] Inspired by the schools they observed in militaristic Prussia, nineteenth-century advocates of government schooling sought to create dutiful, obedient, "enlightened" citizens who would serve the state and constitute a unified, homogeneous, equal society. Liberal Protestants jumped aboard this agenda, even if they didn't share the Unitarians' views on religion or man's nature, because they saw that government schools would help protect America's Protestant character against the new wave of Catholic immigrants. The First Amendment did not yet apply to state and local governments, so the law did not prevent religious teaching in the new schools. In the interest of fostering social unity, only the broadest religious principles were taught—points all Protestants could agree on—but they used the Protestant Bible, and kept Catholic teaching out.[24]

Indeed, anti-Catholic, anti-immigrant bigotry played a leading role in the establishment of compulsory schools. An 1851 *Massachusetts Teacher* article complained of the "poor, the oppressed, and, worse than all, the *ignorant* of the old world" descending on the United States and becoming a "serious alarm to the most intelligent people of our own." It warned that if "left to their [parents'] direction, the young will be brought up in idle, dissolute, vagrant habits, which will make them worse members of society than their parents are." As a result, the article declared, "the children must be gathered up and forced into school, and those who resist or impede this plan, whether parents or *priests*, must be held accountable and punished."[25] Education scholar Andrew Coulson notes that public schools "became an extension of popular bigotry," and textbooks denigrated the Irish and Catholics; some Catholic students were even whipped and beaten for refusing to read from the Protestant Bible.[26] In 1922, Oregon tried to eliminate even *private* Catholic education—the result of a campaign spearheaded by the Ku Klux Klan—by passing a law abolishing private schools. (The U.S. Supreme Court struck the law down.)[27]

Alongside the Unitarians, an "educationist" movement advanced the cause of compulsory government schooling through a network of publications, organizations, and teachers. The movement's members made no secret of their belief that teachers should be superior to parents in instructing children, and that children must learn obedience to the state. For example, the father of North Carolina's government school system, Archibald D. Murphey, said of the schools he envisioned:

> all children will be taught in them . . . in these schools the precepts of morality and religion should be inculcated, and habits of subordination and obedience be formed. . . . The state, in the warmth of her solicitude for their welfare, must take charge of those children, and place them in school where their minds can be enlightened and their hearts can be trained to virtue.[28]

In 1864, the California State Superintendent of Public Instruction said, "The child should be taught to consider his instructor, in many respects, superior to the parent in point of authority. . . . [T]he vulgar impression that parents have a legal right to dictate to teachers is entirely erroneous."[29] In 1865, the Wisconsin State Teachers' Association stated simply that "children are the property of the state."[30] Influential soldier and politician Samuel Smith stated in 1830 that "high considerations of expediency not only justify but dictate the establishment of a system which shall place under a control, *independent of and superior to parental authority*, the education of children."[31]

In the half century after Massachusetts imposed modern compulsory schooling in 1852, most of the rest of the states followed suit, but not without controversy. Many states with a strong tradition of educational freedom held out. For example, Pennsylvania's governor vetoed compulsory education bills in 1891 and 1893 because they interfered with parents' personal liberty.[32] The national platform of the Democratic Party—which was then still America's more libertarian party—stated that the party was "opposed to state interference with parental rights and rights of conscience in the education of children," and that "the largest individual liberty consistent with the rights of others insures the highest type of American citizenship and the best government."[33] In other words, the Democrats recognized that schools were not necessary to make people good citizens. By the end of the century, however, the so-called reformers had won, and almost every state enforced compulsory schooling laws.[34]

COMPULSORY SCHOOLS TODAY

One problem libertarians identify in the present highly centralized government school system is that it attempts to force everyone into a single mold, which is bad for education and social harmony, but good for government.

Mass Instruction

As Murray Rothbard noted, by its very nature "the public school requires the imposition of uniformity and the stamping out of diversity and individuality in education."[35] Many libertarians have emphasized that learning is an inherently individual activity. Every person has unique aptitudes and interests; ideally, each child would be encouraged to develop these at the pace and to the extent that is just right for him or her. One-on-one tutoring would be the ideal way to achieve this, so the teacher could adapt to the student's personal needs as much as possible.

Government schools are about as far as possible from this ideal. Their regimentation tends to discourage individual development by forcing the student to study particular subjects for specified (short) times each day, sticking strictly to the assigned material. By its nature, this type of education cannot adjust to meet individual needs. If you round up all children of a certain age who live in a certain geographical area and force them into a class together, there is no reason to think that they will all excel in the same areas or be capable of proceeding at the same rate. Yet the government-school classroom requires that they *do* proceed at more or less the same level, at the same pace. Such a classroom will cater to the "lowest common denominator," or at best at the level of the *average* student. Then the best students will not fulfill their potential (and may underperform out of boredom), and the slowest students will fail.

No Child Left Behind

The federal No Child Left Behind (NCLB) Act, enacted in 2002 at the urging of both President George W. Bush and Senator Ted Kennedy, imposes the one-size-fits-all approach on an unprecedented scale. It requires that states establish standardized testing and meet various other objective criteria to qualify for federal funding; schools that come up short on the tests are then subject to various remedial actions.

This is not conducive to genuine education. Real education involves learning to reason, to see how the things one learns in different subject areas fit together, and to understand the world. Standardized tests do not and cannot measure or teach this. Instead, they direct students' attention away from genuine learning and make students focus narrowly on learning how to pass particular exams. As nineteenth-century libertarian writer Auberon Herbert put it, to measure performance based on such testing

> necessarily restricts and vulgarizes our conception of education. It reduces everybody concerned, managers, teachers, pupils, to the one aim and object of satisfying certain regulations made for them, of considering success in passing standards and success in education as the same thing. . . . It is needless to say that the higher aims of the teacher, methods of arousing the imagination and developing the reasoning powers, which only bear fruit slowly and cannot be tested by a yearly examination of an inspector . . . must be laid aside as subordinate to the one great aim of driving large batches successfully through the standards.

Herbert concludes:

> Any plan better fitted to reduce managers, teachers, and pupils to one level of commonplace and stupidity could scarcely be found. The state rules a great copybook, and the nation simply copies what it finds between the lines.[36]

Writer and educator John Taylor Gatto takes a similar view, noting that such standards at best teach children how to memorize "dots" of information instead of teaching them how to connect the dots—which is what would make the knowledge actually useful, and what education is really about.[37] And they do nothing to encourage imagination or innovation. Standardized tests may also discourage students who are told that they are failures by test criteria, even though they may simply lack test-taking skills that are irrelevant to real-world success.

As for No Child Left Behind in particular, it has failed even by its own criteria. Since its imposition, test scores have remained flat, declined, or, at best, increased at a lower rate than before. Indeed, even apparent success under NCLB is dubious. When the states established objective standards in response to the Act, they deliberately set the bar *low* to make the results appear better—and when their schools appeared to be failing, they moved it *even lower.* For example, when more than 1,500 Michigan schools turned up on a list of schools needing improvement under NCLB standards, the state simply lowered its standards by, for example, dropping the percentage of students that needed to pass high-school English from 75 percent to 42 percent. Across the country, there are similar stories of ever-lowering standards since NCLB's passage.[38]

With or without No Child Left Behind, government schools are geared primarily toward serving the needs of politicians, bureaucrats, administrators, and teachers, not the needs of students. In private education, as in the market generally, the consumer is king because the consumer has the power to take his dollars elsewhere if the seller fails to satisfy. Government schools face no such threat. The people who run them must instead please the people who control their funding, such as the federal government. And in government, one of the surest ways to get more money is to *fail* and blame a lack of resources. So this incentive structure does not just fail to put children first, it actively harms them.

True, many government-school teachers are genuinely concerned about their students. (The author's father was among that group.) But many have other priorities, especially when they are organized into a labor union, as most are. Teachers' unions express concern for children, but first and foremost do what all labor unions try to do: enrich their members. The teachers, unions reveal their priorities when, for example, they go on strike, attempt to stop a school from firing an incompetent teacher, or resist merit-based pay. And sometimes they spell out their priorities in as many words, as National Education Association (NEA) general counsel Bob Chanin did in a 2009 speech in which he said:

> The NEA and its affiliates are effective advocates because we have power. And we have power because there are more than 3.2 million people who are willing to pay us hundreds of millions of dollars in dues each year because they believe that we are the unions that can most effectively represent them; the union that can protect their rights and advance their interests as education employees.
>
> This is not to say that the concern of NEA and its affiliates with closing achievement gaps, reducing drop rate rates, improving teacher quality, and the like are unimportant or inappropriate. To the contrary these are the goals that guide the work we do. But they need not and must not be achieved at the expense of due process, employee rights, or collective bargaining.
>
> That is simply too high a price to pay.[39]

Unionized teachers have also been known to enlist students in campaigns for more school funding—that is, more government spending that will benefit the teachers at tax-paying parents' expense.[40]

Another problem in the compulsory school is that teachers are, as Rothbard put it, "permanent tyrants" because they have absolute dictatorial control within their jurisdiction, and they may not be removed from office. Teachers may order students around in general, and the Supreme Court has held that despite the First and Fourth Amendments, school officials may search students, stop them from speaking, and even punish them for lawful activities they engage in off school property.[41] Of course it is necessary for teachers to have control for the classroom to function; the problem for libertarians is that children are forced to submit to this small-scale tyranny. And if a teacher abuses his or her power, within very broad limits, there is no means of holding him or her accountable. A parent typically cannot withdraw his or her child from the classroom or the school, and the people cannot vote a teacher out of office as they can with an elected official. Instead, tenure makes it nearly impossible for *anyone* to remove a teacher. This system is not compatible with liberty.

Conflicting Values

Probably most people would agree that if you disagree with the things your neighbor teaches his child, it is not appropriate to kidnap the child and instruct him or her in what you believe to be correct thinking. Yet people use government schools for just this purpose, and in doing so, they create more social conflict than would otherwise exist.

For example, some people want schools to teach the theory of evolution; others want schools to teach creationist ideas on the origin of human life. Some people want schools to teach students about birth-control methods; others want schools to teach only sexual abstinence. Parents also fight about what books shall be assigned or made available, or what films will be shown. In each of these debates, parents on both sides want their children to be educated in the manner they deem best, but the only way they can have this (short of paying for private-school tuition on top of their government-school taxes) is to impose their standards on everyone else.

There is no way to resolve these conflicts under a compulsory school system. One group may succeed in imposing its will on the other for a time, but the struggle for political control will continue because one group will be left unsatisfied. (One can see an example of this in Kansas's frequently changing policies on the teaching of evolution.)

A free market in education resolves this problem because it allows each family to send its children to a school that shares its values. This ends conflicts between groups of people with different beliefs. There are no fights, for example, among parents of Catholic-school students over whether their school should teach students about contraception; parents who want a pro-contraception sex-education curriculum will go elsewhere. Also, one never hears about parents of Catholic-school students campaigning to have, say, Mormon schools teach Catholic beliefs; they have no reason to do this because the market allows both groups to satisfy their preferences. A free market in education would accommodate all value systems, just as the market in general caters to all tastes.

Recognizing this freedom of association would likely lead to greater social harmony overall, as members of different groups would no longer look on one another as enemies who want to force their values on each other's children. Would a small handful of parents—say, Ku Klux Klan members—teach their children anti-social ideas and values the rest of us find abhorrent? Probably. But that problem is also inherent in the freedom to raise one's own children. Libertarians believe that this should be resolved like any other difference of opinion: through persuasion, not force.

Government Promotes Itself

George Orwell wrote in 1984 that "he who controls the past, controls the future." One reason libertarians find government education so troublesome is because, by teaching history, the schools "control the past"—they affect the way Americans view their nation from a young, impressionable age.

Government schools tend to teach an "official" (or "court") version of history. A history class may acknowledge that the government made errors in the past (for example, when it allowed slavery), but it emphasizes that these errors have been corrected. In the schools, American history is presented as a march of progress toward the present moment, when we are the most enlightened we have ever been and, by implication, we have the best government we have ever had. In this official version of history, it is good that we adopted the Constitution; it is good that we fought the Civil War; it is good that we fought other wars; it is good that we broke up Standard Oil; it is good that we enacted the New Deal; and so on. There is never a suggestion that perhaps we might undo any of this. Likewise, all U.S. presidents are presented as great men, and as the most important men in history. (A couple, such as Warren Harding and Richard Nixon, may be singled out as exceptions, but they are presented as just that: exceptions.) All of this serves to instill faith that one's government tends to improve society over time; that the private sector often needs government to correct it; and that we should trust our leaders to do what is right. Schools further reinforce all of this through recitation of the Pledge of Allegiance, the singing of the militaristic "Star Spangled Banner" and other patriotic songs, and other activities designed to induce love of country and, more specifically, love of government.

In addition to shaping children's ideas about history, schools also impress on children politically correct ideas about the need for even more government. For example, few children go through government schools without ample exposure to environmentalist propaganda that calls for government solutions to environmental problems.[42] Schools may also urge children to scold their parents for doing politically incorrect things, such as smoking or not recycling. And they even encourage children to report their parents to their government. For example, in 2007, one Arkansas school urged students to report zoning and building code violations in their parents' homes; and some children have put their own parents in prison after the DARE program urged them to report any drugs they see at home.[43] Regardless of what one thinks of such parents' behavior, propagandizing and encouraging children to inform against their family members have nothing to do with education, and everything to do with government intrusion on families' private lives.

VOUCHERS

Libertarians would of course like to liberate the millions of students who are forced to attend government schools. To achieve this, Milton Friedman suggested government-funded vouchers, which would allow children to use government money to pay for private-school tuition.[44] Then at least parents and students would be allowed to exercise some choice as to where they could attend and escape the worst schools, and, the argument goes, educational quality would improve as schools, including government schools, would have to compete for students and their (government-provided) money.

Although many libertarians have endorsed the voucher idea, vouchers are not necessarily libertarian. They do not strike at the root of the problem with compulsory government schools: the compulsion. They still rely on tax dollars taken by force, still allow children to be forced to attend school, and possibly *increase* the amount of government compulsion with respect to school curricula by imposing new requirements on heretofore private schools.

But are not vouchers at least a step in the right direction because, other things being equal, they give consumers choices? Some libertarians sincerely believe so. But others suggest, with good reason, that vouchers are a step in the wrong direction.

Voucher Programs

In the late twentieth and early twenty-first centuries, the voucher idea became a reality on a limited scale in a few places across the United States. The first major modern voucher program began in Milwaukee in 1990. That program, which still exists, gives students from low-income families (with household incomes at 175 percent of the poverty line or lower) a voucher that is worth up to the amount the student would receive in state funding if the student attended a public school. Private schools in the program must meet certain requirements; for example, they must take all voucher students who apply, and, if the school is religious, it must allow students to opt out of religious teaching if they choose to do so. Ohio implemented a voucher program for Cleveland students in 1995, which pays 75 to 90 percent of participants' private-school tuition, depending on family income, with a maximum voucher value of $3,450.

More recently, some states have implemented voucher programs for particular groups of students. Arizona, for example, provides vouchers for children in foster care; Arizona, Florida, Georgia, and Utah offer vouchers to students with certain disabilities; and Ohio offers vouchers of up to $20,000 to autistic students. Louisiana and Ohio also have programs that give vouchers to students in schools that the state has deemed to be failing.[45]

First Amendment Challenge

One early obstacle to voucher programs was the First Amendment— governments were not sure whether they could fund private religious schools, even indirectly, without violating the Establishment Clause, which the Supreme Court has interpreted to require separation of church and state.

A libertarian public-interest law firm, the Institute for Justice (IJ), took up the cause of defending voucher laws against such challenges. IJ was founded in 1991 by two libertarian lawyers, Clint Bolick and William Mellor, with the mission of advancing various causes in the courts, one of them being "school choice." (We will talk about other facets of IJ's mission in Chapter 8.) When someone challenges a state law in court, the state attorney general (or solicitor general) must defend that law's constitutionality. But when voucher laws are challenged, IJ seeks to intervene, not on behalf of the state, but on behalf of the schools or students who would benefit from vouchers. By becoming involved, IJ's lawyers can make what they believe to be the best arguments on the voucher program's behalf rather than leave it to the government's lawyers, who may have political conflicts and other priorities.[46]

IJ's most important voucher case arose when a group of Ohio citizens challenged the Cleveland program on First Amendment grounds in 1999. In 2002, that case, *Zelman v. Simmons-Harris*, went before the United States Supreme Court, which held that the program did not violate the First Amendment because it simply provided a voucher to parents for the purpose of funding education; that is, it was neutral with respect to religion, and therefore was not unconstitutional.[47]

Vouchers and Libertarianism

Not all libertarians are so enthusiastic about vouchers. To many libertarians, vouchers are just another welfare program and a dangerous threat to independent private education. As the mainstream *American Lawyer* magazine has noted, IJ strays from libertarianism by promoting vouchers because "using government funds to pay for parochial school tuition extends the reach of government, rather than limiting it."[48]

Vouchers as Welfare

One obvious problem with vouchers, in the libertarian view, is that they are a welfare program. That is, vouchers often transfer money from taxpayers to people who do not pay taxes because the programs are targeted toward people with low incomes. As Lew Rockwell has explained, "If the middle and upper-middle class want to send their children to private schools, they must shell out twice: once for public schools for everyone else and once again for the schools they actually use." The voucher recipients, however, just receive a handout.[49] Bolick argues that vouchers simply "empower parents to spend their public education funds on public, private, or religious schools."[50] But this is not so; vouchers in practice empower people to spend *someone else's* "funds."

Libertarian voucher advocates may respond to this by arguing that vouchers do not necessarily require any increase in government spending; under some programs, public schools' budgets are reduced for each student in the district that uses a voucher to go elsewhere. Vouchers may even reduce the amount of tax dollars spent on education overall if the vouchers are worth less than the amount the government spends per child at public schools.[51] But this is not necessarily so, and voucher advocates tend to endorse vouchers even when they do not work this way.

For example, when Hurricane Katrina devastated New Orleans, Bolick—who left IJ in 2004 to found the Alliance for School Choice—called on Congress to allocate $2.8 billion for hurricane victims to attend private schools. After all, he argued, this was just a "tiny share of the $62 billion" that Congress had already appropriated for Katrina relief. This strays far from the traditional libertarian view. For decades, libertarians have celebrated the principled stands taken by Davy Crockett (as a Congressman) and President Grover Cleveland when they resisted appeals to support spending tax dollars on disaster relief—not because they did not want to help people, but because it was not their place to *force* anyone to pay for a matter ordinarily left to the private sector.[52] Following Katrina, however, supposedly libertarian voucher advocates were doing the asking, and asking for far more than anyone ever sought from Crockett or Cleveland. Instead of opposing government spending, these libertarians were—like everyone else in Washington—asking that the government spend money on their pet project.

In calling for government spending, voucher advocates tend to sound more like modern-day liberals than like libertarians. Indeed, although the teachers' unions ensure that the Democrats remain officially opposed to vouchers, voucher advocates have found allies on the left. The liberal *Washington Post*, for one, has endorsed the District of Columbia's voucher program and urged President Obama to support continued funding for it.[53]

Vouchers versus Independent Schools

Even if vouchers did not increase government spending, many libertarians would still oppose them because they threaten independent schools. Government money, after all, usually means government control—and in education, that could mean that private schools would end up looking a lot like government schools.

Current voucher programs have strings attached, just as libertarian voucher critics would predict. For example, the Milwaukee program requires, among other things, that schools allow students to opt out of religious teaching. There is one practical way to comply with such a rule: to relegate religion to a particular course, and scrub all other classes of religious content. Under such a requirement, schools that once applied religious considerations to many different subjects will no longer do so. In this way, the vouchers will prompt schools to stray from their original missions and control what those schools teach.

Schools that accept vouchers must also accept restrictions on *whom* they may admit (or deny admission to) as a student. For example, under the Milwaukee program and most others, schools must accept any student who wants to pay with a voucher—they cannot discriminate in their admissions for any reason, even, for example, religion. The result of this will be a drop in the quality of private school students. The most disruptive students at government schools will now be allowed to drag down the educational environment at private schools. As the late libertarian champion of educational freedom, Marshall Fritz, observed, today's private schools tend to attract a higher quality of student because presumably the student's parents value education and, in many cases, must sacrifice for the child to be there. The parents' attitude is likely to be reflected, to some extent, by the child. On the other hand, students who receive something for nothing are unlikely to appreciate what they receive, and may degrade the experience for everyone else, just as they do now in government schools.[54] (The easier the vouchers are to receive and spend, the more likely this is to be so.)

Voucher advocates may argue that private schools can avoid any threat to their independence by refusing to accept vouchers. But vouchers would put such independent schools at a severe disadvantage in the market. The schools would have to compete against both regular "free" government schools and "free" private schools that accept vouchers. It is easy to imagine independent education mostly disappearing under these circumstances. As economist Gary North has argued, parents who want to educate their child in a truly independent school will have to

> locate other parents equally committed religiously and ideologically to the principle of independent education, and also financially able to put their preference into action. How many concerned parents will do this? How many private school administrators will be able to operate a school while denying admittance to those who would pay with vouchers? How many of these schools with real commitment tò private education will there be? I can tell you: very, very few.[55]

The independent schools would not be killed off by genuine market competition; they would be killed off by government privileges extended to some schools—those willing accept government control—and not others. A program that would do this cannot be called libertarian.

THE HOMESCHOOLING ALTERNATIVE

If not vouchers, then what? The government schools will not go away soon, but many are finding educational freedom anyway through true private education, especially homeschooling.

In those states in which it is unregulated, homeschooling allows people to pursue the libertarian ideal. It entails no coercion except the ordinary "coercion" that parents exercise with respect to their children.[56] In many states, homeschooling parents have no obligation to focus on or administer standardized tests, to follow a particular curriculum, or to teach or not teach certain values.

Homeschooling Results

The results of homeschooling are as libertarians would predict: Homeschooled students perform well above the level of government-schooled students. Although homeschooled students are not required to take standardized tests in many states, a 2009 study found that they score on average 30 or more percentile points higher on those tests than government-schooled students. This held true regardless of:

- family income,
- how much money the family spent on homeschooling,
- whether the parents went to college,
- whether one of the parents was a certified teacher,

- whether the student was male or female, and
- whether the student's state heavily regulated homeschooling.[57]

A 1997 study found similar results, and also noted that the wide performance gap between white and minority students that exists in government schools narrowed to just five percentile points among homeschooled students.[58]

Home education is far less expensive than government education because there is no overhead and no bloated bureaucracy. As of 2009, government schools spent an average of nearly $10,000 per student per year, not including capital expenditures or research and development. The median amount homeschoolers spent on education in 2007–2008 was just $400 to $599 per year.[59] The cost of homeschooling may fall even lower in the years ahead, as high-quality homeschooling materials become available online at little to no cost; for example, one company offers a complete K–12 curriculum on CD-ROMs for $200, and each child in the family can use it at no additional cost.[60]

Some people believe that homeschooling comes at a high social cost, as children are supposedly isolated from the "real world." The evidence suggests this is false. As Chris Klicka, senior counsel for the Home School Legal Defense Association, has noted, homeschooled children *are* living in the real world, and "it is actually the public school children who are not living in the real world." Children in government schools are placed in a highly unnatural situation—they are forced into a room all day every day, exclusively with children their own age, and as a result, their values are strongly influenced by other children rather than by interaction with adults. Homeschooled students, in contrast, interact with adults and children of varying ages, get more "hands on" experience, and view adults, not peers, as their role models. (Indeed, studies show that homeschooled students are less susceptible to peer pressure than non-homeschoolers.) Studies show that, if anything, homeschooled students are *more* involved in outside activities—from clubs to sports to academic competitions to activities with homeschoolers—than their government-school counterparts.[61] This carries over into their adult lives as well: a 2003 study showed that homeschool graduates are far more likely to participate in community service activities than non-homeschoolers (71 percent versus 37 percent), more likely to belong to an organization (80 percent versus 50 percent), and more likely to say they are "very happy" with their lives (58.9 percent versus 27.6 percent).[62]

The evidence also suggests that homeschoolers enjoy more college success than non-homeschoolers. More homeschool graduates age 18 through 24 have taken college-level courses than non-homeschoolers—74 percent versus 46 percent.[63] Admission officers at many colleges now actively recruit homeschoolers. A Dartmouth College admission officer had noted: "The applications [from homeschoolers] I've come across are outstanding. Homeschoolers have a distinct advantage because of the individualized instruction they receive." Stanford University admissions officers have noted that they see "intellectual vitality" unusually often among homeschoolers because of the self-teaching those students have had to do.[64]

Fighting Government Threats

Homeschoolers' success has not stopped state governments from attempting to interfere with their efforts; far from it. At this writing, ten states leave homeschooling entirely unregulated—parents do not even have to give the government notice. Another fourteen states only require that parents notify the government that they intend to homeschool. Twenty states have more regulation, requiring parents to submit test scores, professional student evaluations, or both to the government; six more states impose a high level of regulation, including, for example, state curriculum approval and home inspections.[65] Even in states where homeschooling is fully legal, however, some schools still attempt to enforce truancy laws against homeschoolers. And homeschoolers may face new threats as their success draws attention. For example, the NEA, like any union, seeks to eliminate competition and since 1997 has passed annual anti-homeschooling resolutions, which call for mandatory licensing of homeschooling teachers, imposition of a state-approved curriculum on homeschoolers, and mandatory "assessments to ensure adequate academic progress."[66]

The Home School Legal Defense Association, founded in 1983, helps defend homeschoolers against government attacks on their freedom, through both lawsuits (for example, defending homeschoolers charged with truancy) and efforts to pass laws that facilitate homeschooling or stop laws that would interfere with it. Though it defends the rights of homeschoolers regardless of their religious background, the organization defines itself as Christian. And though it is not officially "libertarian," the HSLDA's fight for educational freedom is a wholly libertarian cause; the group rejects vouchers for many of the reasons we have reviewed above.[67]

Educational Freedom

Probably most homeschoolers are not libertarians, and not all libertarians are homeschoolers (though many are). But the homeschoolers have found a distinctly libertarian means of advancing a libertarian cause. Their method—secession—does not require political action, except of the most defensive kind. To get what they want, homeschoolers do not need to force anyone else to adopt or endorse homeschooling. Rather, they need only *ignore* government to the maximum extent possible as they go about creating their alternative, superior institution.

As more people have seen the success of homeschoolers and the failures of government schools, more people have been persuaded to adopt the home-schooling method. According to the U.S. Department of Education, some 1.5 million students in grades K through 12 were homeschooled in 2007, a 36 percent increase since 2003.[68] If libertarians can create similarly desirable, popular alternatives to additional government schemes, they may find the government a lot less powerful than it has been, as people withdraw their consent and awaken to the idea of just walking away.

Still, homeschooling is not a complete solution; despite its advantages, it's not for everyone. A free market would provide an enormous array of alternatives—as it does for every other type of good and service—and people will not enjoy true educational freedom until government gets out of the way entirely.

NOTES

1. "Prepared Remarks of President Barack Obama Back to School Event," *WhiteHouse.gov*, September 8, 2009, http://www.whitehouse.gov/MediaResources/Prepared SchoolRemarks/.

2. Samuel L. Blumenfeld, *Is Public Education Necessary?* (Boise: The Paradigm Company, 1985), 21.

3. Andrew J. Coulson, *Market Education: The Unknown History* (New Brunswick, NJ: Transaction Publishers, 1999), 74.

4. Robert F. Seybolt, *Source Studies in American Colonial Education: The Private School* (New York: Oxford University Press, 1971), 102, quoted in Sheldon Richman, *Separating School and State: How to Liberate America's Families* (Fairfax, VA: Future of Freedom Foundation, 1994), 38.

5. Joel Spring, *The American School 1642–2000* (Boston: McGraw Hill, 2001), 103.

6. Blumenfeld, *Is Public Education Necessary?* 27; Coulson, *Market Education*, 75.

7. Susan Alder, "Education in America," *The Freeman* (February 1993), http://www.thefreemanonline.org/columns/education-in-america/.

8. Robert A. Peterson, "Education in Colonial America," *The Freeman* (September 1983), http://www.thefreemanonline.org/columns/education-in-colonial-america/.

9. Ibid.

10. Ibid.

11. Quoted in Samuel L. Blumenfeld, "Are Compulsory School Attendance Laws Necessary? Part 1," *Freedom Daily* (March 1991), http://www.fff.org/freedom/0391c.asp.

12. Coulson, *Market Education*, 74.

13. Quoted in Peterson, "Education in Colonial America."

14. Lawrence A. Cremin, *American Education: The Colonial Experience 1607–1783* (New York: Harper & Row, 1970), 544, cited in Blumenfeld, *Is Public Education Necessary?* 20.

15. Barry R. Poulson, "Education and the Family During the Industrial Revolution," in Joseph R. Peden and Fred R. Glahe, eds., *The American Family and State* (San Francisco: Pacific Research Institute, 1986), 183, cited in Richman, *Separating School and State*, 38.

16. John Taylor Gatto, *The Underground History of American Education* (New York: Oxford Village Press, 2006), 52–53.

17. John Taylor Gatto, *Dumbing Us Down: The Hidden Curriculum of Compulsory Schooling* (Gabriola Island, BC: New Society Publishers, 2005 [1992]), 22.

18. See Richman, *Separating School and State*, 38 (citing John Taylor Gatto, "Our Prussian School System," *Cato Policy Report*, March/April 1993); Martin Carnoy and Henry M. Levin, *Schooling and Work in the Democratic State* (San Francisco: Stanford University Press, 1985), 82.

19. Merle Curti, *The Growth of American Thought*, 3rd ed. (New Brunswick, NJ: Transaction Publishers, 1982), 222.

20. Richman, *Separating School and State*, 38 (citing Gatto, "Our Prussian School System"); Gatto, *The Underground History of Education*, 52–53.

21. Sheldon Richman, "Why the State Took Control of 'Education,'" *The Education Liberator* (December 1995/January 1996), http://www.schoolandstate.org/EdLib/Vol1/Richman-StateTookControl.htm.

22. Murray N. Rothbard, *Conceived in Liberty* Vol. 1 (Auburn, AL: The Ludwig von Mises Institute, 1999), 177, 419–20; Blumenfeld, *Is Public Education Necessary?* 18.

23. Blumenfeld, "Are Compulsory School Attendance Laws Necessary? Part 1."

24. Coulson, *Market Education*, 81.

25. "Immigration," *The Massachusetts Teacher* (1851), in Sol Cohen, ed., *Education in the United States: A Documentary History* (New York: Random House, 1974), vol. 2, 995–97 (emphasis in original), quoted in Coulson, *Market Education*, 79–80.

26. Coulson, *Market Education*, 81.

27. See Murray N. Rothbard, *For a New Liberty*, rev. ed. (New York: Collier Books, 1978), 126; *Pierce v. Society of Sisters*, 268 U.S. 510 (1925).

28. Archibald D. Murphey, *The Papers of Archibald D. Murphey*, 2 vols. (Raleigh, NC: E.M. Uzzell, 1914), 53–54, quoted in Rothbard, *Education: Free and Compulsory* (Auburn, AL: Ludwig von Mises Institute, 1999), 45.

29. Coulson, *Market Education*, 82.

30. Ibid., 83.

31. Charles L. Glenn, Jr., *The Myth of the Common School* (Amherst, MA: University of Massachusetts Press, 1988), 75, quoted in Coulson, *Market Education*, 78.

32. Rothbard, *Education: Free and Compulsory*, 43.

33. Ibid., 44.

34. Ibid., 41.

35. Rothbard, *For a New Liberty*, 154.

36. Auberon Herbert, *The Right and Wrong of Compulsion by the State and Other Essays* (Indianapolis: Liberty Fund, 1978 [1885]), 31–32, http://files.libertyfund.org/files/591/Herbert_0146_EBk_v5.pdf.

37. John Taylor Gatto, *Weapons of Mass Instruction: A Schoolteacher's Journey Through the Dark World of Compulsory Schooling* (Gabriola Island, BC: New Society Publishers, 2009), 16.

38. See Neal McCluskey and Andrew J. Coulson, "End It, Don't Mend It: What to Do with No Child Left Behind," *Cato Policy Analysis* No. 599, September 5, 2007, http://www.cato.org/pubs/pas/Pa599.pdf.

39. Tammy Drennan, "NEA Lawyer: It's Not About Kids," *Alliance for the Separation of School and State*, http://www.schoolandstate.org/Knowledge/Drennan/NEALawyer.htm.

40. See James Bovard, "Teachers Unions: Are the Schools Run for Them?" *The Freeman* (July 1996), http://www.thefreemanonline.org/featured/teachers-unions-are-the-schools-run-for-them/; Peter Brimelow, *The Worm in the Apple: How the Teacher Unions are Destroying American Education* (New York: HarperCollins, 2003); G. Gregory Moo, *Power Grab: How the National Education Association Is Betraying Our Children* (Washington, DC: Regnery, 1999).

41. See, e.g., *Morse v. Frederick*, 551 U.S. 393 (2007) (upholding a school's punishment of an 18-year-old student for displaying a banner reading "Bong Hits 4 Jesus" across the street from the school); *New Jersey v. T.L.O.*, 469 U.S. 325 (1985) (allowing school officials to search student lockers without a warrant based on a "reasonable suspicion").

42. Regrettably, this book lacks space to address libertarian solutions to environmental problems. For an introduction, see Terry L. Anderson and Donald R. Leal, *Free Market Environmentalism*, rev. ed. (New York: Palgrave Macmillan, 2001); Murray N. Rothbard, "Law, Property Rights, and Air Pollution," *Cato Journal* (Spring 1982): 55–100, http://mises.org/rothbard/lawproperty.pdf.

43. Radley Balko, "Learning Infractions," *Reason* (April 2007), http://reason.com/archives/2007/04/01/learning-infractions/print; James Bovard, "Destroying Families for the Glory of the Drug War, Part 2," *Freedom Daily* (March 1997), http://www.fff.org/freedom/0397d.asp.

44. See Milton Friedman, *Capitalism and Freedom* (Chicago: University of Chicago Press, 1982 [1962]), 93–98.

45. One can find details on all of these programs at "Current School Choice Programs," *The Friedman Foundation for Educational Choice*, http://www.friedmanfoundation.org/schoolchoice/ShowProgram.do.

46. See Clint Bolick, *Voucher Wars: Waging the Legal Battle Over School Choice* (Washington, DC: Cato Institute, 2003), 81.

47. *Zelman v. Simmons-Harris*, 536 U.S. 639 (2002).

48. Tony Mauro, "Libertarian Litigants," *The American Lawyer*, January 27, 2005, available at http://www.law.com/jsp/article.jsp?id=1106573732639.

49. Llewellyn H. Rockwell, Jr., "Vouchers: Another Name for Welfare," *LewRockwell.com*, July 2, 2002, http://www.lewrockwell.com/rockwell/voucher2.html.

50. Clint Bolick, "Blocking the Exits," *Policy Review*, May/June 1998, available at http://www.hoover.org/publications/policyreview/3566087.html.

51. "Erasing the Myths of School Choice: Vouchers Are Costly and Drain Money from Public Schools," *The Friedman Foundation for Educational Choice*, http://www.friedmanfoundation.org/schoolchoice/myths/detailed_myth5.pdf.

52. See David Crockett, "Not Yours to Give," *FEE.org*, http://fee.org/library/books/not-yours-to-give-2; Lawrence W. Reed, *Government, Poverty, & Self-Reliance* (Midland, MI: Mackinac Center for Public Policy, 2005), 12.

53. "School Vouchers," *The Washington Post*, January 26, 2009, http://www.washingtonpost.com/wp-dyn/content/article/2009/01/25/AR2009012501816.html.

54. See Marshall Fritz, "A Better Brand of Parent," *The Freeman*, September 1999, available at http://www.thefreemanonline.org/featured/a-better-brand-of-parent/.

55. Gary North, "Educational Vouchers: The Double Tax," *The Freeman*, May 1976, http://www.thefreemanonline.org/featured/educational-vouchers-the-double-tax.

56. Libertarians take differing views on the rights of children. For one influential view, see Murray N. Rothbard, "Children and Rights," *Mises.org*, May 9, 2007, http://mises.org/story/2568.

57. Brian D. Ray, *Homeschool Progress Report 2009: Academic Achievement and Demographics*, http://www.hslda.org/docs/study/ray2009/2009_Ray_StudyFINAL.pdf.

58. "Academic Statistics on Homeschooling," *Home School Legal Defense Association*, October 22, 2004, http://www.hslda.org/docs/nche/000010/200410250.asp.

59. Ray, *Homeschool Progress Report 2009*, 4–5.

60. See Gary North, "Why Home Schools Are Superior to Private Schools," *LewRockwell.com*, June 15, 2006, http://www.lewrockwell.com/north/north460.html.

61. All facts to this point in the paragraph are from Chris Klicka, "Socialization: Homeschoolers Are in the Real World," *Home School Legal Defense Association*, March 2007, www.hslda.org/docs/nche/000000/00000068.asp.

62. Brian D. Ray, *Home Educated and Now Adults: Their Community and Civic Involvement, Views About Homeschooling, and Other Traits* (Salem, OR: National Home Education Research Institute, 2003); Ray's study's results are also summarized in "Homeschooling Grows Up," *Home School Legal Defense Association*, http://www.hslda.org/research/ray2003/HomeschoolingGrowsUp.pdf.

63. "Homeschooling Grows Up."

64. This research is summarized in Brian D. Ray, "Homeschoolers on to College: What Research Shows Us," *The Journal of College Admission* (Fall 2004): 5–11, http://www.eric.ed.gov:80/ERICDocs/data/ericdocs2sql/content_storage_01/0000019b/80/29/e6/28.pdf.

65. "Home School Laws," *Home School Legal Defense Association*, http://www.hslda.org/laws/default.asp.

66. See, e.g., *2009–2010 NEA Resolutions*, 37, http://www.nea.org/assets/docs/resolutions2009-2010.pdf.

67. See "Reasons Home Schoolers Should Avoid Government Vouchers," *Home School Legal Defense Association*, November 7, 2002, http://www.hslda.org/docs/nche/000002/00000251.asp.

68. National Center for Education Statistics, "1.5 Million Homeschooled Students in the U.S. in 2007," *Issue Brief* (December 2008), http://nces.ed.gov/pubs2009/2009030.pdf.

FURTHER READING

Gatto, John Taylor. *The Underground History of American Education*. New York: Oxford Village Press, 2006. Gatto shows how government came to dominate education in the United States. This book is available for free online at http://www.johntaylorgatto.com/underground.

Gatto, John Taylor. *Weapons of Mass Instruction: A Schoolteacher's Journey Through the Dark World of Compulsory Schooling*. Gabriola Island, BC: New Society Publishers,

2009. Gatto shows how the "mass instruction" approach of government schools harms children, drawing on his experiences over three decades as a New York City school teacher.

Ostrowski, James. *Government Schools Are Bad For Your Kids*. Buffalo, NY: Cazenovia Books, 2009. Ostrowski makes the case against government schools, and especially for removing one's own children from them.

Richman, Sheldon. *Separating School and State: How to Liberate America's Families*. Fairfax, VA: Future of Freedom Foundation, 1994. Richman shows how government took over education and why it should get out.

Rothbard, Murray N. *Education: Free and Compulsory*. Auburn, AL: Ludwig von Mises Institute, 1999. Rothbard explains the libertarian view of education and describes the history of compulsory education in Europe and the United States. This book is available for free online at http://www.mises.org/books/education.pdf.

7

The Fight for Gun Rights

No Supreme Court case in at least a quarter century has drawn as much attention as *District of Columbia v. Heller*, the 2008 case in which the Court recognized an individual's right to keep and bear arms under the Second Amendment and struck down the D.C. gun ban.

Many people know about the *Heller* decision, but not so many know that the case never would have been brought but for the determined efforts of a small team of libertarian lawyers. And few people know that those libertarians did not just have to fight the government to vindicate Second Amendment rights; they also had to fight the National Rifle Association, which went to great lengths to try to stop the case from going forward.

As the first Supreme Court decision ever to overturn a gun control law under the Second Amendment, *Heller* is historic, and it appears to reach a libertarian result. But not all libertarians are happy with *Heller*. Some see it as sowing the seeds not of greater liberty, but of greater restrictions on gun freedom than ever.

In this chapter, we will consider the libertarian view on guns, the story and implications of the *Heller* case, and what else libertarians are doing in the fight against government gun grabbers.

WHY GUNS?

Like the right to free speech, the right to bear arms is relatively well entrenched in the United States—better than in much of the world. Across the red states, and even to a considerable extent in the blue ones, countless ordinary Americans own guns and do not want the government to take them away. In 2000, historian Michael Bellesiles tried to claim in his book *Arming America: The Origins of a National Gun Culture* that this is a relatively recent phenomenon, and that guns and gun rights are not as firmly rooted in America's past as gun activists would lead one to believe. But Bellesiles's work was exposed as a fraud—he literally made up his facts, as conservative author Clayton E. Cramer showed in his 2006 book, *Armed America: The Story of How and Why Guns Became as American as Apple Pie.* Indeed, so strong is America's libertarian tradition of gun ownership that, as late as 1968, a teenager could go into any hardware store almost anywhere in America and purchase a rifle, no questions asked, and could probably buy a handgun, too.[1]

Why are libertarians so interested in gun rights in particular? On the theoretical level, there is the obvious reason: Libertarians think one should be allowed to own just about *anything,* as long as it is not stolen and one is not using it to aggress against anyone. In addition, gun rights are under constant attack by politicians from both political parties, so it makes sense for libertarians to vehemently defend these rights.

But why the special emphasis? Why do libertarians seem to be disproportionately represented among gun enthusiasts, and vice versa? Two reasons stand out.

Liberty Implies Self-Defense

One reason why libertarians may place special emphasis on gun rights is because the rights to life and liberty imply the right to self-defense. Murray Rothbard explains: "If, as libertarians believe, every individual has the right to own his person and property, it then follows that he has the right to employ violence to defend himself against the violence of criminal aggressors."[2] Otherwise, the right is no right at all. Guns in particular are important to protect one's life and property because *they work.* Leftists who hate and fear guns see them only as instruments of death (except in the hands of government), but the facts bear out libertarians' view that guns are critical to the right to life itself.

Mainstream gun-rights advocates have argued the merits of gun freedom for defense against crime reasonably well, so we do not need to rehash those arguments in detail. But it is still worth briefly reviewing some key facts. Media coverage dwells on crimes committed with guns, but this distorts reality. People see the harm caused by guns, but they do not see the benefits—the many times each year when people use guns defensively, usually without even having to shoot, to prevent crime from happening. Surveys vary in their results, depending on the questions asked, but the most reliable estimates are that Americans use guns defensively to stop a crime from happening more than two million times per year.[3]

Studies by economist John R. Lott (author of *More Guns, Less Crime*) and others have shown that allowing people to carry concealed weapons reduces violent crime rates, and murder rates in particular.[4] Economic logic suggests that this would be so: If a would-be attacker knows that the potential costs of his crime are greater (he is more likely to be shot in self-defense), and the potential rewards of his crime are lower (he is less likely to succeed in his attempted crime), then he will be less likely to attack in the first place. Through this deterrent effect, guns stop crime without even being used. Lott's empirical studies verify this logical conclusion, and even scholars who disagree with Lott about guns *reducing* crime have had to concede that crime *does not increase* where governments respect the freedom to carry concealed weapons.[5]

Opponents of gun rights may argue that we have government police to defend us, as Americans in the founding era did not, so gun rights are obsolete. But to count on the police for help in a life-or-death emergency is suicidal, because there is nothing the police can do for an individual facing an immediate threat. As writer and gun expert Richard W. Stevens illustrates in his book *Dial 911 and Die*, countless people have been killed because they called the police for help and waited, rather than taken matters into their own hands with a firearm. Behaving passively, as the media often advises, is not a viable option, either, because, according to Lott, men who behave passively during a violent crime are 1.4 times as likely to be severely injured than those who have a gun, and passive women are 2.5 times as likely to be severely injured.[6] It is also worth noting that, even though the common defense is the main theoretical justification for government, the U.S. Supreme Court has held that there is no individual right to police protection.[7] So protecting one's life or the life of a family member is something that is ultimately the individual's responsibility—and therefore requires the exercise of an individual right, the right to self-defense through the most effective means available, namely the use of a firearm.

We should add that some libertarians are pacifists and would not use a gun even for self-defense. This is perfectly consistent with libertarianism. Libertarianism does not say that you *must* defend your life with violence, only that government should not prevent you from doing so.

Restraining Government

Another reason gun rights are especially important to libertarians is because they serve as a check on government power. If the government has all the guns in a country, the people are at its mercy. If the people are armed, however, the government will know that if it goes too far in abusing its power, it could meet with armed resistance. That idea is almost unspeakably radical today, but America's founders recognized it as an important safeguard for liberty.

In most of the American colonies, the law *required* every freeman to possess a firearm, and in many of the colonies it required every head of a household to own one, too. Collectively, all of the freemen owning guns constituted the "militia." Instead of having a standing army, as we have today, the colonists relied on themselves for defense if they needed to repel invaders.[8] There is nothing libertarian about forcing people to own guns or participate in a militia, of course, but widespread appreciation for the freedom to own guns would likely achieve a similar result.

The founders and the philosophers who inspired them explicitly acknowledged and celebrated the fact that this kind of militia protected not only against foreign invasion, but also against tyrannical government. James Madison wrote in *The Federalist No. 46* that "ambitious encroachments" by the federal government could not go beyond a certain point because the armed populace would resist:

> Let a regular [standing] army, fully equal to the resources of the country, be formed; and let it be entirely at the devotion of the federal government; still it would not be going too far to say, that the State governments, with the people on their side, would be able to repel the danger. The highest number to which, according to the best computation, a standing army can be carried in any country, does not exceed one hundredth part of the whole number of souls; or one twenty-fifth part of the number able to bear arms. This proportion would not yield, in the United States, an army of more than twenty-five or thirty thousand men. To these would be opposed a militia amounting to near half a million of citizens with arms in their hands, officered by men chosen from among themselves, fighting for their common liberties, and united and conducted by governments possessing their affections and confidence. It may well be doubted, whether a militia thus circumstanced could ever be conquered by such a proportion of regular troops.[9]

Even though Madison speaks of a state militia, it is clear enough that power was essentially with the people because all were armed and ready to resist tyranny.

Algernon Sidney, an eighteenth-century English writer whose *Discourses Concerning Government* influenced America's founders, advanced the idea that gun rights were critical to keep government in line: "Peace is seldom made, and never kept, unless the Subject retain such a power in his hands, as may oblige the Prince to stand to what is agreed.. . ."[10] John Locke took essentially the same view: that the right to self-defense included the right to defense against a government that oversteps its proper boundaries.[11] As summarized by Second Amendment scholar Don B. Kates, the Founders believed that "the right of self-defense exists against murder, rape, robbery, and other crime, whether perpetrated by apolitical criminals or by a tyrant or his agents for political purpose . . ."[12]

At the same time, the Founders did not see a need for perpetual violent revolution against government because, in Kates's words, the "existence of an armed populace will generally avert the necessity of actual resistance, much less revolution, by deterring government and rulers from their inherent tendency to tyrannize and oppress."[13] That is, guns prevent governments from committing crimes in the first place, just as they prevent private crime without anyone having to fire a shot. Today, more gun freedom and more widespread gun ownership would not force the government to fully respect libertarian rights—it did not do so even in the founding era—but it would serve as a preventative measure against the worst possible government offenses.

The twentieth century's tragic history of genocide illustrates the importance of widespread gun ownership as a check on government. Jews for the Preservation of Firearms Ownership, an essentially libertarian gun-rights organization founded and run by Aaron Zelman, emphasizes the connection between gun control and genocide, including but not limited to the Holocaust. In their book *Death by Gun Control*, Zelman and co-author Richard W. Stevens present a formula to illustrate the elements that have historically been necessary for genocide to occur:

Hatred + Government + Disarmed Civilians = Genocide

That is, for genocide to occur, there must generally be hatred toward some group within a country, a government to commit or enable genocide, and disarmed civilians who are powerless to prevent it. *Death by Gun Control* catalogs numerous instances where governments kept guns out of people's hands and then slaughtered them, or allowed them to be slaughtered, en masse. Germany, for example, had strict gun control laws in the first part of the twentieth century, including a complete (if inconsistently enforced) ban on firearms from 1918 through 1928. Following that, it had laws strictly limiting the manufacture and trade of firearms, and explicitly banning gypsies from owning guns. When the Nazis came to power, they further tightened the gun laws, and in 1938 prohibited Jews from entering the firearms business. Finally, later in 1938, Heinrich Himmler issued an order that all Jews' guns be confiscated. Disarmed, the Jews were then unable to put up much resistance when the Nazis finally decided to ship them off to the camps where millions met their deaths.[14]

Nazi Germany committed history's most notorious genocide, but Zelman and Stevens cover many other places where governments or groups empowered by government exterminated disarmed civilians, including Cambodia (more than 2,000,000 killed);[15] China (over 35,000,000 killed);[16] Rwanda (800,000 killed);[17] Uganda (300,000 killed);[18] and the Soviet Union (over 24,000,000 killed).[19] Gun control laws do not cause genocide by themselves, of course, and a lack of gun control laws cannot guarantee that genocide will not occur. But these examples show, at the very least, that disarmed people are more vulnerable to death by government.

Zelman, Stevens, and others also note that gun control laws have harmed minorities in the United States. When Southern states enacted black codes following the Civil War, they also enacted laws designed to keep guns out of blacks' hands.[20] Today, gun laws, which are toughest in some of America's most crime-infested cities, serve to disarm law-abiding black crime victims. As Kates has put it, gun control advocates appear to be "oblivious to the situation of poor and minority people living in areas where the police have given up on crime control."[21] Lott's research indicates that black people living in high-crime areas today benefit the most from carrying or owning a handgun for protection. Laws allowing concealed carry of handguns result in a greater drop in violent crime in counties that are 40 percent African American than in counties that are only five percent African American. Lott's study also found that the drop in murder rates resulting from concealed carry laws was eight times larger in heavily African American counties than in counties with few African Americans.[22]

Heller

Before the *Heller* decision, it was essentially illegal to possess a handgun in the District of Columbia. The law prohibited the carrying of an unregistered firearm, and it prohibited registration of handguns. The law did allow registration of long guns (shotguns, rifles), but it required them to be stored unloaded and disassembled, or bound by a trigger lock or similar device, which made them useless in an emergency. Plus, anyone caught using a long gun in his or her home for self-defense faced the threat of prosecution. This was the toughest gun control law in American history, and on its enactment in 1976, Ron Paul called it "flat out illegal" and presciently predicted that "this law is going to be challenged, and it is going to be thrown out."[23]

Libertarian Lawyers

The judicial and political climates were not right, though, for an immediate court challenge. By 2002, however, some libertarian lawyers decided that the time had come. Clark Neily and Steve Simpson, two attorneys for the libertarian Institute for Justice (IJ) first hatched the idea of a Second Amendment lawsuit in a conversation at a cocktail hour. Because IJ focuses on other areas of the law (see the next chapter), Neily and Simpson realized they would need to look elsewhere for help in bringing a suit. They turned to two other attorneys, Robert Levy and Gene Healy, both of whom were employed by the Cato Institute.[24] Together, they would pursue the case on their own time, not officially on behalf of their institutional employers. Levy, who entered law school at age 50, would fund the suit out of his personal wealth, accumulated during previous careers in portfolio management and software development.[25]

Simpson was too busy with his work for IJ to stay on the case, and before long Healy also had to withdraw to focus on his work. Levy and Neily had fairly full plates, too, so they hired a private attorney, 37-year-old Alan Gura, to be lead counsel in the case.

The Clients

The next step for the three-man team was to find clients—people who wanted to sue the District to vindicate their gun rights. (Finding clients after coming up with your case is common in public-interest law.) To put a good face on the case for the courts and the public, the attorneys took care to choose clients who would come across as sympathetic, ordinary law-abiding citizens who want to protect their lives, not as libertarian extremists, stereotypical "gun nuts," or criminals. The team succeeded in finding six plaintiffs from a variety of backgrounds. For example, Shelly Parker, the original lead plaintiff, was a black woman who had received frequent threats because of her efforts to keep her crime-infested neighborhood safe. (The case was originally called *Parker v. District of Columbia*, but for simplicity we will just refer to it by the short version of its final name, *Heller*.) Gillian St. Lawrence was a young attorney who lived in Georgetown and owned a registered shotgun, which she was forced to render useless in her home. And Dick Heller, whose name ended up on the case, was a trained and licensed special police officer for the District who worked in the Federal Judicial Center. Heller carried a handgun at work every day, as an exception to the law allowed, but the District forbade him from possessing a gun in his home for self-defense.

The U.S. Court of Appeals would ultimately dismiss all of the original six plaintiffs except Heller. The court concluded that the five dismissed plaintiffs lacked standing to sue because they had not actually attempted to register a weapon or get a gun license; they had only claimed, in their complaint filed with the court, that they *wanted* to have a gun but could not have one because the law stood in the way. Heller, on the other hand, had in fact tried to register—a lucky break for his legal team, which had not asked him to do it.[26]

Why D.C.?

The legal team chose to challenge D.C.'s gun law instead of, say, Chicago's, to keep the legal issue as simple as possible. By itself, the Second Amendment, like the other provisions of the Bill of Rights, only constrains the *federal* government. But many protections of the Bill of Rights, such as those of the First and Fourth Amendments, have been applied to the states through the "incorporation doctrine"—the idea that the Fourteenth Amendment's Due Process Clause extends some protections of the Bill of Rights to limit state governments' ability to infringe certain rights. Whether the Second Amendment applies to the states through the incorporation doctrine was unsettled in the law; it would have made the case more difficult if the Supreme Court had to determine both whether the Second Amendment protects an individual right to have a gun in one's house *and* whether that right is enforceable against state and local governments. By challenging the D.C. gun ban—essentially, a law of the federal government—the *Heller* plaintiffs avoided that problem.

Another reason for choosing D.C.'s gun ban was because, as the nation's most stringent gun law, it was the easiest to challenge. The legal team wanted to pursue an incremental strategy. Getting the Court to strike down the worst aspects of the country's worst gun law was a first step. After winning on that issue in this case, they could pursue other issues in other cases to widen the scope of Second Amendment protection.[27]

Why Now?

The lawyers believed the time was right to bring a Second Amendment lawsuit because of three factors that came together. First, much scholarship had arisen in recent decades, even from left-wing legal academics such as Alan Dershowitz, Laurence Tribe, and Akhil Amar, that supported the idea that the Second Amendment protects an individual right.[28] Second, a 2001 decision by the U.S. Court of Appeals for the Fifth Circuit, *United States v. Emerson*, mentioned in passing, in the process of upholding a gun law, that the Second Amendment protects an individual right.[29] Third, the Justice Department under then-Attorney General John Ashcroft, a man not so friendly to liberty in many respects, submitted a brief discouraging Supreme Court review of *Emerson*, agreeing with the court's view of the Second Amendment.[30]

The NRA: Ally or Enemy?

The time seemed right, the team was assembled, and the clients and issues were lined up. Then trouble came from an unexpected source: the National Rifle Association. One would think the NRA would have been a strong supporter from the outset, but it was not—it was an enemy. The NRA tried to crush the suit in several ways. For one, it filed its own lawsuit, *Seegars v. Ashcroft*, in which it sued both the District and the U.S. Department of Justice. The NRA's suit made many arguments challenging the gun ban that did not turn on the Second Amendment. This way, the NRA could give the court an opportunity to strike down the gun ban on another ground and avoid a ruling on the Second Amendment issue. The NRA then tried to take over the *Heller* litigation by moving to have the two cases consolidated, which would have put all of the NRA's issues in play in *Heller*. That attempt failed, and ultimately *Seegars* was dismissed because, unlike Dick Heller, all of the *Seegars* plaintiffs lacked standing.[31] After that strategy failed, the NRA pushed Congress to simply repeal the worst aspects of the D.C. gun ban so the *Heller* suit would become moot. That would help D.C. residents, of course, but it would prevent the *Heller* team from establishing a pro-gun legal precedent. This strategy by the NRA put Levy in the odd position of going to Congress to testify *against* the legislation that would have increased D.C. gun freedom.[32]

Why was the NRA so determined to derail *Heller*? Unlike the *Heller* attorneys, the NRA was not convinced that five Supreme Court justices would vote in favor of gun rights, so it feared that the case could establish a devastating anti-gun precedent. The concern was not totally unwarranted—the *Heller* lawyers did appear to be gambling with Americans' rights. But the *Heller* lawyers' confidence in their own predictions and abilities would of course prove to be well founded. And once it was clear that the case was going forward, the NRA got on the bandwagon.

The NRA, incidentally, has never been a favorite of libertarians because, despite the NRA's reputation among the general public, its approach to gun rights is not always libertarian. Sometimes, for example, the NRA urges strict enforcement of already-existing gun laws as an alternative to passing new gun laws. Libertarians, in contrast, would urge that the old laws be repealed and no new laws be enacted. Some libertarians blame the NRA for committing unnecessary acts of political compromise in "signing off on" two major federal gun control measures, the 1968 Gun Control Act and the Brady Bill.[33] Also, the NRA sometimes appears to put the pro-gun cause above the fundamental libertarian principle of property rights. (Of course, it is property rights, including the property right in one's life, that guns are supposed to protect in the first place.) For example, the NRA opposes private property rights when it supports state laws that would force employers to allow employees to bring guns to work in their cars, on the employer's private property.[34] Libertarians say that if a property owner does not want guns on his property, that is his right; people who do not like it can choose to work elsewhere. So the NRA position is not always the libertarian position. Gun Owners of America and Jews for the Preservation of Firearms Ownership are two organizations that tend to take a more consistent libertarian stance.

The Road to Victory

Through their case, the *Heller* team sought to establish a precedent holding (1) that the Second Amendment protects an individual right to keep and bear arms; (2) that this right at least includes the right to have those arms "readily accessible to be used effectively when necessary" for defense in the home; and (3) that D.C.'s gun ban infringes this right.

In March 2004, the United States District Court for the District of Columbia rejected these propositions.[35] It relied on the last Supreme Court decision to address a Second Amendment challenge, *United States v. Miller* (1939),[36] to conclude that the Second Amendment does not protect an individual right, but only protects firearms possession in the context of a formal, government-organized "Militia" such as a National Guard unit. Because the *Heller* plaintiffs did not purport to be members of a Militia (in that sense), the Court dismissed their claims.

Next, the U.S. Court of Appeals for the District of Columbia Circuit took up the case. Before addressing the Second Amendment issue, the Court held that the five plaintiffs other than Heller lacked standing and dismissed them from the case. The Court (split 2 to 1) then agreed with Heller on the merits, making it the first-ever federal appellate court decision to strike down a law under the Second Amendment.

The government petitioned the Supreme Court to review the Court of Appeals decision, and the Supreme Court took the case. The *Heller* team received advice to let an experienced Supreme Court advocate such as Kenneth Starr or Ted Olsen argue the case, but Levy remained committed to and confident in Gura, who had won in the Court of Appeals and done most of the work on the case.[37] Now that the case was going before the Supreme Court, its profile was extremely high. In addition to the parties' briefs, amicus ("friend of the Court") briefs poured in as well, with 49 of them supporting gun rights and 19 opposed.[38] Gura argued the case in March 2008.

When the Supreme Court issued its decision in late June, most gun-rights supporters and libertarians rejoiced: the Court gave Heller exactly what he asked for. In striking down the law, the Court relied purely on an interpretation of the Second Amendment, not on libertarian principles as such. Justice Antonin Scalia, writing for the majority, noted that the "right of the people" referenced in the Second Amendment must be an individual right, in light of the fact that there are other places in the Constitution where a "right of the people" is mentioned (for example, in the First Amendment) and no one questions that these refer to individual rights, not collective rights. The Court emphasized that the right to keep and bear arms pre-dated the Constitution as a longstanding legal right of Englishmen, and the Second Amendment merely codified it. This follows logically from the Constitution's statement that the right to keep and bear arms "shall not be infringed"—the wording presumes that the right already exists. The Court then turned to the meanings of "keep arms" and "bear arms," and noted that usage of these terms in the founding era showed that they contemplated possession and carrying of firearms *outside* the context of militia service.

The Supreme Court's decision meant that Heller and others like him could finally legally keep handguns in their homes for defense. And although the Supreme Court did not address the incorporation issue, its holding nonetheless made cities across the country rethink their gun laws. Morton Grove, Illinois, which was the first nonfederal municipality to ban handguns, announced that it would repeal its ban. So did another Chicago suburb, Wilmette.[39]

Libertarian Backlash

Heller appears to be a major victory for liberty. But even if they respect and admire the lawyers behind the suit and their motives, not all libertarians are thrilled with the decision. Some even see it as a potential step back for liberty.

How so? The answer lies in certain arguments the legal team did and did not make, and in language in the decision that could seal gun rights' doom rather than preserve them.

In his argument before the Supreme Court, Alan Gura explicitly, deliberately made major concessions to the government's power to restrict gun rights. He told the Court that there is "no question" that the government can ban firearms that are "not appropriate to civilian use," including, he suggested, machine guns.[40] He also conceded that the government has a "great deal of leeway" in regulating guns, and that it would be a "reasonable limitation" for government to require guns to be stored in a safe inside the home.[41] He also told the Court that he had no objection to licensing laws, so long as they were "not enforced in an arbitrary and capricious manner." He said that prerequisites for getting a gun license, including background checks, would be fine.[42]

All of this infuriates libertarians and hardcore gun-rights advocates who see no authorization in the Second Amendment and no other justification for these supposedly "reasonable" limitations on rights. The *Heller* plaintiffs and attorneys were supposed to be the true libertarians, in contrast with the "moderate" NRA, and here they were telling the Supreme Court there was no problem with major qualifications on what's supposed to be an unqualified right.

Gura hit back at these critics, arguing that he had to concede these points for the Court to take him seriously on the relatively narrow point at issue in the case: that, whatever else might be lawful or unlawful under the Second Amendment, a complete ban like D.C.'s goes too far. "We wanted to win," Gura told libertarian journalist Brian Doherty. "And you win constitutional litigation by framing the issues in as narrow a manner as possible. If you ask for too much, you'll lose." He also sees arguing for an unqualified right to be futile: "You cannot tell the Supreme Court there is an absolute right to guns. There are no absolute rights in constitutional law."[43] Probably most of Gura's critics can understand not wanting to ask for too much too soon; what troubles them is conceding important issues that may arise in future cases.

Like Gura's argument, the Supreme Court's decision left a lot of room for government to restrict gun rights. Justice Scalia's majority opinion declares: "Like most rights, the right secured by the Second Amendment is not unlimited." Scalia goes on to state that the Second Amendment only protects those firearms the Court deems to be "in common use for lawful purposes," and does not protect the "right to keep and carry any weapon whatsoever and for whatever purpose."[44]

With such loopholes built in, what did *Heller* really accomplish? Some libertarians have suggested that *Heller* will mostly just help Republicans pretend to be quasi-libertarians as the cause of gun control marches on more or less unimpeded. Libertarian writer William Norman Grigg argues that *Heller* served to "placate key elements of the Republican coalition while suggesting alternative routes to those who seek the eventual abolition of the right that was once protected by the Second Amendment. While Scalia's ruling reinforces one of the few effective rallying points for the demoralized Republican Party ('This year's election is all about the judges!'), it does nothing of substance to defer the day when some judge or president will be able to pronounce the Second Amendment extinct."[45]

The pseudonymous libertarian gun expert "Boston T. Party" finds ominous *Heller*'s statement that "the Second Amendment does not protect those weapons not typically possessed for law-abiding purposes." The trouble, he observes, is that many guns are not "typically possessed" *because they have been outlawed* or the government has made it difficult to get them—creating a "Kafka-esque example of an unconstitutional Act indirectly supporting its own constitutionality."[46]

Some libertarians are concerned that *Heller*'s main effect will be to make it easier for courts to *uphold* gun control laws. Some left-wing gun controllers happily agree. Dennis Henigan of the anti-gun Brady Center to Prevent Gun Violence, for one, predicts that "the lower courts are likely to interpret Heller as giving a constitutional green light to virtually every gun control law short of a handgun ban."[47] Federal district court decisions issued soon after *Heller* bear out this prediction, citing *Heller* to *uphold* gun laws because, after all, even the (supposedly) pro-gun *Heller* case says that Second Amendment rights are not unlimited.[48]

In fairness, though, even a skeptic (such as this author) must admit that before *Heller*, there were *no* federal appellate decisions that found *any* gun control laws unconstitutional under the Second Amendment. And now there is one. It is hard not to view that as a step in the right direction—even if it is a small step and may be uncertain to lead to further steps toward freedom.

THE FIGHT GOES ON

As we have seen, the *Heller* attorneys deliberately kept the case's scope narrow, so the decision only applies to the federal government and does not purport to restrain the states. For Alan Gura and the NRA, the next step has been to take the fight to other cities with gun bans in hopes of persuading courts that the incorporation doctrine extends the Second Amendment to restrain state and local governments. To win on this point, they must convince the courts that gun rights are "fundamental" rights "deeply rooted in this Nation's history and tradition." Unlike Bellesiles, they have substantial evidence, if not much case law, on their side.

As this book goes to press, the Supreme Court is currently considering that issue in *McDonald v. City of Chicago*. If Chicago's gun owners win in that case as many observers predict, the decision's impact could be much greater than *Heller*'s as longstanding gun bans across the country would fall.

Gura has also brought a new lawsuit against the District of Columbia, sponsored by the Second Amendment Foundation (another organization more appealing to libertarians than the NRA), to vindicate the right to carry a firearm on one's person. Having a gun for home defense is a good start, but a right to "bear" arms suggests one should be able to walk around with them. A win on this issue combined with a win in *McDonald* could radically expand gun rights across the country.

Meanwhile, in several states, gun owners have taken a different approach that turns not on the Second Amendment, but on states' rights under the Tenth Amendment. For example, in 2009, Montana's legislature passed, and its Democrat governor signed, a statute that exempts from federal firearm laws any guns, ammunition, and accessories made entirely within the state. At this writing, a lawsuit is pending arguing that the state is entitled to do this because federal regulations on such guns would exceed Congress's powers under the Commerce Clause and therefore violate the Tenth Amendment.[49] We will say more on this approach in the next chapter.

Regardless of how any court cases turn out, though, most libertarians are not counting on the courts to protect their rights. One means by which they advance the cause is by continuing to advocate the most radical interpretation of the right to bear arms, the one that grants citizens, in the words of Grigg, "the unqualified liberty to acquire weapons of any sort, in any quantity they please, for the specific purpose of being able to out-gun the government and its agents when such action would be justified."[50] Libertarian science-fiction author and gun activist L. Neil Smith notes, it is still "up to us [libertarians] to set the tone, just as it always has been. It is up to us to establish the level of discourse, and we can no longer afford to be compromising and conciliatory. It is up to us to establish the meaning of the word 'reasonable' and make it stick"—in the minds of the people, if not in the minds of government-employed life-tenured judges. "We have to make Americans wonder why politicians, bureaucrats, and the media want them helpless and unable to resist the likes of Lenin, Stalin, Hitler, Mao, and Pol Pot."[51]

Another means by which libertarians advance the cause is the same means by which they have always advanced their cause, following Albert Jay Nock's example: one person at a time, beginning with one's self. By learning about guns, using them responsibly, and carrying them (sometimes openly), libertarians take responsibility for protecting their own lives and liberty, show that they do not trust government to do this for them, and set an example of what good citizenship looks like in a free society.

NOTES

1. John R. Lott, Jr., *The Bias Against Guns* (Washington, DC: Regnery, 2003), 81.

2. Murray N. Rothbard, *For a New Liberty: The Libertarian Manifesto*, rev. ed. (Auburn, AL: Ludwig von Mises Institute, 2002 [1978]), 114.

3. Gary Kleck, "The Frequency of Defensive Gun Use," in *Armed: New Perspectives on Gun Control*, by Gary Kleck and Don B. Kates, 213–84 (Amherst, NY: Prometheus Books, 2001), 222.

4. See generally John R. Lott, Jr., *More Guns, Less Crime: Understanding Crime and Gun Control Laws* (Chicago: University of Chicago Press, 1998); John R. Lott, Jr., *The Bias Against Guns* (Washington, DC: Regnery, 2003), 227–43.

5. David Glenn, "'More Guns, Less Crime' Thesis Rests on a Flawed Statistical Design, Scholars Argue," *The Chronicle of Higher Education*, May 9, 2003, A18.

6. Lott, *The Bias Against Guns*, 79.

7. *Deshaney v. Winnebago County Social Services Department*, 489 U.S. 189 (1989).

8. See Clayton E. Cramer, *Armed America: The Story of How and Why Guns Became As American As Apple Pie* (Nashville: Nelson Current, 2006), 3–23.

9. James Madison, *Federalist* No. 46, "The Influence of the State and Federal Governments Compared," available at http://www.constitution.org/fed/federa46.htm.

10. Algernon Sidney, *Discourses Concerning Government* (1698) 134, quoted in Stephen P. Halbrook, *That Every Man Be Armed: The Evolution of a Constitutional Right* (Oakland: Independent Institute, 1994 [1984]), 30.

11. Don B. Kates, "The Second Amendment: A Right to Personal Protection," in *Armed: New Perspectives on Gun Control*, ed. Gary Kleck & Don B. Kates, 343–356 (Amherst, NY: Prometheus Books, 2001), 347.

12. Ibid., 353.

13. Ibid.

14. Stephen P. Halbrook, "Nazi Firearms Law and the Disarming of German Jews," in Aaron Zelman and Richard W. Stevens, *Death By Gun Control: The Human Cost of Victim Disarmament* (Hartford, WI: Mazel Freedom Press, 2001), 75–111.

15. R.J. Rummel, *Death by Government* (New Brunswick, NJ: Transaction Publishers, 1996), 160.

16. Ibid., 98–107.

17. Gerard Prunier, *The Rwanda Crisis: History of a Genocide* (New York: Columbia University Press, 1995) 265, cited in Zelman and Stevens, *Death By Gun Control*, 123.

18. Zelman and Stevens, *Death By Gun Control*, 149.

19. Ibid., 67–73.

20. Ibid., 205–06.

21. Don B. Kates, Jr., "Handgun Control: Prohibition Revisited," *Inquiry* (December 5, 1977), 21, quoted in Rothbard, *For a New Liberty*, 116.

22. Lott, *The Bias Against Guns*, 79.

23. Brian Doherty, *Gun Control on Trial* (Washington, DC: Cato Institute, 2008), 45.

24. Robert A. Levy, "Anatomy of a Lawsuit," *Engage: The Journal of the Federalist Society Practice Groups* (October 2008): 27, available at http://www.fed-soc.org/doclib/20090107_LevyEngage93.pdf.

25. Doherty, *Gun Control on Trial*, 23–25; Levy, "Anatomy of a Lawsuit," 27.

26. Doherty, *Gun Control on Trial*, 65–66.

27. Levy, "Anatomy of a Lawsuit," 29.

28. Ibid. 27–28.

29. 270 F.3d 203 (5th Cir. 2001).

30. Levy, "Anatomy of a Lawsuit," 28.

31. Doherty, *Gun Control on Trial*, 61–64.

32. Ibid., 82–83.

33. L. Neil Smith, "With Friends Like the NRA . . .," *JPFO.org*, http://www.jpfo.org/smith/smith-friends-like-nra.htm.

34. Manuel Lora, "The NRA vs. The Parking Lot," *LewRockwell.com*, November 4, 2005, http://www.lewrockwell.com/orig6/m.lora4.html.

35. *Parker v. District of Columbia*, 311 F. Supp. 2d 103 (D.D.C. 2004).

36. 307 U.S. 174 (1939).

37. Levy, "Anatomy of a Lawsuit," 27.

38. Ibid., 31.

39. Doherty, *Gun Control on Trial*, 115.

40. U.S. Supreme Court, *District of Columbia v. Heller Transcript*, March 18, 2008, 59:12–25, available at http://www.supremecourt.gov/oral_arguments/argument_transcripts/07-290.pdf.

41. Ibid., 63:3–5, 72:17–24.

42. Ibid., 75:22–76:5

43. Doherty, *Gun Control on Trial*, 107.

44. 128 S.Ct. at 2816.

45. William Norman Grigg, "The *Heller* Misdirection," *LewRockwell.com*, June 30, 2008, http://www.lewrockwell.com/grigg/grigg-w32.html.

46. Boston T. Party, *Boston's Gun Bible*, 2008 revised edition (Ignacio, CO: Javelin Press, 2008) 30/13–30/14.

47. Dennis Henigan, "The *Heller* Paradox: A Response to Robert Levy," *Cato Unbound*, July 16, 2008, available at http://www.cato-unbound.org/2008/07/16/dennis-henigan/the-heller-paradox-a-response-to-robert-levy/.

48. Stephan Kinsella, "To Hell With *Heller*," *The LRC Blog*, July 7, 2008, available at http://www.lewrockwell.com/blog/lewrw/archives/021863.html.

49. Declan McCullagh, "Montana Suit Challenges Federal Authority," *Taking Liberties*, October 1, 2009, available at http://www.cbsnews.com/blogs/2009/10/01/taking_liberties/entry5356494.shtml.

50. Grigg, "The *Heller* Misdirection."

51. L. Neil Smith, "Popgun Parade," *JPFO.org*, available at http://www.jpfo.org/smith/smith-popgun.htm.

FURTHER READING

Doherty, Brian. *Gun Control on Trial: Inside the Supreme Court Battle Over the Second Amendment*. Washington, DC: Cato Institute, 2008. Doherty had access to all the players on the pro-freedom side of the *Heller* case and provides a detailed account.

Lott, John R., Jr. *The Bias Against Guns*. Washington, DC: Regnery, 2003. Lott, an economist who also wrote the important study *More Guns, Less Crime*, shows how gun ownership reduces crime and guns are nothing to fear despite the attitudes and propaganda of the left and the media.

Party, Boston T. *Boston's Gun Bible*, 2008 revised edition. Ignacio, CO: Javelin Press, 2008. At more than 800 pages, this book is a favorite of libertarians as a comprehensive guide to firearms and gun control issues.

Zelman, Aaron and Richard W. Stevens. *Death by Gun Control: The Human Cost of Victim Disarmament*. Hartford, WI: Mazel Freedom Press, 2001. The authors show how gun control laws have preceded and enabled history's worst genocides by disarming the victims.

8

Fighting in the Courts

Should the government be allowed to take a person's home by force and then hand it over to private developers? Most people would readily answer *no*. But in 2005, the U.S. Supreme Court outraged the nation by answering *yes* in *Kelo v. City of New London*. That case—probably the second most infamous Supreme Court decision of this century, after the *Heller* gun case—prompted changes in the law across the country as people demanded that their state governments stop abusing their eminent domain power.

As with *Heller*, none of this would have happened but for the efforts of libertarian lawyers. They represented the homeowner in *Kelo* and have used the courts in numerous other cases to argue that various government attacks on freedom, especially on property rights and economic liberty, violate the Constitution. In this chapter, we will look at the brand of "judicial activism" some libertarians have been promoting in the courts, including the theory behind it, their strategy, and particular cases they have pursued. We will also consider the views of other libertarians who are skeptical of this approach—who think the best constitutional strategy is to play the states against the federal government under the Tenth Amendment, or think that libertarians should reject the Constitution entirely.

THE THEORY

Some libertarians want to use the Constitution to advance liberty. But is the Constitution libertarian? Libertarians disagree with each other about this.

Ron Paul, for one, invokes the Constitution constantly, and urges his fellow legislators to follow it. In his book *The Revolution: A Manifesto*, he writes that the Constitution is "not perfect," but is "a pretty good one" because it "defines and limits the scope of government." He adds: "When we get into the habit of disregarding it, we do so at our own peril."[1] The Cato Institute, for its part, publishes and promotes pocket editions of the Constitution, and its Vice President, David Boaz, has stated that the Constitution is "based on the principle that individuals have natural rights that precede the establishment of government and that all the power a government has is delegated to it by individuals for the protection of their rights."[2]

But many libertarians, including this author, do not consider the Constitution to be especially benevolent and see it primarily as an enemy, not a guardian, of liberty because it gives the State an appearance of legitimacy that it does not deserve and empowers it to violate rights. We will consider the dissenters' views on the Constitution later in the chapter. For now, we will focus on the ideas of those who see the Constitution and the courts as a potential force for good.

Of course, even those libertarians who like the Constitution do not like the Constitution *as the government interprets it now*. Instead, they argue that the federal government has twisted the Constitution's meaning, mostly by reading the powers of government too broadly and protections for individual liberty too narrowly, especially since the New Deal era. Provisions that were supposed to protect liberty are treated by courts as though they are not even there. As leading libertarian legal scholar Randy Barnett puts it, a look at today's constitutional law is like holding up the Constitution and finding "empty holes in the parchment where these passages once appeared."[3] The goal of libertarian legal activists is to restore those missing passages, correct misinterpretations of others, and bring back the "lost Constitution" so government will be reduced to the smaller size and scope it had earlier in the nation's history. That would not achieve the libertarian ideal, but it would be closer than what exists now.

Interpreting the Constitution

Before making constitutional arguments, one must decide what method to use to interpret the Constitution. Whether they approve of the Constitution or not, libertarians tend to favor interpreting the Constitution according to its original meaning—that is, according to what a given constitutional provision's words would have meant to the general public at the time it was enacted. ("Original meaning" should not be confused with the framers' "original intent," which could be entirely different and is much harder to discern.) Libertarians prefer this method because it fixes the Constitution's meaning, and a government constrained by fixed rules is likely to be less offensive to liberty than one that can make up the rules as it goes along.

This originalist approach stands in contrast to the "living Constitution" approach favored by many jurists today. Libertarian political economist Thomas DiLorenzo explains why libertarians reject that idea: "[W]henever you hear the phrase 'living Constitution,' just substitute the word 'no' for 'living,' and you'll understand what it means."[4] If the government can change the rules by which it plays by changing the meaning of the Constitution, then government is not constrained at all, and liberty is all the more endangered.

So most libertarians are originalists, but not all originalists are libertarians. Supreme Court Justice Antonin Scalia, for example, is the figure most closely associated with originalism, but he is no libertarian. As we will see, libertarian originalists see broad protections for individual rights—and judicial protection of those rights—in the Constitution's original meaning. But Scalia and other conservative originalists believe that the Constitution leaves most issues up to Congress or state legislatures, with the courts owing the legislative branch a great deal of deference. Also, some libertarians have charged that Scalia is not an originalist at all because he makes many major exceptions to the rule, especially where originalism would produce a result antithetical to his conservative political views, as in the *Raich* medical marijuana case.[5] Justice Clarence Thomas, in contrast, is more consistent in his originalist approach, and although he does not always reach a libertarian result, this appears to be the result of honest interpretation. (Thomas, incidentally, appears to lean toward libertarianism on a number of issues, and says he was influenced in his thinking by free-market economists Thomas Sowell, Walter Williams, and Ludwig von Mises and by the novels of Ayn Rand.)[6] The remaining Supreme Court justices do not claim to be originalists, let alone libertarians.

Abuses of Power

According to libertarian originalism, today's federal government has far exceeded its constitutional authority. Article I of the Constitution gives Congress just 17 specific powers, but today's Congress presumes itself authorized to do practically anything it wants, involving virtually any sphere of human activity, and the courts mostly go along with it. As government grew ever bigger, the Supreme Court did not strike down a single federal law as unconstitutional between 1937 and 1995. According to libertarian originalists, this unchecked government growth occurred in part because the Supreme Court read Congress's powers too broadly, especially through its interpretations of the Necessary and Proper Clause and the Commerce Clause.

The Necessary and Proper Clause

The Necessary and Proper Clause provides that Congress has the power to "make all Laws which shall be necessary and proper for carrying into Execution the foregoing Powers [in Article I], and all other Powers vested by this Constitution in the Government of the United States, or in any Department or Officer thereof." The Supreme Court took this clause in an anti-libertarian direction early in the nation's history, as Chief Justice John Marshall held in the *McCulloch v. Maryland* (1819) decision that "necessary," as that word is used in the Necessary and Proper Clause, doesn't really mean *necessary*. Instead, according to Marshall, the Clause allows Congress to do anything that is "convenient" or "helpful" to Congress in carrying out its other enumerated powers. As long as the ends are "legitimate," then "all means which are appropriate, which are plainly adapted to that end, which are not [explicitly] prohibited, but are consistent with the letter and spirit of the Constitution, are Constitutional." Thus, in *McCulloch*, the Court held that Congress could establish a national bank, even though the Constitution does not actually say so. Since then, the courts have largely deferred to Congress's own determinations of what actions are "convenient" to the exercise of its powers.

Barnett has argued that, based on extensive historical research, the Necessary and Proper Clause does not allow Congress to do whatever it wants. When the Constitution was originally proposed, its opponents expressed concern that the clause would amount to an unlimited grant of power to Congress, but the Federalists—the group that really did want a strong central government—specifically denied the charge. Because of such denials in *The Federalist* and elsewhere, the public understanding of the Necessary and Proper Clause was that "necessary" meant more or less what it appears to mean (though, according to Barnett, "necessary" might arguably mean something less than "absolutely necessary").[7] As for the term "proper," according to Barnett, it entails three criteria: (1) whether the law is in accordance with the Constitutional separation of powers; (2) whether the law respects the principles of federalism; and (3) whether the law respects the background rights retained by the people (about which we will say more below).[8]

Of course, the Supreme Court will never revisit a decision so enshrined in the law as *McCulloch* or reject the long-accepted analysis of a figure so revered as Chief Justice Marshall. As we noted, only two current Court members are originalists. Of them, only one, Justice Thomas, is willing to put aside the doctrine of *stare decisis* to reconsider the meaning of a long-standing precedent if it conflicts with the Constitution's original meaning. But if libertarians could somehow convince courts to strike down some laws at the extremes as being beyond Congress's "Necessary and Proper" powers, liberty would benefit.

The Commerce Clause

The Commerce Clause has been the leading means by which Congress and the courts have expanded and abused federal power. It authorizes Congress "to regulate Commerce with foreign Nations, and among the several States, and with the Indian Tribes," but Congress has taken this as a license to do just about anything since the landmark New Deal era cases of *NLRB v. Jones & Laughlan Steel Corp.*[9] and *Wickard v. Filburn*,[10] on the ground that anything can be said to "affect" commerce between the states—at least indirectly, in a sense that only a lawyer could appreciate. This has prompted U.S. Court of Appeals Judge Alex Kozinski, who sometimes exhibits sympathy for libertarian ideas, to call the Commerce Clause the "Hey, you-can-do-whatever-you-feel-like Clause."[11]

According to Barnett's analysis, when the Constitution refers to "Commerce," it means shipping and trade, not, as Congress and the current Supreme Court would have it, "the production of items to be traded, and certainly not . . . all gainful activity."[12] And "regulate," as that term was understood at the time the Constitution was ratified, did not suggest that Congress could interfere with commerce in any way it chose. Rather, scholars such as Barnett, Richard Epstein, and Roger Pilon have argued that the Commerce Clause, rightly understood, simply allows Congress to make commerce between the states "regular," and not subject to all manner of restrictions by individual state governments.[13] That is, the Clause's language empowers Congress to keep trade free between the states, and to keep trade free *or unfree* with foreign nations if it so chooses.[14] Under the "dormant Commerce Clause" theory, the Commerce Clause implicitly prohibits state governments from erecting barriers to interstate trade—a debatable theory from a strict originalist view, but one that is good for liberty.[15]

These definitions do not allow Congress to prohibit trade in certain items altogether, though Barnett does think of a few possible exceptions. Nor does this understanding of the Commerce Clause allow Congress to prohibit the production, possession, or trade of goods that occurs wholly within a state. Yet the Supreme Court has long allowed Congress to use the Commerce Clause to do just that—recently, for example, in the *Raich* medical marijuana case, where patients were prosecuted for using marijuana that was grown in their own state and never sold to anyone. If the Supreme Court enforced the meaning of the Commerce Clause we have just reviewed, Congress would not be allowed to regulate all the things it regulates today, which would increase liberty—at least, it would until Congress found another provision it could twist and abuse.

Some libertarians were encouraged with respect to the Commerce Clause in 1995, when the Supreme Court held in *United States v. Lopez*[16] that the Gun-Free School Zones Act of 1990, which prohibited anyone from carrying a gun within 1,000 feet of a school, was outside Congress's powers under the Commerce Clause. The government attempted to justify the law by arguing that guns in schools affect the quality of education, and the quality of education, in turn, affects commerce, including interstate commerce. The government also argued that violence increases insurance costs and discourages travel, and these affect commerce. These arguments were too much of a stretch even for a Supreme Court that had not invalidated any federal law under the Commerce Clause since 1937, and it struck down the law. Five years later, the Court struck down portions of the Violence Against Women Act, which allowed victims of gender-based violence to sue their attackers in federal court, in *Morrison v. United States*,[17] because the government could show only an "attenuated" effect on commerce from violence.

The hope that *Lopez* and *Morrison* inspired among fans of limited government was short-lived, as the courts refused to strike down other laws under the Commerce Clause, and *Raich* killed this hope completely. *Lopez* and *Morrison* seem to have been a fluke, not a trend, which cannot be too surprising given how much is at stake for the federal government that, after all, selects and employs federal judges.

The Necessary and Proper Clause and the Commerce Clause are not the only means by which the federal government has increased its power, but they are the only ones we have space to discuss in detail here. Another notable example is the General Welfare Clause, which has been read to allow Congress to spend money on anything it chooses, and to give money to the states with strings attached, effectively allowing Congress to dictate state law. Details on such additional offenses are in some of the books listed in the "Further Reading" section of this chapter.

Individual Rights

In addition to enumerating (and therefore supposedly limiting) the federal government's powers, the Constitution also contains protections for individual rights. Some of these specific protections are well known, such as those in the First and Second Amendments, but libertarian legal scholars have focused on other provisions to argue that the Constitution creates strong protection for a wide array of libertarian rights.

The Takings Clause

One less-noticed provision that could protect individuals from government predation if the Courts fully enforced it is the Takings Clause, found in the Fifth Amendment, which says that private property shall not "be taken for public use, without just compensation." Richard Epstein, a prominent legal scholar at the University of Chicago and New York University, has done groundbreaking work on this issue.[18] According to Epstein, the Takings Clause does not allow the government to take property for any public *purpose* but only for an actual public *use*. That is, the government must put any property it takes toward something that can actually be used by the public, such as a road, not something to be used exclusively by a private party. (He also finds an exception for the rare case of public "necessity.") Under this interpretation, the Takings Clause still remains objectionable for most libertarians, who consider it wrong to force anyone to surrender their private property for *any* purpose. Still, Epstein's interpretation would constrain government considerably by allowing it to take property in fewer cases than it does now. Under Epstein's interpretation, the Takings Clause also applies to more than just the taking of land through eminent domain—the usual context in which it comes up—to protect people who lose the use or value of their property through economic regulation, including wage or price controls. By requiring that the government compensate those who suffer harm because of its programs, Epstein's approach to the Takings Clause, in his words, "invalidates much of the twentieth century legislation"[19]—and from the libertarian view, that's a good thing.

The Ninth Amendment

The Ninth Amendment provides that the "enumeration in the Constitution, of certain rights, shall not be construed to deny or disparage others retained by the people." What does this mean? According to many legal scholars, especially conservatives, it means nothing. In his ill-fated Supreme Court confirmation hearings, conservative jurist Robert Bork famously compared the Ninth Amendment to an "ink blot" and said that he found its meaning so unclear that it would be better to pretend that it does not exist rather than to allow judges to read meaning into it.

Many libertarians, however, find the Ninth Amendment's meaning clear enough. Some 45 years ago, Murray Rothbard argued that the Ninth Amendment should be reinvigorated to protect individual rights.[20] In the past two decades, Barnett has led the way in pursuing this goal with constitutional scholarship. Many of the Constitution's framers, importantly including James Madison, believed that people had a broad range of natural rights, all of which were essentially "liberty rights"—not positive claims on government or others, but "negative" rights such as the right to own property, pursue happiness, and do all manner of peaceful things that did not infringe on anyone else's freedom. The Bill of Rights explicitly protects certain liberty rights—the right to speak freely, to carry firearms, and so on—but most people would agree that the Bill of Rights does not specifically identify all of the rights that people have. The Ninth Amendment was therefore intended as a catch all to protect the additional rights not mentioned and to relieve the concerns of people who feared that listing some rights would imply that other rights were *not* protected and therefore subject to federal infringement.

According to Barnett, who finds support for his view in the words of Madison, the Ninth Amendment even limits the exercise of powers that the Constitution explicitly grants to the government. That is, even where the Constitution grants the government the power to do something, the government must exercise that power in a way that minimizes infringements on liberty. As founding-era commentator St. George Tucker observed, under the Ninth Amendment "every power which concerns the right of the citizen must be construed strictly, where it may operate to infringe or impair his liberty."[21]

The Fourteenth Amendment

The Takings Clause, the Ninth Amendment, and other provisions of the Bill of Rights ostensibly limit the federal government. Libertarian legal scholars have also found broad protections against encroachments on liberty by *state* governments in the Fourteenth Amendment's Privileges or Immunities Clause and Due Process Clause.

The Privileges or Immunities Clause of the Fourteenth Amendment provides that no state "shall make or enforce any law which shall abridge the privileges or immunities of citizens of the United States." What are the "privileges or immunities" it refers to? It is difficult to discern an original public meaning of these terms because they have never been widely used by the general public. But according to libertarian scholars such as Epstein and Barnett, these "privileges or immunities" include natural liberty rights. Their argument gets support from an 1823 decision by Supreme Court Justice Bushrod Washington, sitting as a circuit trial judge in *Corfield v. Coryell*.[22] Interpreting those words as they are used elsewhere in the Constitution (Article IV, section 2), Washington wrote that privileges and immunities include, among other things, "the enjoyment of life and liberty, with the right to acquire and possess property of every kind, and to pursue and obtain happiness and safety; subject nevertheless to such constraints as the government may justly prescribe for the general good of the whole." Barnett also supports this definition with statements from legislators at the time Congress considered the Civil Rights Bill of 1866, which the Fourteenth Amendment was intended to make constitutional, and when it considered the Fourteenth Amendment itself.

But if "privileges or immunities" just meant "natural rights" or "liberty," why doesn't the Fourteenth Amendment just say that? According to Barnett, this is because privileges and immunities include more. In addition to natural rights, Justice Washington's decision in *Corfield* also mentioned certain positive rights—the kind of positive rights that a limited government theoretically is supposed to grant to citizens in exchange for the citizens' surrender of certain liberties—such as "the right to the protection of government and the right to vote."[23]

Despite its supposedly libertarian character, the Privileges or Immunities Clause lost all usefulness as a guardian of liberty very soon after the Fourteenth Amendment's ratification. In the 1873 *Slaughter-House Cases*,[24] the Supreme Court considered a challenge to a Louisiana law that allowed the city of New Orleans to create a corporation with a legal monopoly on slaughterhouse services. (That corporation would be owned, of course, by politically connected businessmen for whose benefit the law was enacted.) Butchers who were forced out of business by this government-created monopoly sued, arguing that the law violated their property rights and economic liberty rights as protected by the Privileges or Immunities Clause. The Supreme Court disagreed, and held that the Privileges or Immunities Clause only protected people's rights *as citizens of the United States*, such as the right to travel to the seat of government, access seaports, and enjoy rights secured by treaties with other nations. The clause did not protect other liberty rights, which the Court said were up to the states to protect (or not) as they saw fit. The Fourteenth Amendment did not place protection of basic liberty rights "under the special care of the federal government."[25]

This decision rendered the Privileges or Immunities Clause useless early on, but the Court later achieved a similar result to that (supposedly) intended by the Privileges or Immunities Clause by interpreting the Due Process Clause in a way that protects libertarian rights. That clause provides that no state shall "deprive any person of life, liberty, or property, without due process of law." It seems plain that the Due Process Clause pertains to *fairness in applying laws* that are otherwise proper. For example, a court must give a defendant all the process he is due—notice of what he is charged with, a trial by jury, etc.—before holding him liable for a violation of an otherwise-constitutional law. By using the word "process," the clause appears to be about procedures, not about substantive rights.[26]

Nonetheless, beginning with the 1905 *Lochner v. New York* decision, the Supreme Court began to find *substantive* protections for liberty in the Due Process Clause. In *Lochner*, the Court struck down a New York law limiting the number of hours per week that bakers could work on the ground that this violated their freedom to contract under the Due Process Clause. In the years that followed, courts struck down nearly two hundred other state laws because they violated so-called "substantive due process." These included, for example, a law that prevented private employment agencies from charging fees, a law that regulated the use of certain materials in mattresses, and a law that required a government permit to manufacture ice.[27]

Three decades later, the New Deal era came in and the *Lochner* era came to an end. Following Franklin Delano Roosevelt's threats to pack the Court with his own appointees, the Supreme Court switched its ideological orientation and dumped *Lochner* in the 1937 *West Coast Hotel v. Parrish* case.[28] The Due Process Clause would no longer be invoked to support economic liberty, though the "substantive due process" idea would make a comeback when the left invoked it to pursue its own agenda in the courts. The Due Process Clause is also still invoked to support the "incorporation doctrine," under which some provisions of the Bill of Rights, such as the First Amendment, are applied to restrain the states, even though the amendments themselves only refer to the federal government.

Today, *Lochner* is widely disdained by legal scholars, who believe the Court overstepped its bounds to advance a pro-business ideological agenda. Many libertarians have trouble swallowing *Lochner*, too, even if they like the results, because it seems to stretch the Due Process Clause too far. It would be better, in their view, to revive the Privileges or Immunities Clause than to try to achieve the same result through the Due Process Clause.[29] Still, given its apparent compatibility with the libertarian agenda, it is safe to say that many libertarians would prefer a return to *Lochner* over the status quo.

The Presumption of Liberty

The libertarian interpretations of the Ninth and Fourteenth Amendment fit in with what Barnett calls the "presumption of liberty." The Constitution was enacted with the widely shared understanding, following the ideas of John Locke, that individuals have natural rights that exist before the formation of government and that people give up a small piece of their rights in order to have a government that will otherwise protect rights. Because natural liberty rights precede government and are not created by it, there is a presumption that people have liberty where they have not explicitly given it up in the Constitution—a presumption that the Ninth Amendment and later the Fourteenth Amendment reinforced.

This presumption of liberty is evident in many Supreme Court decisions from the founding through the *Lochner* era, but today courts have turned things upside down: they assume that an exercise of government power is constitutional unless an individual can show otherwise. In 1938's *United States v. Carolene Products* and cases that followed, the Court held that any regulations of "ordinary commercial transactions" would be upheld provided that they had a "rational basis." In other words, if the government could give a reason—really, *any* reason—for violating economic liberty, then it could do so. Footnote 4 to that case adds that the "presumption of constitutionality" may be narrower if the legislation "appears on its face to be within a specific prohibition of the Constitution, such as those of the first ten amendments."[30] So there are now two classes of rights under constitutional law: those few that are deemed "fundamental," and all the rest that government can ride roughshod over. Following *Carolene Products*, the presumption of constitutionality in cases not involving so-called fundamental rights has only become stronger; all Congress needs to do is to point to some reason (not even the *actual* reason for the legislation) why the law in question *could* have served a government interest, and the courts will give their approval.

Dissent on the Fourteenth Amendment

Probably most libertarians who think about constitutional interpretation agree with the interpretations of the Necessary and Proper Clause, Commerce Clause, and Ninth Amendment discussed above. But not all libertarians agree that the Fourteenth Amendment authorized the federal courts to strike down state laws that violate liberty, or that this would even be desirable. For example, Thomas Woods and Kevin R.C. Gutzman argue that the Fourteenth Amendment was intended only to "ensure that recently freed slaves had the basic rights of citizens"—that is, to make sure that blacks were treated like everyone else.[31] If the Fourteenth Amendment had been intended to radically restructure the relationship between the federal government and the state governments—and essentially impose the whole libertarian program on the states, prohibiting them from doing things they had always done—there surely would have been more debate on the specifics of this at the time it was written and ratified, but there was not.

This argument against a broad reading of the Fourteenth Amendment sounds bad for liberty, but giving more power to federal judges also threatens liberty. If courts begin using the Fourteenth Amendment to enforce libertarian natural rights, it would be but a small step for them to start using it to enforce non-libertarian positive rights. This happened, for example, in the years following *Brown v. Board of Education*, when the courts went beyond the prohibition on governmental race discrimination and forced state and local governments to raise and spend tax dollars on racial-integration efforts.[32] If libertarians do not want courts to twist the Constitution like this, it may make sense to urge courts to stick to the narrower interpretation even when it does not go the libertarian way.

As libertarian lawyer and writer Gene Healy has observed, even a reinvigorated Ninth Amendment could be subject to judicial abuse. What would stop a court from interpreting the Ninth Amendment's unspecified rights to include welfare rights?[33] Given the courts' track record, and the tendency of government to always take more power for itself by whatever means are available, it might be better to let the sleeping dog lie.

The Decentralist Approach

Many libertarians, including this author, strongly favor decentralization—so-called "states' rights"—as an additional or alternative means of checking government power. Of course, libertarians do not believe that state governments should have any rights at all (only individuals have rights), but as long as we have a federal system, it may be better for liberty if the states have certain *legal* rights with respect to the federal government than if the federal government can dominate both the states and the people.

It is true that in American history, state governments have sometimes invoked "states' rights" to do bad things to their people, as the Southern states did in the Jim Crow era, for example. But decentralists believe that the effects of states' rights are likely to be good for liberty on balance. One reason for this is competition among states. If one state is too oppressive, it is relatively easy to move to another—easier, anyway, than escaping the reach of the federal government.

But decentralism is not primarily about empowering states—it is about limiting the federal government. The legal basis for limiting federal power over the states derives from the Tenth Amendment, which provides that "powers not delegated to the United States by the Constitution, nor prohibited by it to the States, are reserved to the States respectively, or to the people." The Amendment means that the federal government can only do things the Constitution specifically says it can do. All other powers belong to the states or the people.

How can states enforce their rights under the Tenth Amendment? Libertarians suggest reviving the idea of *nullification*—allowing any state to nullify any federal law it believes violates the Constitution by declaring the law unconstitutional and protecting state citizens from its enforcement. As it stands, the states generally do not assert their right of nullification, so the federal government alone gets to interpret the rules by which it is supposed to be bound, and of course it has read its own powers broadly. Nullification would give others a say. As Woods puts it, "If the federal government has the exclusive right to judge the extent of its own powers . . . it will continue to grow—regardless of elections, the separation of powers, and other much-touted limits on government power."[34]

Thomas Jefferson—one of the more libertarian Founding Fathers, his slave-holding notwithstanding—was a champion of nullification. In 1798, he anonymously wrote the Kentucky Resolutions, which declared that the Alien and Sedition Acts (which prohibited speech criticizing the government) were unconstitutional and that nullification would be the appropriate remedy. That same year, James Madison wrote the Virginia Resolutions, which made the same argument. In 1832 and 1833, South Carolina nullified a tariff imposed by the federal government (and almost faced a federal invasion as a result). Some Northern states later effectively nullified fugitive slave laws by ignoring them.[35]

There are more recent examples of states standing up to the federal government. For example, 25 states have passed either binding laws or resolutions refusing to implement the Bush Administration's 2005 REAL ID Act, which included a requirement that states implement national standards for driver's licenses, creating a de facto national ID card. Libertarians and many others concerned about privacy opposed this. State governments heard their citizens' complaints, and also did not like the high costs the program would have imposed on them—so they defied, and effectively nullified, the law.

Some liberty-minded Americans have succeeded in getting their state governments to pass "state sovereignty resolutions" asserting their rights under the Tenth Amendment. For example, Tennessee's legislature passed a resolution in February 2009 that states in part:

> [W]e hereby affirm Tennessee's sovereignty under the Tenth Amendment to the Constitution of the United States over all powers not otherwise enumerated and granted to the federal government by the Constitution of the United States. We also demand the federal government to halt and reverse its practice of assuming powers and of imposing mandates on the states for purposes not enumerated by the Constitution of the United States.[36]

At of this writing, seven states have passed resolutions along these lines, and legislatures in most of the rest of the states are considering doing so. These resolutions are not binding (they don't actually nullify any federal law), but according to the Tenth Amendment Center, an organization that promotes states' rights issues from a libertarian perspective, the resolutions are intended to serve as a "notice and demand" to the federal government that it must cease and desist or face further resistance.[37]

Decentralist libertarians also tend to favor the next step down the decentralist path: secession. That means that states should be allowed to secede from the Union, or any smaller unit of government should be allowed to secede from a larger one. Of course many people associate secession with the (unlibertarian) Confederacy, but the idea has also received support from many much more respectable sources, such as Jefferson, Lord Acton, and Mises. A credible threat of secession can keep the federal government in check, and actual secession could be necessary to free a state's people from an oppressive central government.

Politically impossible? Probably, for now. But as the federal government becomes more burdensome, more people in more states may consider it, especially in the event of a complete monetary or financial collapse. Texas Governor Rick Perry probably was not serious when he mentioned in an April 2009 speech that Texas could secede from the Union if Washington's taxing and spending do not improve. But polls soon thereafter of Texas Republicans showed that 35 percent thought the state would be better off as an independent nation.[38] If the federal government continues to encroach, the number could rise.

THE STRATEGY

For the people we might call libertarian centralists[39]—those who emphasize using the federal government against the states—the strategy for advancing libertarian legal theories in the courts can be summarized in two words: judicial activism. People often use those words derisively, but libertarian legal activists embrace them. If constitutional limitations on government power and protections for individual rights are to be judicially enforced at all, it will have to be by courts that are willing to *actively* enforce them and not passively accept whatever Congress and the executive branch do. The trick for libertarian lawyers is: How to persuade them to do it?

The lawyers at the Institute for Justice (IJ), a libertarian public-interest law firm, have been working on that problem for nearly two decades. Founded in 1991 by lawyers Clint Bolick and William Mellor, IJ has been pursuing a strategy to establish libertarian legal precedents that will work the theories we have described back into the law. As part of its strategy, IJ carefully selects cases that have the potential to create a precedent that moves the cause forward, and which have a sympathetic client.

A sympathetic client is critical, because it helps win the case in the court of public opinion—and, for IJ, that is half the battle. Wherever it has a case, IJ aggressively pursues media attention through op-eds, interviews, and any other means available. There are several reasons for this. One is that, despite their insistence to the contrary, many judges do pay attention to the public's views on cases and issues—especially, it seems safe to say, state-court judges who must stand for reelection. Another reason is because, even if IJ loses a case, the public will be educated about the issue, and sometimes, as they did after the *Kelo* eminent-domain case, people may even push the government to change the law.

IJ litigates in four areas: private property rights, economic liberty, free speech, and school choice. We will leave out school choice in the rest of our discussion because we covered that issue in Chapter 6. For each of the other issues, we will look at what IJ has done—and it is quite a lot.

THE CASES

Private Property Rights

We mentioned the *Kelo* case at the beginning of the chapter. Suzette Kelo was forced to leave her New London, Connecticut property because Pfizer Corporation wanted to build a research facility adjacent to her neighborhood, and the city wanted to give her land to a private developer to build other projects to support the Pfizer project, such as office space and parking lots. New London's practice was not unusual; cities across the country had been doing the same thing for years, often claiming that perfectly well-maintained property was "blighted," then taking it to give it to private interests to try to increase the tax base. In *Kelo*, the Supreme Court said this was fine. Although handing land over to private developers is not what most of us would think of as a "public use," that did not matter. As Justice John Paul Stevens noted in his majority opinion, the view that "public use" in the Takings Clause actually means "public use" had "steadily eroded over time" because it was "impractical given the diverse and always evolving needs of society." Instead, a "public purpose" would suffice. What counts as a "public purpose"? Practically anything the government says—the Court said it would show "deference to legislative judgments in this field."

Kelo appeared to be a big loss for liberty. But it turned out to be a major win—at least with respect to outraging and educating the public about the issue of eminent domain. The outcome seemed so unfair—and seemed to be such an obvious case of "Robin Hood in reverse," as Bolick put it[40]—that it became the most talked-about Supreme Court decision since *Bush v. Gore*, and was condemned by voices across the political spectrum. A Saint Index national survey showed that 81 percent of Americans opposed the decision, and that about the same percentage of blacks, whites, men, women, Republicans, Democrats, liberals, and conservatives opposed it.[41]

Even if they do not care about libertarian principles in the abstract, most people do not want what happened to Suzette Kelo to happen to them, so there was outcry for state governments to protect liberty where the federal government had refused to do so. The *Kelo* backlash prompted at least 43 states to change their eminent-domain laws—probably the biggest-ever state-level legislative response to a Supreme Court decision.[42] A close review shows that many of these reforms are only superficial; for example, many of the new laws include definitions of "blight" that still allow governments to declare property "blighted" even if it is perfectly well-maintained but, in the government's opinion, stands in the way of economic development.[43] Presumably politicians hope people will forget about *Kelo* before they have a chance to notice.

But some of the measures may have more teeth. Libertarian law professor Ilya Somin reports that fourteen state legislatures enacted laws "that either abolish or significantly constrain economic development takings," and the people of at least six more states enacted such laws by ballot measure.[44] State courts may improve on *Kelo*, too. After *Kelo*, IJ took an eminent-domain case, *Norwood v. Horney*, to the Ohio Supreme Court. There, the City of Norwood wanted to take the property of IJ's clients to give it to a developer who wanted to put up stores, condos, and office space. The Ohio court gave IJ the sort of decision it wished it had received from the U.S. Supreme Court, including surprisingly libertarian rhetoric and citations to libertarian scholars such as Epstein and Bernard Siegan. The Court wrote:

> Believed to be derived fundamentally from a higher authority and natural law, property rights were so sacred [historically] that they could not be entrusted lightly to "the uncertain virtue of those who govern. As such, property rights were believed to supersede constitutional principles. . . . To be protected and secure in the possession of [one's] property is a right inalienable, a right which a written constitution may recognize or declare, but which existed independently of and before such recognition, and which no government can destroy.
>
> The right of private property is an original and fundamental right, existing anterior to the formation of the government itself; the civil rights, privileges and immunities authorized by law, are derivative—mere incidents to the political institutions of the country, conferred with a view to the public welfare, and therefore trusts of civil power, to be exercised for the public benefit. . . . Government is the necessary burden imposed on man as the only means of securing the protection of his rights. And this protection—the primary and only legitimate purpose of civil government, is accomplished by protecting man in his rights of personal security, personal liberty, and private property.[45]

Interpreting the Ohio Constitution, the Court concluded that takings for economic development do *not* constitute a "public use," and that the use of eminent domain should be subject to heightened scrutiny. It may not be a coincidence that the Ohio Supreme Court's members are elected and, unlike federal judges, can be held accountable for their offenses against liberty.

Meanwhile, back in New London, the City has yet to do anything at all with Suzette Kelo's former property—other than kick her off it—despite its win.

Economic Liberty

IJ's lawyers have been fighting for economic liberty on multiple fronts.

One area in which IJ enjoyed Supreme Court success was in protecting consumers' freedom to buy products from states other than their own. Before IJ took action, New York and other states prohibited out-of-state wineries from shipping wine directly to consumers, but allowed in-state wineries to do so. The purpose of these laws was obvious: to benefit local wine producers at the expense of both out-of-state wineries and wine consumers. Juanita Swedenburg, a Virginia winemaker then in her 70s, wanted to be able to ship to customers in New York, and some customers in New York wanted her to be able to ship to them. So with IJ's help, they sued the state—and won. They argued that the "dormant" Commerce Clause prevents states from erecting barriers to trade between the states, and New York's law did exactly that. The Court agreed,[46] and today winemakers in any state can ship to customers in any other state, and there is nothing any state government can do about it. Getting to buy wine from another state may not be the most pressing issue facing the nation—it is not as fundamental as monetary freedom or gun rights—but there can be no doubt that liberty has increased in a real way for countless buyers and sellers across the country. And the precedent should force states to think twice before enacting any other protectionist schemes.

IJ has also worked to advance economic liberty through cases over the right to pursue a living. Every state has laws that require people in various professions and businesses to have licenses. Libertarians would argue that *none* of these laws are justified—not even those requiring licensing for doctors, as we noted in Chapter 5. For the most part, such occupational licensure laws do not really serve to protect the public so much as they serve to protect the interests of established members of a given profession. If you have to jump through expensive hoops to get into a particular business, fewer people will enter that business—and those already in it will make more money as a result. For example, if anyone could be a barber without a license, more people would open barber shops or cut people's hair on the side at home, and because of the increased competition, haircuts would cost less.

Given a body of federal law that has mostly approved of state-law restrictions on the right to earn a living since the *Slaughter-House Cases*, and especially since the end of the *Lochner* era, challenging occupational-licensure laws has been tough. Under the *Carolene Products* distinction between fundamental rights and economic-liberty rights, such laws only have to survive the "rational basis" test to be valid, and it is usually easy enough for states to come up with bogus "health and safety" excuses for their laws. Yet IJ has had some success, in and out of court.

One relatively easy target is laws that require African hairbraiders to have state cosmetology licenses before they can sell their services. African hair-braiding is a unique art that has little in common with most of the things one learns in cosmetology school. Besides, many of its practitioners cannot afford the thousands of dollars cosmetology schooling would cost. So IJ has sued in numerous states to vindicate hairbraiders' rights. To date, the courts have not issued many rulings on this because they have not needed to—the states have backed off and repealed their restrictions on hairbraiders rather than face liti-gation and the potential of a court ruling that could place other state regula-tions in danger. This is good for the client, but less than ideal for IJ's strategy.

Another target has been funeral casket sales. Numerous states have laws that allow only licensed funeral directors to sell caskets, which allow funeral directors to keep prices artificially high. IJ won on this issue in the United States Court of Appeals for the Sixth Circuit, which held that Tennessee's casket-selling law could not even satisfy the rational-basis test because the law had no conceivable purpose except to line the pockets of funeral directors, which the court held was not a legitimate state interest. In another case, the Tenth Circuit Court of Appeals reached the opposite conclusion, stating that economic protectionism for a particular industry *is* a legitimate state purpose—and that it is not the Court's place to establish a "libertarian para-dise," even if that's a "worthy goal."[47]

IJ has pursued economic liberty for people in various other occupations and businesses, including taxicab drivers, jitney van providers, shoe shiners, florists, and even people who file horses' teeth. Each case is a small step in a path IJ hopes will eventually lead to a Supreme Court reversal of the *Slaughter-House Cases*. A Supreme Court decision on that issue would create a precedent that could be used to attack all manner of economic regulations, or, if it goes the wrong way, it could create a precedent that permanently declares such regulations lawful.

Free Speech

On free speech, the First Amendment is already fairly libertarian. Americans have a lot more freedom in what they may say than citizens of many other countries. There are exceptions, of course, such as the "McCain-Feingold" law restricting campaign speech. Libertarians, notably including former Federal Elec-tion Commission Chair Bradley A. Smith, have attacked McCain-Feingold,[48] but IJ has been especially focused on an area of speech that has received less protection from courts than political speech: commercial speech.

To curb the speech of someone who is advertising a product, the government need only show that it has a "substantial interest" in doing so, that its restriction "materially advances that interest," and that the restriction is narrowly drawn—and suddenly the right to free speech is no right at all.[49] This distinction cannot be found in the First Amendment's text, which just says "speech" and doesn't appear to leave room for courts to favor speech in politics—where false advertising runs rampant and unpunished—over speech related to the ordinary business of voluntarily buying and selling in the marketplace.

We saw one example of this in Chapter 5, with the government's restrictions on advertising for natural supplements. Another example is the case of Christopher Pagan, a Cincinnati-area man who wanted to sell his 1970 Mercury Cougar by keeping it parked on the street with a "For Sale" sign in the window. Local regulations said a "For Sale" sign cannot be in a window of a car parked on the street, so IJ helped Pagan challenge the law under the First Amendment (long applied to the states under the incorporation doctrine). After a hearing in the trial court, the U.S. Court of Appeals for the Sixth Circuit held that the local government had failed to show any evidence that its rule served a legitimate concern; an affidavit from a police chief claiming that it served "aesthetic concerns" wasn't enough.[50] That is a favorable decision, but it will probably serve mostly as a warning to local governments that they just need to drum up lots of evidence of their "substantial interest" in restricting speech before they go to court. So there is much work to be done before commercial speech will get the protection the First Amendment's text promises to all speech.

DISSENT ON THE CONSTITUTION

So far this chapter has been about libertarians using the Constitution, one way or another, to attempt to beat back government encroachments on rights. Not all libertarians are on board with this approach. In fact, many consider it a useless exercise, or worse.

One major libertarian objection to the Constitution is that, on its face, it is not libertarian, even if one accepts all the originalist arguments we have discussed above. For one thing, the Constitution establishes *a government*. According to John Locke and others who believe in the "social contract," governments theoretically derive their power from the consent of the governed. But of course most of the American people living at the time the Constitution was adopted had no say in it at all, and no one alive today did—so the governed have not, in fact, consented. As nineteenth-century anarchist libertarian legal theorist Lysander Spooner observed in his *Constitution of No Authority*, the Constitution at best bound those who actually signed it; there is no compelling reason why it should bind anyone else.

Not all libertarians are anarchists, of course, but even many libertarians who accept some government see major problems with the Constitution. For one, it gives the federal government a lot of power. Indeed, having a more powerful federal government was the whole point of scrapping the Constitution's more-libertarian predecessor, the Articles of Confederation. The federal government's constitutional powers go beyond mere defense, dispute resolution, or elimination of state trade barriers. They include the power to coin money, to grant monopoly rights in the form of copyrights and patents, to establish a post office and post roads, to seize private property for "public use," to declare war, and to restrain international trade. And, of course, the Constitution long tolerated the wholly unlibertarian institution of slavery.[51] And it creates a powerful executive.

Some libertarians question whether "originalist" constitutional interpretation is even possible. Georgetown University legal scholar John Hasnas argues that it is not—that words do not have a "plain meaning," so courts can never reach "correct" answers and the law will never be consistent.[52] In his view, to pretend that correct or consistent constitutional interpretation is possible subtly reinforces the idea that we are somehow ruled by impartial laws and not, in fact, by *other people* who use violence and threats of violence to control us. As an anarchist, Hasnas proposes a free market in law as in everything else—a topic we regrettably lack space to address.[53]

Another obvious libertarian problem with the Constitution is that it gave rise to the government *we have now*—which is the largest government in human history, and which violates rights on a massive scale. Even if the Constitution reflects a sincere effort by its framers to limit government and preserve rights (a questionable proposition),[54] it is a failure. Spooner could see this even in 1870, when he wrote that the Constitution "has either authorized such a government as we have had, or has been powerless to prevent it. In either case, it is unfit to exist."[55]

One obvious reason for this is because the Constitution allows the three branches of the very government that it is supposed to restrain, especially the courts, to interpret the limits of government power. If an institution gets to decide the limits of its own power, it cannot be too surprising when that institution decides that there actually are not very many limits on its power. The Constitution's checks and balances are supposed to mitigate this problem, and surely they have done so, but not enough to prevent government from growing ever bigger and ever further beyond the bounds the Constitution appears to impose on it. State nullification of federal laws should help, but states have mostly refused to assert their rights—in part because the federal government has decided that it has the authority to bribe the states by giving them money with strings attached.

A problem with libertarian legal activism, from the libertarian skeptic's view, is that it assumes that putting the right arguments in front of the right judges will set things straight. To their credit, IJ and others have had successes, but it is difficult to see how they will win the bigger prizes they are after. What president would appoint a Supreme Court justice who will impose limits on executive power? What Senate would approve a Supreme Court nominee who doesn't think Congress can just do whatever it wants? The system appears to be a rigged game that special interests and the federal government are sure to win. Robert Levy (mentioned in the previous chapter) and IJ co-founder Mellor have criticized this author for being "too cynical" in making this argument,[56] but cynicism about the State is at the heart of libertarianism. (Notably, the decentralist approach does not suffer as much from this flaw because it does not depend on the enlightenment of government officials, and instead harnesses politicians' selfish desire to protect their turf and compete with other states for citizens.)

But there is perhaps one way out under our system: for large numbers of citizens to demand that politicians respect liberty and to punish those politicians who do not. But for liberty to become so important to people, education about liberty must come first. To try to achieve results through politics or the courts as a first step—forcing liberty from the top down—is to put the cart before the horse. This point was emphasized by Albert Jay Nock and by the libertarian movement's progenitors at the Foundation for Economic Education (FEE)—and is mostly forgotten by most libertarians who go to Washington. Sheldon Richman, the present editor of FEE's magazine, *The Freeman*, suggests that for "the sake of freedom, there is no substitute for getting right *the constitution within*," which requires "self-education and an articulate passion for liberty."[57] Still, as Ron Paul's campaign and IJ's efforts show, sometimes political and legal efforts can be educational in themselves. And if they give some people a bit more freedom along the way—to buy wine, braid hair, or stay in their home—few libertarians could object to that.

NOTES

1. Ron Paul, *The Revolution: A Manifesto* (New York: Grand Central Press, 2008), 67.

2. David Boaz, *Libertarianism: A Primer* (New York: Free Press, 1997), 44.

3. Randy E. Barnett, *Restoring the Lost Constitution* (Princeton, NJ: Princeton University Press, 2004), 354.

4. Ilana Mercer, "Obama Presidency: Hamiltonian Curse or Marxist Mess?" *World NetDaily*, November 7, 2008, http://www.wnd.com/index.php?fa=PAGE.view&pageId= 80301.

5. See Randy E. Barnett, "Scalia's Infidelity: A Critique of Faint-Hearted Originalism," *University of Cincinnati Law Review* 35 (2006): 7, http://papers.ssrn.com/sol3/papers .cfm?abstract_id=880112.

6. Clarence Thomas, *My Grandfather's Son* (New York: Harper, 2007), 62, 125–26; Timothy Sandefur, "Justice Thomas at Chapman," *Freespace*, December 18, 2007, http://sandefur.typepad.com/freespace/2007/12/justice-thomas.html.

7. See Barnett, *Restoring the Lost Constitution*, 158–84.

8. Ibid., 184–89.

9. 301 U.S. 1 (1937).

10. 317 U.S. 111 (1942).

11. Alex Kozinski, "Introduction to Volume Nineteen," *Harvard Journal of Law & Public Policy* 19 (1995), 5.

12. Barnett, *Restoring the Lost Constitution*, 281.

13. See, e.g., ibid., 303; Richard A. Epstein, "The Proper Scope of the Commerce Clause," *Virginia Law Review* 73 (1987), 1387; Roger Pilon, "A Court Without a Compass," *New York Law School Law Review* 40 (1996), 999, 1005.

14. Richard A. Epstein, *How Progressives Rewrote the Constitution* (Washington, DC: Cato Institute, 2006), 22–24.

15. Ibid., 27–29.

16. 514 U.S. 549 (1995).

17. 529 U.S. 598 (2000).

18. See Richard A. Epstein, *Takings: Private Property and the Power of Eminent Domain* (Cambridge, MA: Harvard University Press, 1985).

19. Ibid., 281.

20. Murray N. Rothbard, "Discovering the Ninth Amendment," *Left and Right*, Vol. 1 No. 2 (1965): 8–12, http://mises.org/journals/lar/pdfs/1_2/1_2_2.pdf.

21. Quoted in Barnett, *Restoring the Lost Constitution*, 241–42.

22. 5 F.Cas. 546, 551–52.

23. Barnett, *Restoring the Lost Constitution*, 63.

24. 83 U.S. 36 (1873).

25. Ibid., 78.

26. See Randy E. Barnett, "Foreword: What's So Wicked About *Lochner?*" *NYU Journal of Law and Liberty* 1 (2005): 325–333, http://www.law.nyu.edu/journals/lawliberty/pdfarchive/vol1no1lochner/ECM_PRO_060899.

27. See Andrew P. Napolitano, *The Constitution in Exile: How the Federal Government Has Seized Power by Rewriting the Supreme Law of the Land* (Nashville: Nelson Current, 2006), 111–13.

28. 300 U.S. 379 (1937).

29. Barnett, "Foreword: What's So Wicked About *Lochner?*"

30. 304 U.S. 144, 152 (1938).

31. Thomas E. Woods, Jr., and Kevin R.C. Gutzman, *Who Killed the Constitution? The Fate of American Liberty from World War I to George W. Bush* (New York: Crown Forum, 2008), 45.

32. For more details and a strong argument against "libertarian centralism," see Gene Healy, "The Fourteenth Amendment and the Perils of Libertarian Centralism," http://mises.org/journals/scholar/Healy6.PDF.

33. Ibid.

34. See Thomas E. Woods, Jr., "The States' Rights Tradition Nobody Knows," *LewRockwell.com*, June 29, 2005, http://www.lewrockwell.com/woods/woods44.html.

35. Ibid.

36. HJR 0108 (2009), http://www.tenthamendmentcenter.com/2009/02/19/tennessee-sovereignty-resolution.

37. "Tenth Amendment Resolutions," *The Tenth Amendment Center*, http://www.tenthamendmentcenter.com/nullification/10th-amendment-resolutions/.

38. Eric Kleefeld, "Poll: Texas Republicans Approve of Rick Perry's Secession Remarks," *TPMDC*, April 23, 2009, http://tpmdc.talkingpointsmemo.com/2009/04/poll-texas-republicans-approve-of-rick-perrys-secession-remarks.php.

39. See Healy, "Fourteenth Amendment."

40. Clint Bolick, *David's Hammer: The Case for an Activist Judiciary* (Washington, DC: Cato Institute, 2007), 114.

41. Ilya Somin, "The Limits of Backlash: Assessing the Response to *Kelo*," *Minnesota Law Review* 93 (2009), 2109–10, http://papers.ssrn.com/sol3/papers.cfm?abstract_id=976298 rec=1&srcabs=979201#.

42. Ibid., 2102.

43. See Ibid., 2120–31.

44. Ibid., 2138.

45. *Norwood v. Horney*, 110 Ohio St. 3d 352, 362 (2006).

46. *Granholm v. Heald*, 544 U.S. 460 (2005).

47. *Powers v. Harris*, 379 F.3d 1208, 1220 (10th Cir. 2004).

48. See Bradley A. Smith, *Unfree Speech: The Folly of Campaign Finance Reform* (Princeton, NJ: Princeton University Press, 2003).

49. See *Central Hudson Gas & Electric Corp. v. Public Service Commission*, 447 U.S. 557 (1980).

50. *Pagan v. Fruchey*, 492 F.3d 766 (6th Cir. 2007) (en banc).

51. For a libertarian discussion of federal promotion of slavery and race discrimination, see Andrew P. Napolitano, *Dred Scott's Revenge: A Legal History of Race and Freedom in America* (Nashville: Nelson Current, 2009).

52. John Hasnas, "The Myth of the Rule of Law," *Wisconsin Law Review* 1995 (1995), 199, http://faculty.msb.edu/hasnasj/GTWebSite/MythWeb.htm.

53. For ideas on how free-market law might work, see, for a start, Bruce Benson, *The Enterprise of Law: Justice Without the State* (San Francisco: Pacific Research Institute, 1990); Edward Stringham, ed., *Anarchy and the Law* (New Brunswick, NJ: Transaction Publishers, 2006); Morris Tannehill and Linda Tannehill, *The Market for Liberty* (Lansing, MI: self-published, 1970), http://freekeene.com/files/marketforliberty.pdf.

54. For a populist but well-researched libertarian take on the Founders' impure motives, see Kenneth W. Royce, *Hologram of Liberty: The Constitution's Shocking Alliance With Big Government* (Austin, TX: Javelin Press, 1997). On Alexander Hamilton in particular, see Thomas J. DiLorenzo, *Hamilton's Curse: How Jefferson's Archenemy Betrayed the American Revolution—and What It Means for America Today* (New York: Crown Forum, 2008).

55. Lysander Spooner, *No Treason No. VI: The Constitution of No Authority* (1870), http://www.lysanderspooner.org/node/64.

56. Robert Levy and William Mellor, "To Judge or Not to Judge," *Liberty* (December 2008), http://findarticles.com/p/articles/mi_7651/is_200812/ai_n32307109/?tag=content; coll.

57. Sheldon Richman, "The Constitution Within," *The Freeman* (September 2007), 28–29, http://www.fee.org/pdf/the-freeman/9%2007%20Richman.pdf.

FURTHER READING

Barnett, Randy E. *Restoring the Lost Constitution: The Presumption of Liberty*. Princeton, NJ: Princeton University Press, 2004. Barnett expounds his view that the Constitution, rightly understood, contains strong protections for liberty.

Bolick, Clint. *David's Hammer: The Case for an Activist Judiciary*. Washington, DC: Cato Institute, 2007. Bolick makes a case for using the courts to advance liberty.

Epstein, Richard A. *How Progressives Rewrote the Constitution*. Washington, DC: Cato Institute, 2006. Epstein documents how Progressives deliberately changed the courts' view of the Constitution to advance their agenda.

Napolitano, Andrew P. *The Constitution in Exile: How the Federal Government Has Seized Power by Rewriting the Supreme Law of the Land*. Nashville: Nelson Current, 2006. Judge Napolitano catalogs the ways in which the Supreme Court has twisted the Constitution to expand federal power.

Woods, Thomas E., Jr. *Nullification: How to Resist Federal Tyranny in the 21st Century*. Washington, DC: Regnery, 2010. Woods argues that state governments can and should strike down oppressive federal laws.

Woods, Thomas E., Jr. and Kevin R.C. Gutzman. *Who Killed the Constitution? The Fate of American Liberty from World War I to George W. Bush*. New York: Crown Forum, 2008. Woods and Gutzman pronounce the Constitution "dead," show how all three branches of government have ignored its putative restrictions on their power, and express doubt that any other result was possible.

9

The Fight for Peace

WHY LIBERTARIANS OPPOSE WAR

Libertarianism and war are not compatible. One reason why should be obvious: In war, governments commit legalized mass murder. In modern warfare especially, war is not just waged among voluntary combatants, but kills, maims, and otherwise harms innocent people. Then, of course, wars must be funded through taxes, which are extracted from U.S. citizens by force—a form of legalized theft, as far as libertarians are concerned. And, historically, the United States has used conscription—legalized slavery—to force people to fight and die. In addition, an interventionist foreign policy makes civilians targets for retaliation, so governments indirectly cause more violence against their own people when they become involved in other countries' affairs. In addition, war is always accompanied by many other new restrictions on liberty, many of which are sold as supposedly temporary wartime measures but then never go away.

War Involves Mass Murder

Today, people mostly accept that innocent civilians die in wars, and it does not seem to bother them too much as long as it is happening to other people on the other side of the world. The military calls this "collateral damage" and the American media mostly ignores it, but libertarians call attention to it and call it what it is: mass murder.

Historically, war did not necessarily involve killing innocents on a large scale. War was always terrible and undesirable, but by the eighteenth century, Europe had developed rules of "civilized warfare," and wars were generally fought only between armies, with civilians off-limits.[1] From the libertarian perspective, this type of war is not so much of a problem; if people choose to engage in mortal combat with each other, that may be foolish, self-destructive, and even immoral, but it is not aggression in the libertarian sense. (Of course, those wars still have objectionable *ends*—generally, the right to dominate a particular territory—but at least the *means* are not so offensive.)

Modern warfare is another story. Modern governments, including but not limited to democracies, claim to represent "the people," so modern wars are seen as being fought, not just between rulers, but between *whole peoples.* By this way of thinking, it is not two governments fighting; it is "all of us versus all of them."[2] This is how politicians and some conservative pundits talk: either one is rooting "for America" or one "wants America to lose"—they do not distinguish between the country's government and its citizens. If their view is correct—if governments really do represent the people—then it follows (more easily) that the people are fair game in war.

Of course, libertarians reject this view of government and democracy. Governments do not actually represent their people—they *prey on* their people. Many people in any given country, democratic or otherwise, do not support all of their government's policies, and do not deserve to be punished, let alone killed, for what their government does. But many are unwillingly implicated in their government's crimes through taxation, conscription, and other ways in which they are forced to directly and indirectly support the war effort.

The United States led the way in destroying the historic prohibition on targeting civilians. In the Civil War, with Abraham Lincoln's approval, General William Tecumseh Sherman unleashed "total war" in the South, burning cities and towns to the ground and destroying huge amounts of civilian property—food, housing, tools—mostly for no reason except to terrorize the "enemy" population.[3]

Britain also played its part, thanks to Winston Churchill. In World War I, as First Lord of the Admiralty, Churchill implemented a blockade that caused about 750,000 German civilians to die of hunger or malnutrition.[4] In World War II, Churchill urged the deliberate bombing of civilians in German cities, which killed 600,000 people and severely injured some 800,000 more.[5]

President Harry S. Truman contributed as well, killing more than 200,000 people with the atomic bombs dropped on Hiroshima and Nagasaki—the first and so far only nuclear attacks by any country. The United States also killed more than 100,000 more civilians in raids on Tokyo, including one major raid that took place *after* the atomic bombs had been dropped and Japan had indicated its willingness to surrender.[6] Libertarians would consider the killing of all those civilians to be an unjustifiable war crime in any event, but libertarian historian Ralph Raico has argued that, contrary to popular belief, the atomic bombs were not even necessary to save American soldiers' lives or win the war.[7]

In the Cold War, the United States (and the Soviets) continued to produce and accumulate nuclear weapons, which, if used, would destroy enormous civilian populations. Even now, as it condemns other countries for wanting even one nuclear weapon, the United States maintains a huge nuclear arsenal, with nearly 4,000 nuclear missiles ready to use.[8] Unlike guns and other traditional weapons, nuclear weapons have no legitimate defensive purpose; they cannot even theoretically be limited to target only enemy combatants. True, they serve as a "deterrent" without being detonated, but this provides little comfort because it assumes that the President of the United States is, in fact, ready, willing, and able to bring a nuclear holocaust on millions of people if put to the test. For these reasons, libertarianism calls for immediate, total nuclear disarmament.[9] Libertarians might also point out that the very existence of nuclear weapons provides a powerful argument against large governments. Without big government, there is no reason why these weapons, which have the potential to destroy the entire human race, would ever have existed.

Sometimes the U.S. foreign policy kills people indirectly. For example, from 1990 through March 1998, sanctions against Iraq kept food and medicine out of that country and caused at least 350,000 excess deaths of Iraqi children under the age of five ("excess deaths" meaning deaths above the normal death rate).[10] In 1996, when asked on 60 *Minutes* whether it was worth allowing hundreds of thousands of children to die to achieve U.S. foreign policy goals, Madeleine Albright (the future Secretary of State, who was then U.S. Ambassador to the United Nations) infamously said, "We think the price is worth it."[11]

The Iraq war itself has also killed many thousands of people, causing at least 90,000 documented Iraqi civilian deaths by October 2009.[12] Other estimates put the figure much higher, such as an October 2006 study from the medical journal *The Lancet*, which estimated that the war had caused, directly and indirectly, more than 650,000 excess Iraqi deaths.[13] For perspective, one might recall that the September 11 attacks that led—quite indirectly—to the Iraq war killed 2,976 Americans.[14]

War Is Anti-Market

Many on the right see no contradiction between their (nominal) support for capitalism and their support for war. Many on the left believe capitalism and militarism go hand in hand. Libertarians say they are both wrong because war interferes with the free market.

War and the Economy

War disrupts the market by directing society's resources away from productive uses and toward *destructive* uses, or at least toward things that people did not voluntarily demand. Nonetheless, the myth persists that war is good for the economy. For example, many people still insist that World War II ended the Great Depression, but libertarians have pointed out why this is false.

The idea that war makes for prosperity is an instance of the "broken window fallacy" that the great libertarian economist Frederic Bastiat identified in the nineteenth century.[15] We mentioned this concept briefly in Chapter 1: if a window breaks, this "creates jobs" for the people who make and install windows. But if the window had not broken, the window's owner could have spent his or her money on something else instead—and society would be wealthier because we would have not only the unbroken window, but also the additional goods and services produced.

War is nothing but "breaking windows" on a massive scale. It creates jobs for the people doing the breaking, and for the people who do the cleanup— but if there were no war jobs, those people would do something else that would be creative instead of destructive. Yes, unemployment plummeted during World War II, but ending unemployment is easy if you draft millions of people into the military. Slavery is indeed a "full employment" program, but not a very desirable one, especially when it can get you killed. And it is difficult to see how American soldiers were economically better off for being sent into the line of fire, or how their families were made better off by having fathers and sons sent away, possibly never to return.[16]

Merchants of Death

Wars are not good for the economy, but they are good for some businesses: those that produce military equipment and weaponry, such as Lockheed Martin, Raytheon, and Northrop Grumman; those that provide "infrastructure" in occupied territory, such as Halliburton and KBR; and those that provide "private" military services, such as Blackwater. These "merchants of death"[17] are not "free-market" entities; without a government buying their goods and services to wage war, they would not exist as we know them. They are economic parasites, who take society's resources but do not produce anything for civilian use in return. Libertarians have consistently echoed President Dwight D. Eisenhower's warning about the dangers of the "military-industrial complex"—a warning that

Republican and Democrat politicians have almost universally ignored as the war profiteers successfully lobby them year after year.[18]

The government's extensive use of outside contractors to carry out the Iraq war has helped sully the idea of "privatization." True privatization, which libertarians advocate, just entails getting the government out of some business that it is already in. An example would be abolishing the U.S. Postal Service's monopoly on mail delivery and allowing any private carriers to compete freely to deliver letters and packages. It would not be true privatization if the government were to maintain the Postal Service's monopoly but turn over the operation of the Service to a "private" company. In that case, the activity would maintain its monopolistic, governmental character and just be under different management. And so it is with war contracting: the underlying activity of warfare is not private at all, and with so-called privatization, it is just being carried out by people who are nominally employed by a third party. This false privatization may be especially pernicious because, unlike regular soldiers who fear for their lives and have some sense of justice, contracting firms do not have any incentive to question the war's merits; fighting wars is their business, and when there is a war, business is good. The substitution of private contractors for regular troops also allows government to make it appear as though it is withdrawing troops and scaling back the war, when it is not actually doing so.[19]

Paying for War

Governments pay for the military and wars through taxes, of course. The amounts are not trivial, especially in the United States, which spends about as much on its military as all other countries combined spend on theirs.[20] The president's proposed defense budget for fiscal year 2009 was $515 billion (not counting war funding), plus an additional $70 billion to fund the wars in Iraq and Afghanistan for the first part of the year.[21] As economic historian Robert Higgs has observed, these numbers do not even include many other parts of the federal budget that pertain to defense and war, such as the Department of Homeland Security's budget, and parts of the Justice Department's budget.[22] As of this writing, America's wars have cost nearly $1 trillion since 2001.[23]

Governments also pay for war by borrowing and printing money. As we saw in Chapter 3, libertarians see this as a form of theft, too—one that impoverishes the country and can lead to economic disaster. Funding war in this way hides the costs of war. As Ron Paul has put it, "If every American taxpayer had to submit an extra five or ten thousand dollars to the IRS this April to pay for the [Iraq] war, I'm quite certain it would end very quickly."[24] On the other hand, when the government funds its wars through inflation and debt, people who do not understand monetary economics do not see the connection between the economy and the war.

Other Economic Intervention

Wars also tend to include many other interventions into the economy. For example, Higgs describes some of the interventions that accompanied World War I:

> [The federal government] virtually nationalized the ocean shipping industry. It did nationalize the railroad, telephone, domestic telegraph, and international telegraphic cable industries. It became deeply engaged in manipulating labor-management relations, securities sales, agricultural production and marketing, the distribution of coal and oil, international commerce, and markets for raw materials and manufactured products. Its Liberty Bond drives dominated the financial capital markets. . . . In view of the more than 5,000 mobilization agencies of various sorts—boards, committees, corporations, administrations—contemporaries who described the 1918 government as "war socialism" were well justified.[25]

After the war, the government repealed many of its worst intrusions into the economy—but some stuck around in some form, and the precedent was set for the government to pursue a similar interventionist route when the next crisis, the Great Depression, arrived.

When World War II came, the New Deal had already greatly expanded government, but the war led to even more economic intervention. The government set price controls and imposed rationing for a wide range of goods deemed to be "necessities," such as gasoline, tires, coffee, canned foods, meats, sugar, and typewriters.[26] As we saw in Chapter 5, it imposed wage controls, including maximum wages on employees of private businesses. (So much for wartime prosperity.) Once again, most of the economic interventions were repealed when the war ended, but not all were. For example, as we saw in Chapter 5, the tax code remained skewed after the war in a way that pushed people to favor health insurance over direct payment for health services, which has led in turn to today's high healthcare costs.

Another policy introduced in World War II was the withholding of taxes from paychecks.[27] This began as a supposedly temporary wartime measure, but of course it was never repealed, and today people take it for granted. Income-tax withholding helped the government grow as it did during and after the war; because automatic withholding spreads the pain of tax payments out over a year, people are less likely to feel the burden of taxation as much as they would if they had to write a big check on April 15. This helps mask how much government steals from people, and it even makes people feel like they get a "gift" from the government when they receive a refund check.[28]

Conscription Is Slavery

Libertarians oppose conscription—a military draft—under any circumstances, and call for a permanent end to every form of it. As long as conscription does exist, libertarians view draft-dodging and military desertion not as crimes, but as heroic refusals to participate in *government* crimes.

For the libertarian, forcing anyone into any kind of slave labor is bad enough, but military conscription is especially objectionable. The draftee is forced into not just any job, but one that requires him to take unconscionable actions, experience extreme psychological trauma, and face a high risk of death or severe, permanent injury. And, as with many government policies, the poor and powerless (especially African Americans) suffer first and most, while the rich and powerful suffer last and least, because the poor are less likely to receive college deferments or have other connections or opportunities that would help them escape.[29]

Through most of the twentieth century, the United States relied on conscription to have enough men to fight its wars. For example, in World War I, the government forced 2.8 million men to serve in the military, and conscripts made up 70 percent of Army troops.[30] In World War II, the government forced some 10 million men into service, and conscripts made up about 62.5 percent of the troops.[31] In the Vietnam era, the government forced 2.2 million people to serve.[32] These numbers include only people who were actually drafted. Many others undoubtedly joined the military "voluntarily" because of the *threat* of being drafted; by doing so, they could at least choose a specialty and type of service that would hopefully keep them off the front lines. Some scholars estimate that during the Vietnam War as many as four million men "voluntarily" joined the military for this reason.[33]

How Libertarians Helped End the Draft

Today, the worst type of conscription no longer exists in the United States. Young men who do not volunteer for the military do not have to fear being forced to fight. For this, they owe thanks in part to libertarians, who played a critical role in ending the draft.

Free-market economist Martin Anderson suggested this idea to Richard Nixon (himself no free-marketer) as one of Nixon's economic advisers during the 1968 presidential campaign.[34] Nixon liked the proposal because he wanted

to end domestic unrest over the draft if it were economically and militarily fea-
sible. So in 1969, Nixon set up a commission to study the issue, which included
among its 15 members Milton Friedman, free-market scholar W. Allen Wallis,
and Ayn Rand associate Alan Greenspan, who had not yet completed his fall
from libertarian grace.[35]

Reportedly, Friedman played a critical role in winning over skeptical
Commission members. When General William Westmoreland, commander of
U.S. Vietnam operations from 1964 through 1968, told the group that he was
not interested in leading "an army of mercenaries," Friedman asked him, "Would
you rather command an army of slaves?" Westmoreland replied: "I don't like to
hear our patriotic draftees referred to as slaves." Friedman then responded:
"I don't like to hear our patriotic volunteers referred to as mercenaries. If they are
mercenaries, then I, sir, am a mercenary professor, and you, sir, are a mercenary
general; we are served by mercenary physicians, we use a mercenary lawyer, and
we get our meat from a mercenary butcher."[36] The group unanimously recommended that the government end the draft, and Congress did so on July 1, 1973.

Conscription Today

Despite that victory for freedom, conscription is not dead in America. All
men between ages 18 and 25 must still register with the Selective Service System or face criminal penalties. This system continues for one reason: so the
government can easily begin drafting troops for combat again if those in power
deem it necessary.[37]

Also, even if a person voluntarily joins the military, he or she is thereafter
enslaved. In most regular jobs, one can simply quit and be done. Some people
have an employment contract in which they promise to work for some specified period of time, but the law still allows them to quit, though they may be
liable to the employer for damages if they do. Under the law as it applies to
regular employment contracts—and under libertarianism as most libertarians
understand it—one cannot sell oneself into slavery.[38]

In the military, however, one cannot quit, so one does effectively sell oneself
into slavery. There, quitting is a crime called desertion and, in wartime, it is theoretically punishable by death. In practice today it is punished by imprisonment.
Since 2001, some 20,000 soldiers have left their posts because they decided the
war was illegal or unjustified, because they became conscientious objectors, or
because they simply decided it was no longer what they wanted to do. Of those,
the military prosecutes about ten percent, some of whom are sentenced to prison
terms of a year or more.[39] The military also forces many soldiers to stay longer
than they bargained for through "stop-loss" orders that require them to stay for
up to 18 months beyond their original enlistment term.[40]

Politicians occasionally suggest reinstating the draft, but this seems unlikely to occur soon; the government does not want to face the same sort of massive resistance and flouting of its laws that occurred during Vietnam, because this tends to undermine respect for government in general. Nonetheless, large-scale conscription could make a comeback in the form of mandatory "national service." For example, White House Chief of Staff Rahm Emanuel has proposed three months of compulsory national service for all Americans ages 18 through 25.[41] The Edward M. Kennedy Serve America Act, which President Obama signed into law in April 2009, provides for greatly expanded voluntary service opportunities, but, as Ron Paul has noted, the Act could provide federal funding for state or local programs (which already exist) that require young people to perform community service to graduate from high school, itself a form of conscription.[42] Libertarians find such programs objectionable on a number of grounds—for example, they require compulsory funding, imply that government-approved "service" is somehow superior to participating in the private sector, and imply that young people owe something to the State. Above all, however, libertarians are concerned that a voluntary service program, like a voluntary military, could become non-voluntary.

War Makes Civilians Targets

When a government goes to war, it kills civilians in another country, but it also puts its own civilians at a much greater risk of being killed by an enemy's retaliation. Governments also do this to their citizens when they intervene in other countries' affairs without actually going to war. For example, if the United States enters an alliance with another country such as Israel (to pick a non-controversial example), Israel's enemies will now see the United States as an enemy as well. Likewise, if the United States supplies monetary and military aid to a foreign government, people who hate that government may then hate the United States—and U.S. citizens will be put at risk as a result.

The United States has not technically suffered many civilian casualties in its wars because the United States mostly only fights countries with little or no means of retaliating. (Americans were fortunate, of course, to survive the Cold War, which put everyone at risk.) But libertarians would point out that Americans have suffered greatly as a result of U.S. foreign intervention in the Middle East, especially on September 11, 2001. As Ron Paul noted in a 2008 Republican presidential debate, referring to the history of U.S. intervention in the Middle East, "They attack us because we've been over there. . . . We need to look at what we do from the perspective of what would happen if somebody else did it to us." To this, former New York Mayor Rudolph Giuliani replied, to applause from the GOP faithful, "That's an extraordinary statement . . . that we invited the attack because we were attacking Iraq. I don't think I've ever heard that before and I've heard some pretty absurd explanations for September 11."[43]

But Paul had strong support for his claim, and he was hardly the first to make it. In a press release issued shortly after the debate, Paul offered Giuliani a reading list of books that showed that the September 11 attacks were indeed "blowback" against America's foreign policy in the Middle East, including the government's own *9-11 Commission Report*, which noted that Osama Bin Laden was motivated in substantial part by U.S. troops' presence in Saudi Arabia and by the sanctions against Iraq; former CIA consultant Chalmers Johnson's book *Blowback*; former CIA anti-terrorism expert Michael Scheuer's book *Imperial Hubris*; and suicide-terrorism expert Robert Pape's book *Dying to Win*.[44]

Paul did not come up with this theory after the fact; he had been pointing out the likely consequences of America's aggressive foreign policy for years before September 11. For example, when President Bill Clinton ordered four days of bombing in Iraq in 1998, Paul told a reporter that "our national security is more jeopardized by permitting this to happen because we're liable to start a war. . . . We're liable to have more attacks on us by terrorists."[45] On February 8, 2001, Paul warned Congress: "If one were truly concerned about our security and enhancing peace, one would always opt for a less militaristic policy. It is not a coincidence that U.S. territory and U.S. citizens are the most vulnerable in the world to terrorist attacks."[46]

None of this, of course, denies or mitigates the culpability of the September 11 attackers or of anyone else who retaliates against civilians; they are aggressors and have no justification for their actions. But the U.S. government could avoid such attacks on its citizens if, as libertarians urge, it simply stayed out of other countries' affairs, militarily and otherwise.

War Is the Health of the State

Randolph Bourne's famous quote, "War is the health of the State,"[47] appears a lot in libertarian literature, with good reason. As we have seen, there are certain government interventions that are inherent in any modern war: killing, taxation, and often conscription. These, however, are just the beginning. Wars also allow governments to impose many other policies and programs, which are often introduced as temporary measures, but then never go away.

In his groundbreaking book *Crisis and Leviathan*, Higgs describes the permanent increase in government power following a war or other crisis as a "ratchet effect." During a crisis, the government greatly increases its size and power as people demand that it "do something." Once the crisis is past, the government's powers shrink to some extent, but never back to where they would have been if the crisis had not occurred.[48]

According to Higgs, this happens because crises create "permanent shifts in the tolerable limits of the true size of government."[49] Government expansion during war changes people's ideological perspective and creates a precedent in favor of big government, as it leads people to think that government is not all bad and can get things done. But much of this popular belief is a product of the *post hoc, ergo propter hoc* fallacy: "we won; therefore government's collectivist war policies must have been necessary and proper."[50] Also, special interests take advantage of government expansions during a crisis, and once they have their programs in place, they are difficult to get rid of, and government becomes permanently bigger. Today, government leaders are consciously aware of their ability to exploit crises to increase power in this way; Rahm Emanuel, for one, has noted, "You never want a serious crisis to go to waste. . . . This crisis provides the opportunity for us to do things that you could not do before."[51]

War Hurts Liberty at Home

One way government expands at home during a war is through increased restrictions on civil liberties.

For example, in World War I, President Wilson signed the Espionage Act and the Sedition Act, which made it a crime to speak out against the draft or the war and sent people to prison just for exercising their free-speech rights. Charles T. Schenk, for one, was sentenced to six months in prison for distributing pamphlets that argued that the draft was unconstitutional, and Socialist Party leader Eugene V. Debs received a ten-year sentence for criticizing the war. Thomas E. Woods, Jr. and Kevin R.C. Gutzman relate some other examples of how government attacked free speech:

> A movie about the American War for Independence called *The Spirit of '76*, which portrayed the British in an unflattering light, got its makers in trouble with the law: because the United States was now allied with Britain, such images could promote discontent in the American armed forces and interfere with recruitment. They received a prison sentence of ten years. A Christian minister in Vermont was sentenced to fifteen years for writing a pamphlet, which he distributed to five people, arguing that Christ had been a pacifist and that Christians should not participate in war. . . . A man was arrested under the Minnesota Espionage Act for saying in reference to women who knitted socks for soldiers, "No soldier ever sees these socks."[52]

Despite the First Amendment, the Supreme Court approved of this as it upheld the prison sentences of Debs and Schenck. (The relatively libertarian President Warren G. Harding freed Debs in 1920.)[53]

During World War II, the government perpetrated one of its most notorious attacks on the rights of peaceful people: the imprisonment of some 120,000 people of Japanese ancestry, most of whom were American citizens, in "relocation camps" for nearly two years. Once again, the Supreme Court allowed the Executive Branch of government to trample on Americans' rights because the Court, like most everyone else, is willing to allow government more power in wartime.[54] Free speech suffered again, too, as many newspapers were denied access to the mail under the Espionage Act (which was still in effect), some newspapers were banned entirely, and an "Office of Censorship" censored press reports and radio broadcasts as well as personal mail entering or leaving the country. In addition, the government put almost 6,000 conscientious objectors to war in prison for refusing to comply with the draft.[55]

War and Liberty Today

Today's so-called War on Terror has also harmed liberty. Following September 11, 2001, pollster John Zogby found that, as in previous wars, "the willingness [of Americans] to give up personal liberties is stunning because the level of fear is so high."[56] The government did not hesitate to take advantage of this.

There is one respect, however, in which this war is different from previous wars: there is no end in sight. Because the War on Terror theoretically may continue as long as there are terrorists in the world (i.e., forever), there is no foreseeable point at which the United States will declare victory and then begin to roll back its domestic interventions as it has after other wars. Instead, as with the drug war, the interventions only seem to increase over time (with occasional setbacks from the Supreme Court, which, to its credit, has not been quite as deferential as it was in the days of the Espionage Act and Japanese internment).

One way the government has infringed rights since 2001 is by spying on Americans. For example, President George W. Bush authorized the National Security Administration (NSA) to spy on Americans through wiretaps without a warrant, probable cause, or notice. When legal scholars attempted to challenge this program in federal court, the U.S. Court of Appeals for the Sixth Circuit dismissed the case because the scholars could not show that they were actually victims of the program. Of course, *no one* could show this because the wiretaps were secret—which meant that Americans had no way to challenge this intrusion upon their privacy and their rights in court.[57] The NSA suspended the program in 2007, but in 2008, Congress passed the FISA Amendments Act of 2008, which immunized telecommunications companies from liability for their complicity in government wiretaps, authorized the government to conduct surveillance of a person for up to a week before getting a court order, and eliminated any requirement that government agents seeking permission to conduct a wiretap specify what they are seeking.

The government has also violated citizens' privacy under the Patriot Act by sending hundreds of thousands of "National Security Letters" to businesses, demanding information on their clients. The clients never learn of this invasion of their privacy because the law prohibits businesses that receive these letters from stating that they received the letter or turned over the customer's information.[58] The Patriot Act also authorized "sneak-and-peek" warrants, which allow law enforcement to break into homes and search them without notifying the occupants. Though introduced as necessary to fight terror, they have since been used extensively to investigate other crimes, mostly drug offenses.[59]

TSA Transgressions

Americans who travel suffer violations of their privacy and liberty when they are forced to submit to intrusive searches by the Transportation Security Administration (TSA) before boarding an airplane. People take off their shoes, follow orders, and submit to pat-downs—and they mostly do so with minimal complaint, knowing that asking questions may only lead to more hassle, a missed flight, or even criminal charges. Frequently people have their property confiscated or are barred from boarding a plane for arbitrary reasons.

On top of all this, the TSA recently added another indignity: Americans at many airports must now walk through "millimeter-wave scanners," which allow TSA agents to see through their clothes and essentially view their naked bodies. Originally, the TSA promised that these scanners would only serve as an *option* for people who set off the metal detector and did not want to submit to a pat-down search. In 2009, however, the TSA predictably changed its policy; now it wants everyone to submit to the scans as a matter of course.[60] The TSA has promised to blur facial images on the scans, and not to save the images to computers, but given the TSA's track record, Americans have little reason to believe this promise will be kept or that TSA employees will reliably follow any such policy. Indeed, TSA employees have become notorious for taking passengers' personal belongings for themselves.[61]

Despite all these intrusions, there is little evidence that the TSA has made anyone safer by scanning shoes or confiscating fingernail clippers, shampoo, and the like. Indeed, one 20-year-old college student put the system to the test by successfully smuggling box-cutter components and fake bomb-making materials onto planes. (After notifying the TSA of their failure, he was charged with a felony and ultimately received probation.)[62]

While the majority of Americans just do as they are told, libertarians have been among the TSA's most vociferous critics. Andrew Napolitano, a Fox News legal analyst, criticized the TSA in his book with the fitting title *A Nation of Sheep*. James Bovard, a libertarian journalist and prominent critic of War on Terror measures generally, has also done so in books and articles, and on his blog.[63] Libertarian writer Becky Akers has also decried and discussed the TSA's offenses extensively in a series of columns for *LewRockwell.com* and elsewhere.[64] So have Robert Higgs and other writers at the Independent Institute.

Libertarians say the government should exit the air-security business entirely and allow airlines to impose whatever precautions they deem appropriate. After all, the planes' owners have the strongest of incentives to keep them from crashing and to avoid potential lawsuits from passengers or their families. And unlike the TSA, the airlines would have an incentive to find methods of screening that work without excessively inconveniencing innocent passengers.

Libertarians' objections to the TSA are about far more than travel hassles or what will keep planes safest. Libertarians find the TSA so disturbing in part because it accustoms Americans to obeying orders from uniformed government agents without question and to submitting to gross violations of privacy and dignity. If a government agent can search you before traveling on a plane, why not let him do so on the street? Or in your house? Libertarians hope their fellow Americans draw the line now so that never becomes an issue.

Kidnapping, Detention, and Torture

It is well known that the government in the post-9/11 era has also disregarded both the Constitution and international law in kidnapping, detaining, and torturing alleged terror suspects who have not been convicted of any crime, some of whom are certainly innocent. For most of three years, the Bush Administration believed it could declare U.S. citizens it suspected of involvement with terrorism "enemy combatants" and detain them indefinitely at its prison at Guantanamo Bay without any hearing or trial. After that, it attempted to use military tribunals to declare non-citizens "enemy combatants" and then hold them indefinitely without a hearing or trial at Guantanamo. The U.S. Supreme Court finally ended this practice in 2008, when it declared in *Boumediene v. Bush* that detainees were entitled to seek habeas corpus relief in federal courts.[65] (That is, the prisoners were allowed to go to court to force the government to show that it had a lawful basis for holding them.) Once the prisoner in that case, Lakhdar Boumediene, finally received his hearing, a court determined there was no credible evidence to justify holding him and he was released—after nearly seven years of imprisonment and torture.[66]

Despite this favorable development, anyone who thinks that the *Boudmediene* decision and the election of Barack Obama put an end to such concerns would be wrong. The Obama Administration has claimed the right to do essentially the same thing that the Bush Administration did—hold prisoners indefinitely without any opportunity for judicial review, ever—only at the Bagram Theater Internment Facility in Afghanistan instead of at Guantanamo.[67]

The libertarian view is that the government has no right to lock up anyone whom it has not proven guilty of a crime, regardless of whether they are American, what they are accused of, where they were arrested, or where they are being held. It would be a crime for any private citizen to abduct and imprison someone whom he or she merely suspected of wrongdoing, and so it is for government. Could such a policy result in some would-be terrorists going free? Of course. A free society always entails that risk; the only alternative is to preemptively put *everyone* in prison.

More Military at Home

Americans also face the specter of more liberty violations as the military increasingly threatens to interject itself into their lives. From its passage in 1878 until 2006, the Posse Comitatus Act barred the military from deploying troops to enforce the law within the United States. In 2006, Congress changed this and authorized the president to deploy troops domestically when he deems it necessary to respond to an emergency. Congress repealed that provision in 2008, but the military has proceeded with plans to deploy troops in the United States anyway. In late 2008, the *Washington Post* reported that the military "expects to have 20,000 uniformed troops inside the United States by 2011 trained to help state and local officials respond to a nuclear terrorist attack or other domestic catastrophe."[68] This prospect troubles libertarians because soldiers are not trained to be police, but are trained to be warriors, meaning they are trained to kill; and it is difficult to imagine a country that is both dominated by the military and free.[69]

Can Any War Be Libertarian?

Is there *any* war a libertarian can support? In theory, perhaps, but in practice, almost no U.S. war has satisfied libertarian criteria for a justified war, and few wars could.

Just War Theory

Libertarians who believe in minimal government for defensive purposes would say that a genuinely defensive war is just. A person may defend himself against an ordinary criminal with violence, so people may band together to defend themselves against an attack by a foreign invader. But to be consistent with libertarianism and avoid the problems we have discussed above, a war would have to be fought with, as Murray Rothbard put it, "(a) weapons limited so that no civilians were injured in their persons or property; (b) volunteer rather than conscript armies; and also (c) financing by voluntary methods instead of taxation."[70] In addition, many libertarians would say that a war should satisfy the principles of traditional Just War Theory. Ron Paul takes this view, and summarizes those principles as follows:

1. War should be fought only in self-defense;

2. War should be undertaken only as a last resort;

3. A decision to enter war should be made only by a legitimate authority;

4. All military responses must be proportional to the threat;

5. There must be a reasonable chance of success; and

6. A public declaration notifying all parties concerned is required.[71]

America's Wars

Applying these criteria, very few if any of America's wars have been justified.

The American Revolution is the probably the least objectionable war because it involved casting off an oppressive government and was targeted at that government, not at civilians back in England.[72] Even the Revolution, though, relied on inflation, economic controls, and conscription.[73]

Following the Revolution, the libertarian policy of non-intervention and neutrality was the American norm. Although the United States did assert a right to intervene in the Western Hemisphere under the Monroe Doctrine in 1823, few interventions came of it until the late nineteenth century. America's foreign policy wasn't perfect in the early Republic, but as libertarian historian Joseph Stromberg has put it, "the lapses were deviations."[74]

This changed over the course of the nineteenth century, most notably with the Civil War. Although no libertarian could endorse the Confederate government or its protection of slavery, the Union did not fight the Civil War in self-defense; it invaded another country that had, like the colonies in 1776, declared its independence and wanted to be left alone. Some may argue that the Confederacy wanted to be left alone *to do something evil*—protect the institution of slavery—but of course all governments do things that harm their citizens. The Union, for one, did not have clean hands, even with respect to slavery—after all, slavery was legal under the Constitution (and even in several Union states during the Civil War), and the Union's courts upheld the Fugitive Slave Act. Another country's bad domestic policies are not enough, in the libertarian view, to justify a war against it. Regardless of its merits, the Civil War was exceptionally bloody, killing over 600,000 soldiers between the two sides—more American deaths than all other U.S. wars combined. As noted above, the Union Army also killed innocent civilians and destroyed private property on an unprecedented scale. And the war came with large liberty costs, as Abraham Lincoln violated civil liberties and dramatically increased the federal government's power through, for example, suppression of free speech, suspension of habeas corpus, and his insistence on federal supremacy over the states.[75] (Lincoln has been a favorite target of many libertarians since economic historian Thomas DiLorenzo exposed his misdeeds in his 2002 book, *The Real Lincoln*.)

Over the nineteenth century, America began fighting wars to expand its territory in North America and overseas because of popular belief in Manifest Destiny and the idea that expanding into new territory was necessary for economic prosperity. These wars—for example, those against Mexico, Spain, and the Philippines—were wars of aggression with no libertarian justification. (Probably few Americans today know that their government temporarily possessed the Philippines and then killed some 220,000 Filipinos when the country demanded its independence.)[76]

World War I had no libertarian justification, either, because the United States faced no threat at all from the fight between European powers.[77] World War II was essentially a result and an extension of World War I. After the Great War, the Allies punished the Germans in the Treaty of Versailles by, among many other things, taking territory away from Germany that was populated by German-speaking people who wanted to be part of Germany. This humiliation and loss of territory helped set the stage for Hitler to take power in 1933.[78] Though Hitler's evil was great, he posed no imminent threat to the United States. In fact, he could not even succeed in his attempt get past the English Channel, let alone across the Atlantic, and even his wildest fantasies of eventual world domination did not involve attacking the United States until about 1980. Had Britain and the United States not intervened when Hitler attempted to expand Germany's territory eastward, Hitler and Stalin might have fought each other to the death, bringing a relatively swift end to both Nazism and the even more murderous Soviet regime.[79]

The lack of justification for more recent U.S. wars has perhaps been more obvious to more people (though still too few people, too late, to prevent the wars from happening). Vietnam posed no direct or indirect threat to the United States, and the "loss" of that war did not harm the American people. Afghanistan and especially Iraq, about which more below, posed no threat to the United States that would justify a war, either.

LIBERTARIANS FOR WAR?

Despite everything we have said in this chapter about liberty and war, some libertarians nonetheless believe that modern wars, even present U.S. wars, may be justified. Most prominently, a 2007 *Wall Street Journal* op-ed by Randy Barnett (whom we mentioned in Chapters 4 and 8) declared: "Ron Paul doesn't speak for all of us."[80]

Barnett's article asked: "Does being a libertarian commit one to a particular stance toward the Iraq war? The simple answer is 'no.'" He explained his view:

> [Some libertarians] supported the war in Iraq because they viewed it as part of a larger war of self-defense against Islamic jihadists who were organizationally independent of any government. They viewed radical Islamic fundamentalism as resulting in part from the corrupt dictatorial regimes that inhabit the Middle East, which have effectively repressed indigenous democratic reformers. Although opposed to nation building generally, these libertarians believed that a strategy of fomenting democratic regimes in the Middle East . . . might well be the best way to take the fight to the enemy rather than solely trying to ward off the next attack.

Many of Barnett's fellow libertarians were shocked and disappointed that he would take such a view and were quick to disavow it. Anyone who has read this chapter so far can imagine why. For one thing, as Walter Block explained, Barnett's description of the Iraq war as defensive made little sense:

> To construe our invasion of Iraq as "defensive" is so totally to misconstrue what "defense" is as to violate not only libertarian principle, but even common sense. Iraq, as opposed to the perpetrators of the unjustified bloodbath of 9/11, not only never attacked us, they never even threatened to do so. For us to *initiate* an invasion of their country was thus not *defense*; it was *offense*.
>
> Preemptive war of the sort advocated by . . . Barnett is the foreign analog of domestic preventive detention. I note that males between the ages of 15 and 25 commit a disproportionately high number of crimes. Why wait to "ward off the next attack" by this age sex cohort? Why not take the fight to (this domestic) enemy? Can I as a libertarian advocate that we lock up *every* male in the country at age 15, regardless of whether they have committed a crime, and set them free at age 25? I cannot, and still remain a libertarian. Well, then, neither can Barnett . . .[81]

Libertarian writer Sheldon Richman noted that Barnett's position is "ahistorical" in that it makes assumptions that ignore both the history of libertarian thought and the history of the world:

> Nowhere in Barnett's article does one find a hint that the leading, pioneering classical liberals of the nineteenth and early twentieth centuries were not just skeptical of the government's war-making power; rather they were forthrightly *antiwar, anti-empire,* and *pro-peace.* These include Frederic Bastiat, Richard Cobden, John Bright, Herbert Spencer, Auberon Herbert, and William Graham Sumner. This is no coincidence. These men were not ivory-tower theorists; they were *historians* as well as keen observers of contemporary events, applying libertarian principles to the historical conduct of politicians, bureaucrats, and diplomats. It was Sumner, echoing many before him, who pointed out that "national defense" means "war, debt, taxation, diplomacy, a grand governmental system, pomp, glory, a big army and navy, lavish expenditures, politically jobbery." *The liberals unfailingly understood that war means the mass murder of innocents and regimentation at home.* Nothing is easier for a politician than conjuring up a "self-defense" justification for war, but the great classical liberals would have nothing to do with it.[82]

Barnett's article also claimed that "libertarian principles tell us little about what constitutes appropriate and effective self-defense after an attack." The Cato Institute's Gene Healy found this questionable, asking whether libertarianism is "really a political philosophy that tells you what to think about mandatory recycling and restrictions on the interstate shipment of wine, but has virtually nothing of interest to say about when it might be morally permissible to use daisy cutters and thermobaric bombs."[83] Richman pointed out that even if libertarian principles didn't say much on the appropriate methods of legitimate self-defense, they certainly do "tell us what constitutes *inappropriate* 'self-defense' after an attack." Specifically, libertarian principles offer the following guidance: "don't commit mass murder, don't destroy a people's infrastructure so they will die of starvation and disease, and don't violate the rights of the people allegedly being defended. The principles also provide guidance in how to avoid attacks and the need for self-defense in the first place. Such as: Don't prop up and arm dictators, don't overthrow elected regimes, don't aid those who oppress others . . ."[84] Of course, U.S. policy toward Iraq before and during the war violated all these principles.

Barnett was not the only person in the libertarian camp (broadly defined) to endorse the Iraq war. The Cato Institute's Brink Lindsey, for example, strongly supported the war at the outset.[85] Objectivists such as Ayn Rand Institute founder Leonard Peikoff and president Yaron Brook have favored war, even urging that the United States not be squeamish about killing civilians, apparently on the ground that saving our own lives is more important than respecting anyone else's.[86]

Such views, however, are the exception. Most libertarians have vehemently opposed the war for all the reasons we have reviewed in this chapter. Indeed, some anti-war libertarians such as Block would argue that people who take the pro-war view cannot even be called libertarians because supporting a war of aggression such as the Iraq war goes too far. Whether that is an appropriate judgment or not, one can safely say that the pro-war position is in direct opposition to libertarianism as we have defined it in this book, as most libertarians define it, as most leading thinkers at major libertarian organizations define it, and as nearly all of the major libertarian thinkers of the past have defined it. In sum, support for the Iraq war is deviation from libertarianism.

LIBERTARIANS AGAINST WAR

In fact, libertarians have been the most consistent opponents of war, particularly since September 11, 2001.

It is tempting to say that Republicans support wars started by their presidents, and Democrats support wars started by theirs, but this really has not been so. Rather, both parties overwhelmingly support almost all wars, regardless of who starts them. For example, Democrats supported the Iraq invasion from the outset. (Barack Obama, an Illinois state senator at the time, was an exception.) Once the war turned disastrous, Democrats were happy to scold George W. Bush for supposedly fooling them with faulty intelligence, but they made no serious push to withdraw the troops.

And what about Obama? He ran as an anti-war candidate, proudly contrasting himself with the unabashed hawk, Hillary Clinton. Obama's popular support among young people was based in no small part on their assumption that he opposed President Bush's war; at the time of this writing, one can still see cars displaying campaign bumper stickers on which the "O" in "Obama" is a peace symbol. In practice, however, Obama's conduct has been essentially as aggressive as Bush's. As a candidate, Obama promised troops out of Iraq within 16 months of taking office.[87] At the time of this writing, it is clear that troops will remain in Iraq at least through the third year of Obama's presidency. Meanwhile, the war in Afghanistan has only escalated. In Pakistan, unmanned drones have bombed targets and killed many innocent people—but Obama has faced little outcry from most of the liberals who hated Bush so much for his wars. And conservatives need not have feared that Obama would capitulate to Iranian president Mahmoud Ahmadinejad; despite Obama's receipt of a Nobel Peace Prize, the United States has continued to threaten Iran and move toward another war.

Republicans, for their part, have not taken their defeat in 2008, or the intense interest Ron Paul received, as a sign that anything was wrong with their foreign policy. They criticize Obama for his profligate spending, but not for the hundreds of billions spent on the military and war. If they mention war at all, it is only to call for even more of it. There are no signs that the Republicans will return to the less interventionist stance they took when they opposed President Clinton's war in the Balkans, or when Bush promised "no nation building" in his 2000 campaign.

If Democrats and Republicans both support war, who does this leave to oppose it? It leaves a handful of principled paleoconservatives and far-left liberals, and it leaves libertarians. Libertarians, with the exceptions we have noted, never fell for Iraq war propaganda because libertarians are inherently less susceptible to believing *any* propaganda. If one thinks government is a criminal organization, why would one believe it when it says it needs more money and maybe also one's life to go fight some *other* criminal? Also, libertarians tend to be aware of America's history of going to war based on flimsy pretenses, from the sinking of the *Maine* (which probably was not attacked by the Spanish)[88] to the Gulf of Tonkin incident (which was entirely fabricated).[89] And even if the worst of the Iraq war propaganda had been true—if Saddam Hussein had possessed weapons of mass destruction—this still would not have satisfied the criteria for a just war.

If many libertarians are not the type one sees holding signs at anti-war protests (though some are), they more than make up for this through writing and online activism. We noted some leading writers on the War on Terror above. In addition, the popular anti-war website *Antiwar.com*, led by founders Eric Garris and Justin Raimondo, has published anti-war news and commentary since 1995; the writers come from varied political backgrounds, but its mission statement proclaims that its politics are libertarian. Also, in the days and years following September 11, several libertarian organizations held especially firm against war hysteria: the Ludwig von Mises Institute; the Independent Institute, a think tank based in Oakland, California; and the Future of Freedom Foundation, an advocacy group based in Fairfax, Virginia.

To succeed in convincing their fellow citizens to roll back the warfare state, libertarians will need to sway members of the right and the left to the antiwar view. They will need to get past many conservatives' extreme distaste for Islam and belief in the righteousness of war to convince them that "big-government" schemes to invade other countries are no less costly, problematic, or socialistic than proposals for, say, universal healthcare. And they will need to convince liberals that wars are no less atrocious, no less painful for their victims, when carried out by Democrats. All of this persuasion will, of course, have to be at the grassroots level because most Washington politicians are beholden to the merchants of death and will not disappoint their patrons unless seriously threatened by the voters.

If libertarian ideology alone will not push voters in the anti-war direction, the economy might. If foreign governments stop lending to the United States, the government will have no way to finance its wars except to raise taxes on Americans who are already financially strapped, or it will have to resort to the printing press, which will further wreck the economy. If reality at last disciplines the government, or awakens people to the combined destructiveness of its foreign and monetary policies, we could see a rare historic case where freedom, not government, advances in a time of crisis.

NOTES

1. See Hans-Hermann Hoppe, *Democracy—The God That Failed: The Economics and Politics of Monarchy, Democracy, and Natural Order* (New Brunswick, NJ: Transaction Publishers, 2000), 34–37.

2. See Ibid., 36–39.

3. Clyde Wilson, "War, Reconstruction, and the End of the Old Republic," in John V. Denson, ed., *The Costs of War: America's Pyrrhic Victories* (New Brunswick, NJ: Transaction Publishers, 1999), 163–64; Thomas J. DiLorenzo, "Targeting Civilians," *LewRockwell.com*, September 17, 2001, http://www.lewrockwell.com/dilorenzo/dilorenzo8.html.

4. See Ralph Raico, "Rethinking Churchill," in Denson, *The Costs of War*, 331, http://www.lewrockwell.com/raico/churchill-full.html.

5. Ibid., 351. Though Patrick J. Buchanan is no libertarian, his book *Churchill, Hitler, and the "Unnecessary War": How Britain Lost Its Empire and the West Lost the World* (New York: Crown Forum, 2008) documents well Churchill's love of war and deliberate targeting of civilians.

6. Laurence M. Vance, "Bombings Worse than Nagasaki and Hiroshima," *Future of Freedom Foundation*, August 14, 2009, http://www.fff.org/comment/com0908j.asp.

7. See Ralph Raico, "Harry S. Truman: Advancing the Revolution," in John V. Denson, ed., *Reassessing the Presidency: The Rise of the Executive State and the Decline of Freedom* (Auburn, AL: Ludwig von Mises Institute, 2001), http://mises.org/Books/reassessingpresidency.pdf.

8. "2007 Annual Report on Implementation of the Moscow Treaty," *U.S. Department of State*, http://www.state.gov/t/vci/rls/rpt/88187.htm.

9. Murray N. Rothbard, "War, Peace, and the State," in Hans-Hermann Hoppe, ed., *The Myth of National Defense* (Auburn, AL: Ludwig von Mises Institute, 2003), 68–69, http://mises.org/etexts/defensemyth.pdf.

10. See Chris Suellentrop, "Are 1 Million Children Dying in Iraq?" *Slate*, October 9, 2001, http://slate.msn.com/?id=1008414.

11. "Punishing Saddam," *60 Minutes*, May 12, 1996, http://www.youtube.com/watch?v=FbIX1CP9qr4.

12. *Iraq Body Count*, http://www.iraqbodycount.org/.

13. Gilbert Burnham, Riyadh Lafta, Shannon Doocy, and Les Roberts, "Mortality After the 2003 Invasion of Iraq: A Cross-sectional Cluster Sample Survey," *The Lancet*, October 16, 2006, http://brusselstribunal.org/pdf/lancet111006.pdf.

14. "September 11 Attacks," *Encyclopædia Britannica Online*, http://www.britannica.com/EBchecked/topic/762320/September-11-attacks.

15. Frederic Bastiat, "What Is Seen and What Is Not Seen" (1850), in Frederic Bastiat, *The Bastiat Collection*, Vol. 1 (Auburn, AL: Ludwig von Mises Institute, 2007), http://mises.org/books/bastiat1.pdf.

16. For more, see Robert P. Murphy, *The Politically Incorrect Guide to the Great Depression and the New Deal* (Washington, DC: Regnery, 2009), 145–64; Thomas E. Woods, Jr., "The Myth of Wartime Prosperity," *The Freeman*, December 2004, http://www.thefreemanonline.org/featured/the-myth-of-wartime-prosperity.

17. The phrase was made popular by an early book on the phenomenon by H.C. Engelbrecht and F.C. Hanighen, *The Merchants of Death: A Study of the International Armament Industry* (New York: Dodd, Mead, & Co., 1934), http://mises.org/books/merchantsofdeath.pdf. The next year saw publication of a short classic on the subject, Smedley Butler, *War Is a Racket* (New York: Round Table Press, Inc., 1935), http://www.lexrex.com/enlightened/articles/warisaracket.htm.

18. See, e.g., Dwight D. Eisenhower, "Farewell Address," January 17, 1961, http://www.independent.org/issues/article.asp?id=1133; Robert Higgs, *Depression, War, and Cold War* (New York: Oxford University Press, 2006); Karen Kwiatkowski, "Military Industrial Complexes," *LewRockwell.com*, May 3, 2004, http://www.lewrockwell.com/kwiatkowski/kwiatkowski72.html.

19. See John Byrne, "US Actually Increasing Personnel in Iraq: More Contractors, Fewer Troops," *The Raw Story*, September 9, 2009, http://rawstory.com/blog/2009/09/us-replacing-iraq-troops-with-private-contractors/.

20. Christopher Hellman and Travis Sharp, "The FY 2009 Pentagon Spending Request—Global Military Spending," *Center for Arms Control and Non-Proliferation*, February 22, 2008, http://www.armscontrolcenter.org/policy/securityspending/articles/fy09_dod_request_global/.

21. "Budget FY 2009," *Office of Management and Budget*, http://www.whitehouse.gov/omb/rewrite/budget/fy2009/defense.html.

22. Robert Higgs, "The Defense Budget Is Bigger than You Think," *San Francisco Chronicle*, January 18, 2004, http://www.independent.org/newsroom/article.asp?id=1253.

23. *Costofwar.com*, October 24, 2009.

24. Ron Paul, "Inflation and War Finance," *LewRockwell.com*, January 30, 2007, http://www.lewrockwell.com/paul/paul364.html.

25. Higgs, "How War Amplified Federal Power in the Twentieth Century," *The Freeman*, July 1999, http://www.thefreemanonline.org/featured/how-war-amplified-federal-power-in-the-twentieth-century/. See also Murray N. Rothbard, "War Collectivism in World War I," *LewRockwell.com*, http://www.lewrockwell.com/rothbard/rothbard91.html.

26. Robert Higgs, *Crisis and Leviathan: Critical Episodes in the Growth of American Government* (New York: Oxford University Press, 1987), 209.

27. Milton Friedman, a Treasury Department official at the time, played a role in introducing the withholding tax, earning many libertarians' undying scorn. See Brian Doherty, "Best of Both Worlds," *Reason* (June 1995), http://reason.com/archives/1995/06/01/best-of-both-worlds/singlepage; Murray N. Rothbard, "Milton Friedman Unraveled," *Journal of Libertarian Studies* (Fall 2002): 37–54, http://mises.org/journals/jls/16_4/16_4_3.pdf.

28. See Robert Higgs, "Wartime Origins of Modern Income-Tax Withholding," *The Freeman*, November 2007, http://www.thefreemanonline.org/columns/our-economic-past-wartime-origins-of-modern-income-tax-withholding.

29. This came to the public's attention particularly during the Vietnam War. See, e.g., James E. Westheider, *The Vietnam War* (Westport, CT: Greenwood Press, 2007), 33–35.

30. Higgs, *Crisis and Leviathan*, 134.

31. Ibid., 202.

32. Westheider, *Vietnam War*, 31.

33. Brett E. Morris, *The Effects of the Draft on U.S. Presidential Approval Ratings During the Vietnam War, 1954–1975* (dissertation, University of Alabama, 2006), 42, citing M. Useem, *Conscription, Protest and Social Conflict: The Life and Death of a Draft Resistance Movement* (New York: Wiley, 1973) and W. Oi, "The Economic Cost of the Draft," in Martin Anderson, ed., *The Military Draft: Readings on Conscription* (Stanford, CA: Hoover Institution, 1982).

34. Martin Anderson is best known among libertarians for his book *The Federal Bulldozer* (Cambridge, MA: MIT Press, 1964), which describes how government "urban renewal" programs destroyed poor people's housing for the benefit of wealthy special interests.

35. Gary North, "The Libertarian Roots of the All-Volunteer Military," *LewRockwell .com*, December 20, 2003, http://www.lewrockwell.com/north/north235.html.

36. David R. Henderson, "Thank You, William H. Meckling," *Red Herring* (January 1999), http://www.davidrhenderson.com/articles/0199_thankyou.html.

37. So said the U.S. Supreme Court in *Rostker v. Goldberg*, 453 U.S. 57 (1981).

38. Murray Rothbard argues that one cannot sell oneself into slavery in *The Ethics of Liberty* (New York: New York University Press, 1998 [1982]), 40–41, http://mises.org/rothbard/ethics.pdf. Walter Block disagrees on this point (though he still would argue for a right to quit the military) in "A Libertarian Theory of Inalienability," *Journal of Libertarian Studies* (Spring 2003): 39–85, http://mises.org/journals/jls/17_2/17_2_3.pdf.

39. Gretel C. Kovach, "Canada's New Leaf," *Newsweek*, June 6, 2009, http://www.newsweek.com/id/200860/output/print.

40. See Charles V. Peña, "Backdoor Draft," *Antiwar.com*, August 30, 2006, http://www.anti-war.com/pena/?articleid=9622; Justin Raimondo, "The 'Stop Loss' Scam," *Antiwar.com*, December 9, 2004, http://original.antiwar.com/justin/2004/12/08/the-stop-loss-scam/; Michael Schwartz and Tom Engelhardt, "Letting in the Draft?" *Antiwar.com*, April 28, 2005, http://www.anti-war.com/engelhardt/?articleid=5759.

41. Rahm Emanuel and Bruce Reed, *The Plan: Ideas for America* (New York: Public Affairs, 2006), 61–62.

42. Ron Paul, "Statement in Opposition to HR 1388—National Service," *Ron Paul's Speeches and Statements*, March 18, 2009, http://www.house.gov/apps/list/speech/tx14_paul/natservoppose.shtml.

43. "Republican Debate Transcript, South Carolina," *CFR.org*, May 15, 2007, http://www.cfr.org/publication/13338/.

44. Ron Brynaert, "Paul Campaign Hopes 'Reading for Rudy' Will 'Educate' Giuliani," *The Raw Story*, May 24, 2007, http://www.rawstory.com/news/2007/Paul_campaign_hopes_Reading_for_Rudy_0524.html.

45. Llewellyn H. Rockwell, Jr., "Did Ron Paul Predict 9/11?" *The LRC Blog*, September 5, 2009, http://www.lewrockwell.com/blog/lewrw/archives/35093.html.

46. Ron Paul, *A Foreign Policy of Freedom: Peace Commerce, and Honest Friendship* (Lake Jackson, TX: Foundation for Rational Economics and Education, Inc., 2007), 140.

47. Randolph Bourne, "The State" (1918), in Murray Polner and Thomas E. Woods, Jr., eds., *We Who Dared to Say No to War* (New York: Basic Books, 2008), 135, http://fair-use.org/randolph-bourne/the-state.

48. See generally Higgs, *Crisis and Leviathan*.

49. Ibid., 73.

50. Ibid., 260.

51. Gerald F. Seib, "In Crisis, Opportunity for Barack Obama," *Wall Street Journal*, November 21, 2008, A2, http://online.wsj.com/article/SB122721278056345271.html.

52. Ibid., 9 (internal citations omitted).

53. Thomas E. Woods, Jr. and Kevin R.C. Gutzman, *Who Killed the Constitution? The Fate of American Liberty From World War I to George W. Bush* (New York: Crown Forum, 2008), 15–20.

54. *Korematsu v. United States*, 323 U.S. 214 (1944).

55. Higgs, "How War Amplified Federal Power in the Twentieth Century."

56. Quoted in Robert Higgs, *Resurgence of the Warfare State: The Crisis Since 9/11* (Oakland, CA: Independent Institute, 2005), 22.

57. See Andrew P. Napolitano, *A Nation of Sheep* (Nashville, TN: Thomas Nelson, 2007), 87–90; *American Civil Liberties Union v. National Security Agency*, 493 F.3d 644 (6th Cir. 2007).

58. See Napolitano, *A Nation of Sheep*, 91–97.

59. Daniel Tencer, "Feingold: 'Sneak-and-Peek' Searches Being Used for Regular Crimes," *The Raw Story*, September 23, 2009, http://rawstory.com/blog/2009/09/patriot-act-regular-crimes/.

60. See William Saletan, "Deeper Digital Penetration," *Slate*, April 18, 2009, http://slate.msn.com/id/2215687.

61. See James Bovard, "Bag It," *New York Times*, August 18, 2004, http://www.nytimes.com/2004/08/18/opinion/18bovard.html.

62. Eric Rich, "Student Who Hid Box Cutters on BWI Flight Gets Probation," *Washington Post*, June 25, 2004, http://www.washingtonpost.com/wp-dyn/articles/A3739-2004Jun24.html.

63. See, e.g., James Bovard, *Terrorism and Tyranny: Trampling Freedom, Justice, and Peace to Rid the World of Evil* (New York: Palgrave Macmillan, 2004); *Bovard* [blog], http://jimbovard.com/blog; *idem.* "Bag It"; idem. "Federal Attitude Policy," *LewRockwell.com*, August 29, 2008, http://www.lewrockwell.com/bovard/bovard59.html; James Bovard, "Dominate. Intimidate. Control." *Reason* (February 2004), http://reason.com/archives/2004/02/01/dominate-intimidate-control.

64. See "Becky Akers: Archives," *LewRockwell.com*, http://www.lewrockwell.com/akers/akers-arch.html; Becky Akers, "Big Brother Is Watching as He's Never Watched Before," *The Freeman* (July 2008), http://www.thefreemanonline.org/featured/big-brother-is-watching-as-hes-never-watched-before/.

65. 553 U.S. ___, 128 S. Ct. 2229.

66. See Glenn Greenwald, "ABC News' Interview with Lakhdar Boumediene and Our Current Policies," *Salon.com*, June 8, 2009, http://www.salon.com/opinion/greenwald/2009/06/08/boumediene/.

67. See Glenn Greenwald, "Bagram: The Sham of Closing Guantanamo," *Salon.com*, September 15, 2009, http://www.salon.com/opinion/greenwald/2009/09/15/bagram/.

68. Spenser S. Hsu and Ann Scott Tyson, "Pentagon to Detail Troops to Bolster Domestic Security," December 1, 2008, http://www.washingtonpost.com/wp-dyn/content/article/2008/11/30/AR2008113002217_pf.html.

69. On libertarian concerns about troops deployed in the United States, see, e.g., William Norman Grigg, "Rubicon in the Rear-View, Part I: Militarizing the Police," *LewRockwell.com*, October 6, 2008, http://www.lewrockwell.com/grigg/grigg-w49.html; idem., "Rubicon in the Rear-View, Part II: Perpetual War, Here and Abroad," *LewRockwell.com*, October 7, 2008, available at http://www.lewrockwell.com/grigg/grigg-w51.html; idem., "En Route to Military Rule," *LewRockwell.com*, December 27, 2008, http://www.lewrockwell.com/grigg/grigg-w68.html.

70. Murray N. Rothbard, *For a New Liberty: The Libertarian Manifesto*, rev. ed. (Auburn, AL: Ludwig von Mises Institute, 2006 [1978]), 275.

71. Ron Paul, "Why Are Americans So Angry?" *LewRockwell.com*, June 29, 2006, http://www.lewrockwell.com/paul/paul331.html.

72. See Murray N. Rothbard, "America's Two Just Wars: 1775 and 1861," in Denson, *The Costs of War*, 119–134.

73. See Jeffrey Rogers Hummel, "The American Militia and the Origin of Conscription: A Reassessment," *Journal of Libertarian Studies* (Fall 2001): 29–77, http://mises.org/journals/jls/15_4/15_4_2.pdf; idem. "The Constitution as Counter-Revolution: A Tribute to the Anti-Federalists," *Free Life: The Journal of the Libertarian Alliance* 5 (undated), http://www.la-articles.org.uk/FL-5-4-3.pdf.

74. Joseph R. Stromberg, "Imperialism, Noninterventionism, and Revolution," in Robert Higgs and Carl P. Close, eds., *Opposing the Crusader State: Alternatives to Global Interventionism* (Oakland, CA: Independent Institute, 2007), 4.

75. For libertarian perspectives on Lincoln and the Civil War, see Thomas J. DiLorenzo, *The Real Lincoln: A New Look at Abraham Lincoln, His Agenda, and an Unnecessary War* (Roseville, CA: Prima, 2002) and Jeffrey Rogers Hummel, *Emancipating Slaves, Enslaving Free Men: A History of the American Civil War* (Chicago: Open Court, 1996). Not all

libertarians object to the Civil War, particularly those who take a less stringent view of what is necessary to justify war. See, e.g., David N. Mayer, "A Bicentennial Defense of Abraham Lincoln," *MayerBlog*, February 4, 2009, http://users.law.capital.edu/dmayer/Blog/blogIndex.asp?entry=20090204.asp.

76. See Stromberg, "Imperialism, Noninterventionism, and Revolution," 8; see also idem. "The Spanish-American War as Trial Run, or Empire As Its Own Justification," in Denson, *The Costs of War*.

77. For a libertarian historian's view of World War I and its consequences, see Jim Powell, *Wilson's War: How Woodrow Wilson's Great Blunder Led to Hitler, Lenin, Stalin, & World War II* (New York: Crown Forum, 2005).

78. See Buchanan, *Churchill, Hitler*; Powell, *Wilson's War*.

79. See Buchanan, *Churchill, Hitler*.

80. Randy E. Barnett, "Libertarians and the War," *The Wall Street Journal*, July 17, 2007, http://www.opinionjournal.com/editorial/feature.html?id=110010344.

81. Walter Block, "Randy Barnett: Pro War Libertarian?" *LewRockwell.com*, July 23, 2007, http://www.lewrockwell.com/block/block79.html.

82. Sheldon Richman, "Ahistorical 'Libertarian' Warmongers," *Liberty & Power*, July 18, 2007, http://hnn.us/blogs/entries/41068.html.

83. Gene Healy, "Randy Barnett and the Iraq War," *Cato-at-Liberty*, July 18, 2007, http://www.cato-at-liberty.org/2007/07/18/randy-barnett-and-the-iraq-war/.

84. Sheldon Richman, "More on Barnett," *Free Association*, July 19, 2007, http://sheldonfreeassociation.blogspot.com/2007/07/more-on-barnett.html.

85. Brink Lindsey, "No More 9/11s," *Reason.com*, October 29, 2002, http://reason.com/archives/2002/10/29/no-more-9-11s.

86. See Justin Raimondo, "The Objectivist Death Cult," *LewRockwell.com*, October 12, 2004, http://www.lewrockwell.com/orig5/raimondo1.html.

87. Tom Shanker, "Campaign Promise on Ending the War in Iraq Now Muted by Reality," *New York Times*, December 3, 2008, http://www.nytimes.com/2008/12/04/us/politics/04military.html.

88. See Stromberg, "The Spanish-American War as Trial Run," 180.

89. John V. Denson, "War and American Freedom," in Denson, *The Costs of War*, 43.

FURTHER READING

Denson, John V., ed. *The Costs of War: America's Pyrrhic Victories*, 2nd ed. New Brunswick, NJ: Transaction Publishers, 1999. This volume collects essays, mostly by libertarian scholars, showing how most of America's wars have been extremely costly and unnecessary.

Eland, Ivan. *The Empire Has No Clothes: U.S. Foreign Policy Exposed.* Oakland, CA: Independent Institute, 2008. Eland describes the United States' expansion into an empire and the threat it poses to Americans.

Higgs, Robert. *Crisis and Leviathan: Critical Episodes in the Growth of American Government.* New York: Oxford University Press, 1987. Higgs shows how the U.S. government has exploited crises, especially wars, to permanently increase its power.

Napolitano, Andrew P. *A Nation of Sheep*, Nashville, TN: Thomas Nelson, 2007. The libertarian Fox News legal analyst and former judge examines the many attacks on Americans' liberty since the War on Terror began.

Paul, Ron. *A Foreign Policy of Freedom: Peace, Commerce, and Honest Friendship*. Lake Jackson, TX: Foundation for Rational Economics and Education, 2007. This book collects many of Paul's speeches in Congress opposing foreign intervention.

10

The Fight against Intellectual Property

When the Recording Industry Association of America (RIAA) wins a $1.92 million verdict against a 32-year-old Minnesota woman for sharing 24 songs online, is that good for liberty? When Disney and other big media companies got Congress to extend copyright protection for Mickey Mouse (and everything else) far into the future, should libertarians have cheered? When a patent holding company threatened to shut down the BlackBerry network unless BlackBerry's creator paid it hundreds of millions of dollars in licensing fees, was this a win for property rights, or was it just extortion?[1]

For a long time, libertarians were conflicted about "intellectual property" (IP). On the one hand, libertarians support property rights, so IP sounds like something they should favor. On the other hand, IP empowers some people to use government to limit other people's speech and actions. Libertarian giants of the past such as Ayn Rand and Ludwig von Mises endorsed IP, either as a moral matter (for Rand), or to encourage the production of creative works and inventions (for Mises). But more recent libertarian thinking attacks the idea that so-called intellectual property is either justified or necessary.

OLDER LIBERTARIAN VIEWS

To call the ideas protected by patents and copyrights "property" is misleading. Historically, "property rights" referred only to interests in real property (land, buildings) and personal property (tangible objects). This kind of property right existed before there even were governments, as people homesteaded land, produced goods, and traded. Government came into existence later, to protect these property rights; it did not invent them.

Intellectual property has origins that are far different and far more recent. As law professor Lawrence Lessig has put it, some people's desire to treat IP rights just like we treat other property rights has "*no* reasonable connection to our actual legal tradition."[2] Rather, intellectual property rights are the product of government fiat—of statutes that grant inventors, writers, and artists a monopoly privilege to use certain ideas for certain lengths of time. The people who enacted IP laws in the first place knew this well—that they were not recognizing some preexisting natural property right, but just granting a temporary *privilege*. This is clear in the wording of Article I, section 8, clause 8 of the U.S. Constitution, which gives Congress "the power to promote the Progress of Science and the useful Arts, by securing for limited Times to Authors and Inventors the exclusive Right to their respective Writings and Discoveries." The language shows that Congress would be granting a positive right to serve a specific purpose, not recognizing some preexisting natural right. We can contrast this, for example, with the First and Second Amendments, which state that certain rights "shall not be infringed," implying that those rights already exist. Congress did not need to *grant* those rights because those rights derived from individuals' rights to their lives and property and therefore preceded the formation of the government.

If IP rights really were just like other property rights, they would not present a controversial or difficult issue for libertarians. After all, libertarianism is founded on property rights. So, in that case, libertarians could simply agree with the late Motion Picture Association of America (MPAA) head Jack Valenti, who declared before Congress: "Creative property owners must be accorded the same rights and protection resident in all other property owners in the nation."[3] And libertarians would also then have to agree with present-day representatives of the recording industry who claim that, when a person illegally downloads an album online, it is no different than if the person went into a store, took a copy of the CD off the shelf, and walked out with it. And maybe libertarians would find those huge verdicts against file sharers justified.

But even in the days when a greater proportion of libertarians supported IP, it was never quite that simple.

Ayn Rand considered the legal protection of a patent or copyright necessary to protect the rights of an idea's creator because of "man's right to the product of his mind." But Rand recognized that ideas could not really be treated just like other property. Rights to ordinary property exist in perpetuity—you can pass the property on to your heirs, and they to their heirs, and so on forever. But Rand believed that IP rights could only be recognized for some limited period of time. She could see that if people retained permanent property rights in ideas, this would "paralyze" society as research and innovation would grind to a halt and people would be forced to pay royalties for virtually everything they use to the layabout heirs of long-dead inventors. So Rand recognized that some time limit would have to be established that balanced the inventor's rights with the ability of others to pursue further research.[4] Rand maintained that her philosophy and her views on IP were a product of her moral views on man's rights, so limiting the duration of IP rights to encourage innovation seems uncharacteristically utilitarian. But anyone who believes that IP rights are natural property rights will have to contend with this difficulty.

Ludwig von Mises was not concerned with natural rights, so he did not run into this problem. He simply considered IP necessary to motivate people to create useful books and technological innovations. He wrote in *Human Action* that it is "unlikely that people would undertake the laborious task of writing" such things as "textbooks, manuals, handbooks, and other nonfiction works," if "everyone were free to reproduce them," and that it is "very probable that technological progress would be seriously retarded" if inventors and those who finance their work could not have a patent's help to recoup their expenses.[5]

Murray Rothbard began to chip away at the IP idea but still clung to parts of it.[6] He attempted to justify copyrights and, in a limited sense, patents by rooting them in the traditional Lockean system of property rights, even though IP did not actually arise out of that tradition. For Rothbard, a believer in natural law and natural rights, copyright could not be justified on utilitarian grounds or legitimately established by government fiat. But Rothbard thought copyright could be justified if it were the product of contract. For example, if, when Smith sells Jones a book, Smith marks it "copyright," then Jones would only receive from Smith the right to possess and use that physical book, but *not* the right to copy it. In other words, by giving Jones notice of copyright, Smith does not include the right to make and sell copies of the book in the bundle of rights that he sells to Jones. Because a person cannot transfer any greater rights in something than he or she owns, any third parties who later got the book after Jones would be subject to the same restriction Jones faced. Under this line of thinking, anyone who copied a copyrighted book without permission would be stealing by exercising a right that still belonged to the book's original owner because he or she had never given it up.

Rothbard justified patents of a sort on similar grounds. If Smith sells Jones a new kind of vacuum cleaner and marks it "patented" (or, as Rothbard would have it, "copyrighted"), that tells Jones that he is only receiving the right to the physical object, not the right to make copies of it. The patent/copyright creates a contractual limitation, just as in the copyright context. This type of "patent" would not, however, prevent another inventor who comes up with the same device *completely on his own* from producing and distributing his device. As it stands, patent law grants exclusive rights to the first inventor of a good, and later inventors—even if they never saw or heard about the original invention—are bound by the patent. For Rothbard, this was unjust because the later inventor did not violate any property rights of the first inventor when he thought up and created the invention on his own. (This problem does not arise in the copyright context because it is safe to assume that two people will not independently write the exact same novel, play, or piece of music, Shakespeare-typing monkeys notwithstanding.)

REJECTING INTELLECTUAL PROPERTY

IP remained a questionable issue among libertarians for decades, but in the first years of the twenty-first century, opinion seems to have shifted strongly against the legitimacy of IP for natural-rights libertarians and consequentialist libertarians alike. (Here, and throughout the chapter, when we refer to IP rights, we refer to patents and copyrights; trademarks, another concept typically grouped with IP rights, are relatively uncontroversial.)

IP Violates Property Rights

The current generation's libertarian scholars in the natural-rights tradition have largely rejected the legitimacy of IP. The most influential figure in this intellectual revolution has been lawyer and legal scholar Stephan Kinsella, whose article, "Against Intellectual Property," appeared in the *Journal of Libertarian Studies* in 2001 and was published separately as a monograph in 2008.[7] According to Kinsella, the problem with IP is that it is not grounded in property rights—as all libertarian rights must be—and in fact requires government to *violate* property rights for its enforcement.

Under the Lockean libertarian theory of property rights, people create private property in land (assuming it is unowned when they find it) by occupying it and making it theirs. Then, they are entitled to do what they please with that land—live there, enjoy what they produce on it, sell it to someone else, give it away—as long as they do not aggress against anyone else or anyone else's property in the process.

Land and tangible items are subject to becoming private property in this way because they are *scarce*. That is, they are limited in quantity, and one person's use of a piece of property prevents someone else from using it. Two people cannot occupy the same space or eat the same orange. Without property rights, there would be irresolvable conflicts over who can use what land and objects, and how they may use them. With property rights, these conflicts are avoided. On the other hand, if certain things were not scarce—if we could reproduce them infinitely at no cost, or if they were somehow abundant— there would be no conflicts over those things, and no need for ethical rules, property rights, or laws to govern such conflicts.

As it happens, *ideas* fall into this latter category. If two people want to have the same idea in their minds, or put that same idea to use, there is no conflict between them—they both can do it. And they can pass on an idea to as many people as they want without diminishing their own possession of the idea. Kinsella uses the example of a book:

[I]f you copy a book I have written, I still have the original (tangible) book, and I also still "have" the pattern of words that constitute the book. Thus, authored works are not scarce in the same sense that a piece of land or a car are scarce. If you take my car, I no longer have it. But if you "take" a book-pattern and use it to make your own physical book, I still have my own copy.[8]

Thomas Jefferson had essentially the same insight some two hundred years earlier:

If nature has made any one thing less susceptible than all others of exclusive property, it is the action of the thinking power called an idea, which an individual may exclusively possess as long as he keeps it to himself; but the moment it is divulged, it forces itself into the possession of every one, and the receiver cannot dispossess himself of it. Its peculiar character, too, is that no one possesses the less, because every other possesses the whole of it. He who receives an idea from me, receives instruction himself *without lessening mine*; as he who lights his taper at mine, receives light without darkening me.[9]

So IP rights cannot be true "property rights." And when government grants IP rights, it is not really granting a property right in an idea, but is instead granting a *monopoly* on the right to *use* an idea for certain profitable purposes. If one owns a copyright in a book, only that person (or someone to whom that person gives permission) can produce and sell copies of that book. If one owns a patent on an invention, only that person (or someone to whom that person gives permission) can produce and sell the invention for a certain period of time.

This means that IP rights are not property rights, but are in fact a power to *stop other people* from exercising *their own* property rights.[10] If I own a copyright in a book, I can use the force of government to stop someone from using their own paper and ink to produce their own copies of the book. If I own a patent on an invention, I can use the force of government to shut down someone else's factory that produces copies of my invention, even though the other person is using his or her own equipment, machinery, and components. I can even do this if the other person is *not* using a "copy" of my invention, but independently invented it all on his or her own. For a libertarian, this is unjust because it is using aggressive force against peaceful people. As law professor Tom W. Bell has put it:

> By invoking state power, a copyright or patent owner can impose prior restraint, fines, imprisonment, and confiscation on those engaged in peaceful expression and the quiet enjoyment of tangible property. Because it thus gags our voices, ties our hands, and demolishes our presses, *the law of copyrights and patents violates the very rights Locke defended.*[11]

So according to libertarian theory, IP rights are not "property rights" at all, but are a government-issued *license to attack* property rights—and therefore should be abolished.

Rand's attempt to justify IP fails under this framework because it presumes that ownership of ideas is possible and legitimate. So does Rothbard's attempt to ground IP in contract. We can see why by comparing Rothbard's contract-based copyright to a case in which Jones makes a contract with Smith to tell him a secret. A contract to keep a secret, standing alone, is legitimate—people can always make deals to do or not do things. If Smith tells everyone Jones's secret, Jones rightly can sue Smith because he broke their deal. Jones cannot, however, sue everyone else in the world who now knows the secret to stop them from repeating it; he did not have contracts with those people and therefore cannot claim any rightful ownership over them, the ideas in their heads, or their property. And so it is with copyright: a seller can make his buyers agree not to copy a book, but he may not stop others who happen to see it from doing so.[12] Likewise, an inventor may not stop someone who sees his or her invention (say, a machine) from using this knowledge to make a similar or better machine.

All this analysis may sound academic, but it illustrates how libertarians approach issues by going back to their philosophical first principles in a way that most adherents to the more nebulous political philosophies of conservatism and liberalism do not. And it is important for libertarians, as champions of property rights, to explain why IP rights are not property rights because to call IP "property" is not only Orwellian, it also sullies the reputation of true property rights. This is why Bell suggests we instead refer to IP as a "privilege," not as "property,"[13] and why the two authors on whom we will focus in the next section, Michele Boldrin and David K. Levine, suggest an even more blunt term for IP: "intellectual monopoly."

IP, Creation, and Innovation

Of course, our argument about property rights might not matter to a utilitarian. Libertarian thinkers such as Mises or, today, Richard Epstein, would argue that even if IP rights are not property rights in the usual sense, we should make an exception to the usual rule of liberty and property rights for IP because it presents a rare case where the benefits to society of a government intervention far outweigh the costs.[14] If such claims by IP supporters were true, they might present a compelling argument in favor of IP. But the facts show that this is not true, and that IP not only is not necessary for creation and innovation to occur, it also actively harms these things.

The leaders in debunking the myth of IP's necessity have been Boldrin and Levine, whose 2008 book, *Against Intellectual Monopoly*, argues that patents and copyrights are not necessary for progress and creativity, and, in fact, have greatly harmed it. (Boldrin and Levine may not be strict libertarians across the board, but they are close, they have influenced libertarians, and they are pure libertarians on the subjects of patent and copyright, so that is good enough for our purposes.)

Copyrights

Many IP advocates take it as self-evident, as the framers of the U.S. Constitution did, that copyrights are necessary to motivate people to produce creative works. Supposedly, writers, musicians, and filmmakers would not bother to produce books, music, and films if other people could come along and copy and take the benefits of their work—or at least, creative people would not produce "enough" of these types of works, whatever that means. But it is not self-evident that this is the case, and the evidence shows that it is just wrong.

After all, for most of history, there were no copyrights, but people still created great literature, art, and music. Suppose Shakespeare had lived in a world where copyright existed. As one writer put it, "his legal bills would have been staggering."[15] Shakespeare made a unique contribution to Western civilization by putting words together in a way that no human being had before or has since, but he was not a pure original. He took many stories, characters, and ideas from other works by other people—which he would not have been able to do if the creators of those previous works had possessed and enforced copyrights. And what of copyright protection for Shakespeare's own plays? He authored 38 plays without any incentive or protection from copyright law, and he managed to prosper besides. It is difficult to see how copyright would have prompted him to create more. One can imagine, though, that if copyright had existed in Shakespeare's day, he might have spent his some of his time and effort suing people who sold transcriptions of his plays or performed them without permission, and devoted less of his time to writing, and we would all be immeasurably poorer for it. A rich public domain allowed Shakespeare to become what he was, and it has allowed the world to benefit in turn from Shakespeare. It seems likely that IP rights would only have resulted in less for him to draw upon and less for us to enjoy.

Writers today could make money without copyrights even if they are not modern-day Shakespeares. Of course, even with copyright protection, most authors whose names are not Stephen King or J.K. Rowling do not make much money from book royalties. Instead, publishing a book gives an author prestige and opportunities to do other things. Publishing in academic journals (for no pay) creates opportunities to get teaching jobs. Publishing books for a popular audience (usually for low pay) may raise one's profile as an expert and create opportunities to give speeches or do other things for money.

Still, even without copyrights, many authors would make *some* money from book sales, and some authors would make a lot of money. One reason we can be confident of this is because books by foreign authors did not receive copyright protection in the United States for most of the nineteenth century, yet the authors made money here anyway. A publisher would pay an author to be the first to receive a copy of the author's manuscript, which would allow the publisher to be first publisher to reach the market with the book.[16] Even without copyright protection, there is great value in being the first publisher to sell a book. The first publisher will have the market to itself for a while because it will take competitors time to come out with their own editions. Plus, other publishers are unlikely to find it worthwhile to copy that book unless it proves to be a success for the first publisher. Once the first publisher has success, then it *might* be worthwhile for others to copy and sell it, if they believe they can profitably sell enough additional copies. But in any event the first publisher is likely to reap the biggest profits, especially because books on average make 80 percent of their profits in their first three months.[17]

So that's the nineteenth century. What about now? In this century, the government gave W.W. Norton the right to be the first to publish the *9-11 Commission Report*. As a government work, the 568-page report would immediately enter the public domain, and others would be free to copy and sell it. Despite this lack of copyright protection—and even though the report was also available online for free and downloaded millions of times—Norton's edition of the Report became a bestseller and earned Norton profits approaching $1 million.[18] Two weeks after Norton's edition came out, St. Martin's released its own edition, with additional articles and analysis included, and it too became a best seller. Based on this and similar cases, Boldrin and Levine estimate that J.K. Rowling could have received multimillion-dollar advances for later books in her Harry Potter series— not enough, perhaps, to make her one of England's richest women, as copyright protection did, but surely enough to keep her writing.

What about the music industry? Here we know what happens because artists have already effectively lost copyright protection for their recordings as millions of people trade them for free on the Internet instead of buying them. This has simply pushed artists into other ways of making money, especially performances. Even before the Internet age, most rock musicians, even successful ones, made comparatively little from their album sales. So, like books, recordings have been a way for their creators to attract attention and make money through other projects.

In the realm of serious music, many of the great composers' works were never protected by copyright. England began protecting musical compositions with copyrights in 1777, yet relatively few composers lived or worked in England after that time, despite England's relative prosperity overall. Beethoven, for one, lived in Germany, which offered no copyright protection, yet he made enough money to survive and felt sufficiently motivated to create some of the greatest musical works ever.[19] Like Shakespeare, pre-IP composers were able to draw on previous composers' works and alter and adapt them freely. Today, that requires permission from copyright holders that may or may not be granted.

Like the record labels, movie studios face rampant piracy, yet they remain in business. This is so in part because people are willing to pay for the experience of seeing a film in a theater; for many people, a DVD or downloaded version is no substitute. This would not change in the absence of copyrights. Studios could use contracts, technology, and security to make sure their films are only exhibited in theaters that pay for copies of them. Like book publishers, studios would also profit from being the first to market with a DVD. We could also note, as Boldrin and Levine do, that the pornographic film industry has always thrived and constantly innovated even though it essentially operates outside the protection of IP law because of its lack of social respectability.[20]

Another point that applies to all media is that many people create just for the joy of doing it, without concern for further benefits; no government policy is necessary to "incentivize" them. For example, one of the most important American composers, Charles Ives, spent his days making money as an insurance executive and wrote serious music on the side, for which he received minimal recognition (let alone money) during his lifetime. Today, countless individuals produce countless written, audio, and visual works, at all levels of quality, for an Internet audience, with no expectation of payment. Many even do so anonymously, with no expectation of personal recognition; Wikipedia provides one example. Increasingly, people are not just passive consumers of content from big media companies, but producers of original work themselves, and compensation is not their motive.

Copyrights in general are questionable; the kinds of copyright-term extensions we have seen in recent years are entirely indefensible. The Sonny Bono Copyright Term Extension Act of 1998 (CTEA) increased copyright terms by 40 percent. Copyrights were extended (retroactively) to cover the life of an author plus 70 years, or, in the case of a work for hire, the earlier of 95 years after the date of publication or 120 years after the date of creation. Did this extension create additional incentives for writers, musicians, and filmmakers to produce more? Of course not. What difference does it make to artists if you extend their copyright protection for some number of years *long after they are dead?* In fact, economists have determined that the CTEA increases creators' revenue by just 0.33 percent.[21] So copyright extensions don't benefit artists; instead, they benefit big media companies that own really old properties and do not want to lose them to the public domain. In fact, the CTEA was pushed by one such entity in particular, Disney, which did not want to lose its copyright on Mickey Mouse.

While copyright extension offers no benefits to anyone but big media, the costs to the rest of society are tremendous. There is no "cultural commons" for creative people to draw from, as Shakespeare did—and as Disney did when it made movies out of stories in the public domain such as *Snow White and the Seven Dwarfs, Pinocchio,* and *Sleeping Beauty.*[22] Countless thousands of books, recordings, and software titles go out of print and remain out of print because the rights holders cannot be found, refuse to take advantage of their rights, or refuse to release their rights. We are all poorer as a result.[23]

Patents

It is also not obvious that patents are necessary to inspire innovation—and there is much reason to believe that they *prevent* innovation.

If you own a patent on a mechanical rice picker, that means you can stop other people from building a better rice picker that is based on yours. For a number of years, your potential competitors legally *cannot* innovate and improve your product—or at least, if they do, they cannot bring their innovation to market without your permission until the patent expires. At the same time, *you* do not have much incentive to improve your product because you can just milk your old invention free from competition—enforcing your patents becomes a substitute for research and development.[24] This forces your competitors to waste effort trying to "invent around" your ideas to make competing products, perhaps inferior ones, without infringing on yours. And it also gives you, the patent holder, an incentive to take out a cluster of broadly worded patents for products similar to your own, to discourage others from even trying to enter your field and to legally block them if necessary.[25] The potential to infringe on one of these patents and then get sued scares many would-be competitors out of the market.

On the other hand, what if there were no patents? The first person to implement an idea would still receive exclusive benefits for some period of time because even without patents, it would take a while for the competition to figure out how to imitate the invention and catch up. But competitors probably would figure it out before too long, so the original inventor could not rest on his or her laurels. Everyone would have to constantly improve to stay competitive.

We see that idea at work in the many innovations businesses make where patent law does not protect them. The people who invented shopping malls, 24-hour convenience stores, supermarkets, fast-food franchising, and the extra-value meal did not have any exclusive rights to their ideas. Neither do the people who invent perfumes, recipes, clothing designs, furniture, or car bodies.[26] But people do come up with these things because they want to outpace their rivals. Without IP privileges, they have to be focused on what they can do to attract and please customers better—not what they can do with the legal system to crush other businesses.

Historically, there have been many cases where patents allowed their holders to *stop* innovating and to *stop others* from innovating. Consider the supposedly heroic Wright brothers. They created their first airplane by slightly improving the unpatented ideas of others who came before them, such as British engineer Sir George Cayley and German Otto Lilienthal. Their 1902 patent was for the system of flight control resulting from "wing warping" and the use of a rudder. Glenn Curtiss improved on the Wright brothers' design by replacing the wing-warping technique with movable control surfaces, the means by which airplanes to this day control their movements. For this, the Wright brothers—who did not sell many airplanes at the time—sued Curtiss to try to stop him from selling airplanes. The Wrights' litigiousness stunted the growth of the aviation industry in the United States as they focused more on suing Curtiss and other competitors than on making better planes. As a result, airplane development then took off in France, where the Wright brothers "had little legal clout."[27]

Another example Boldrin and Levine point out concerns James Watt's steam engine. During the period in the late eighteenth century that Watt and his business partner, Matthew Boulton, held their steam-engine patent, innovation in steam engines practically ceased. When Jonathan Hornblower built a better engine in 1790, Watt and Boulton sued and stopped him from bringing it to market. Other competitors invented their own improvements, but kept them off the market while waiting out Watt's patent term; they did not want to be sued like Hornblower. Watt himself was distracted from improving his product both because he did not need to do so—he had monopoly protection—and because he was preoccupied with using the legal system against his competitors. As a result, while his patent was in place, the United Kingdom added only about 750 horsepower of steam engines per year; in the 30 years after Watt's patent expired, horsepower was added at a rate of more than 4,000 per year. Similarly, fuel efficiency improved little, if at all, during the years of Watt's patent (1769–1800), but increased by approximately a factor of five between 1810 and 1835.[28]

What about pharmaceuticals? Some people argue that we need pharmaceutical patents because drugs require expensive research and development to develop, but then can be cheaply reverse engineered. So, the thinking goes, if we do not give drug makers patent protection, they won't bother to produce drugs in the first place.

Numerous facts undermine this argument. Boldrin and Levine have found that the pharmaceutical industry historically grew "faster in those countries where patents were fewer and weaker."[29] Italy, for one, provided no patent protection for pharmaceuticals before 1978, but had a thriving pharmaceutical industry. Between 1961 and 1980, it accounted for about nine percent of all new active chemical compounds for drugs. After patents arrived, Italy saw no significant increase in the number of new drugs discovered there—contrary, one supposes, to the IP advocates' predictions.[30]

Another fact the conventional view overlooks is that patentable drugs are not the only medical innovations possible. Boldrin and Levine looked to a poll of the *British Medical Journal*'s readers on the top medical milestones in history, and found that almost none had anything to do with patents. Penicillin, x-rays, tissue culture, anesthetic, chlorpromazine, public sanitation, germ theory, evidence-based medicine, vaccines, the birth-control pill, computers, oral rehydration theory, DNA structure, monoclonal antibody technology, and the discovery of the health risks of smoking—of these top fifteen entries, only two had anything to do with patents.[31] Similarly, *nothing* on the U.S. Centers for Disease Control's list of the top ten public-health achievements of the twentieth century had any connection to patents. And even a review of the most important pharmaceuticals reveals that many came about without the motive and/or possibility of acquiring a patent, including, for example, aspirin, azidothymidine (AZT), cyclosporine, digoxin, ether, fluoride, insulin, isoniazid, medical marijuana, methadone, morphine, oxytocin, penicillin, phenobarbital, prontosil, quinine, Ritalin, salvarsan, vaccines, and vitamins.[32]

Patent law does create one incentive for researchers: to pursue more of the kind of research that will lead to patentable drugs, and less of the kind of research that might lead to other types of breakthroughs that cannot be patented—even though, as we have just seen, the latter category may include some of the most important.[33] If patent law were abolished, we would probably see fewer artificial chemical drugs and more discoveries related to remedies from natural substances such as vitamins, minerals, and plants. Given the harmful side effects of many prescription drugs, it is not at all obvious that this would be a bad thing.

Boldrin and Levine also show that patents are not essential to success in the pharmaceutical industry by pointing to the analogous paint and dye industries (which also depended on chemical formulas) in the nineteenth century. Germany offered no patent protection for paints and dyes at all until 1877, and even then only for the process involved in producing them, not for the products themselves. Nonetheless, German companies' market share rose from next to nothing in 1862 to 50 percent by 1873 and 80 percent in 1913. Britain and France, on the other hand, had patent protection for both products and processes all along and saw their market shares fall from about 50 percent and 40 percent, respectively, in 1862 to between 13 percent and 17 percent in 1873.[34] The Germans eventually benefited from patents, but it is clear that patents were not essential to their rise to the top.

Costs and Benefits

So we have seen that copyrights and patents have costs that most people do not think about. How to balance this against their benefits? Austrian economists would say this is impossible. Costs and benefits are subjective; they exist inside people's heads and cannot be measured or compared to each other to find out what is economically optimal. The only way to know what is optimal is to look at what people actually do in the marketplace through their voluntary choices using their own actual tangible property.[35] Because IP rights by their nature interfere with private property and voluntary exchange, they necessarily move us away from what is optimal.

Putting aside that problem, any attempt by non-Austrian economists to measure the costs and benefits of IP will necessarily leave out countless important factors. One such factor is human liberty. Even if we could determine that IP makes us *materially* better off in some respects—in terms of economic growth or the number of different products produced, for example—IP laws require a government empowered to interfere with individuals' peaceful use of their own property. You do not have to believe in natural rights to value liberty and view its loss as a high cost.

Still, even if one measures IP's effects just in terms of economic growth—a rough measure of prosperity—economists are mostly undecided as to whether IP has even made this greater than it otherwise would be. Boston University law professors James Bessen and Michael J. Meurer have found that "intellectual property rights appear to have at best only a weak and indirect relationship to economic growth, the relationship appears to apply only to certain groups of countries or certain specifications, and the direction of causality is unclear."[36] This last point is critical. To the small extent that patents *may* show a correlation with economic growth, we cannot even say whether patents caused the growth, or if the growth caused people to pursue patent protection.

THE END OF IP

Libertarians may not have to appeal to rights theory, economics, or history to win the war on IP. Libertarians are already winning as people around the globe incessantly violate the legal rights of copyright holders by sharing music through bit torrent programs and by uploading (and remixing and mashing up) videos of copyrighted material to YouTube without the slightest feeling of guilt. People cheered the Swedish proprietors of *The Pirate Bay* website as they went on trial for helping people freely trade music, movies, and software. (*The Pirate Bay*'s anti-IP, pro-privacy views are so popular that they have even inspired a Pirate Party that has won one of Sweden's seats in the European Parliament.) As the RIAA and MPAA crack down on file sharers and website operators with ever bigger threats, these organizations only look more like villains to the young people who have always operated under the assumption that they should be allowed to do as they please with their own computers as long as they do not invade anyone else's.

More thinkers outside of libertarianism are challenging IP, too. Lessig and others in the "free culture" movement have informed a large audience of how lengthy copyright terms and other especially oppressive aspects of IP impoverish us, and how an ever-growing "cultural commons" (public domain) would enrich us. Through the Creative Commons license invented by Lessig, people are deliberately giving up their exclusive rights under copyright law because they believe IP is not in their interests as creators and they want their ideas to spread.

Along similar lines, the "Free Software" and "Open Source" movements have created software products that people are permitted to download, alter, and distribute freely. Contrary to IP advocates' predictions, people make improvements to these software projects even though they do not stand to profit personally. And many of these products, such as the Linux operating system and the Firefox Web browser, are competing successfully against such IP-dependent dinosaurs as Microsoft.

Harvard law professor Yochai Benkler—not a libertarian himself, but a leading thinker in the "free culture" movement—has observed that because of the Internet, we "are at a moment in history at which the terms of freedom and justice are up for grabs," especially in the context of IP.[37] Because libertarians have the intellectual ammunition to show people that what they are feeling and doing online is right, and what the big media companies and government want to do to them through IP laws is wrong, this moment presents a unique opportunity for libertarians to provide those definitions and advance their cause.

NOTES

1. For these stories, see David Kravets, "Feds Support $1.92 Million RIAA File Sharing Verdict," *Threat Level*, August 14, 2009, http://www.wired.com/threatlevel/2009/08/feds-support-192-million-file-sharing-verdict/; Lawrence Lessig, *Free Culture: How Big Media Uses Technology and the Law to Lock Down Culture and Control Creativity* (New York: Penguin, 2004), 213–45, http://www.free-culture.cc/freeculture.pdf; Rob Kelley, "BlackBerry Maker, NTP Ink $612 Million Settlement," *CNNMoney.com*, March 3, 2006, http://money.cnn.com/2006/03/03/technology/rimm_ntp/index.htm.

2. Lessig, *Free Culture*, 118.

3. Ibid., 117.

4. Ayn Rand, "Patents and Copyrights," in Ayn Rand, *Capitalism: The Unknown Ideal* (New York: Signet, 1967) 130–34.

5. Ludwig von Mises, *Human Action: A Treatise on Economics*, 4th ed. (San Francisco: Fox & Wilkes, 1996), 661–62, http://mises.org/Books/humanaction.pdf.

6. Rothbard's ideas on IP are presented in Murray N. Rothbard, *Man, Economy, and State* (Auburn, AL: Ludwig von Mises Institute, 1993 [1962]), 652–660; Murray N. Rothbard, *Power and Market: Government and the Economy*, 4th ed. (Auburn, AL: Ludwig von Mises Institute, 2006 [1970]), http://mises.org/Books/powermarket.pdf; Murray N. Rothbard, *The Ethics of Liberty* (New York: New York University Press, 1998 [1982]), 123–24, http://mises.org/rothbard/ethics.pdf.

7. Kinsella has not been alone. See also, for example, Roderick T. Long, "The Libertarian Case Against Intellectual Property Rights," *Formulations* 3, no. 1 (Autumn 1995), http://libertariannation.org/a/f31l1.html; Wendy McElroy, "Contra Copyright," *The Voluntaryist* (June 1985), 1–3, http://www.voluntaryist.com/backissues/016.pdf; Tom G. Palmer, "Are Patents and Copyrights Morally Justified? The Philosophy of Property Rights and Ideal Objects," *Harvard Journal of Law and Public Policy* 13 (1990), 817–65; Timothy Sandefur, "A Critique of Ayn Rand's Theory of Intellectual Property

Rights," *Journal of Ayn Rand Studies* 9:1 (Fall 2007), 139–61, http://ssrn.com/abstract=1117269.

8. N. Stephan Kinsella, *Against Intellectual Property* (Auburn, AL: Ludwig von Mises Institute, 2008), 32, http://mises.org/books/against.pdf.

9. Thomas Jefferson to Isaac McPherson, Monticello, August 13, 1813, http://press-pubs.uchicago.edu/founders/documents/a1_8_8s12.html (emphasis added).

10. For an argument that rejects this analysis, see Adam Mossoff, "Is Copyright Property?" 42, *San Diego Law Review* 42 (2005), 29, http://papers.ssrn.com/sol3/papers.cfm?abstract_id=491466.

11. Tom W. Bell, "Indelicate Imbalancing in Copyright and Patent Law," in Adam Thierer and Clyde Wayne Crews, Jr., eds., *Copy Fights: The Future of Intellectual Property in the Information Age* (Washington, DC: Cato Institute, 2002), 4 (internal footnotes omitted, emphasis added), http://papers.ssrn.com/sol3/papers.cfm?abstract_id=984085.

12. "Trade secrets"—a relatively minor part of IP law—may present a special case. If a third party *induces* someone to give away a company secret, they may be considered liable in the same way that a co-conspirator to any wrongdoing is jointly liable. See Kinsella, *Against Intellectual Property*, 56–57. Perhaps someone who induced a contractual-copyright breach could be held liable as well—but this still would not be enough to stop the information from getting out, so the attempted copyright protection would not really be effective.

13. Tom W. Bell, "Copyright as Intellectual Property Privilege," *Syracuse Law Review* 58 (2008), 541, http://papers.ssrn.com/sol3/papers.cfm?abstract_id=1023735.

14. Epstein argues that IP rights can be considered property rights, and has attempted to tie Locke's system to utilitarianism and IP. See Richard A. Epstein, "Liberty versus Property? Cracks in the Foundations of Copyright Law," *San Diego Law Review* 42 (2005), 1, http://papers.ssrn.com/sol3/papers.cfm?abstract_id=529943.

15. Tom G. Palmer, "Intellectual Property: A Non-Posnerian Law and Economics Approach," *Hamline Law Review* 12 (1989), 302.

16. Michele Boldrin and David K. Levine, *Against Intellectual Monopoly* (New York: Cambridge University Press, 2008), 22–23, http://www.dklevine.com/general/intellectual/againstfinal.htm.

17. Ibid., 141.

18. Ibid., 25.

19. Ibid., 187–89.

20. Ibid., 36–38.

21. Ibid., 101.

22. Ibid., 31.

23. On this, see Lessig, *Free Culture*; and see Jeffrey A. Tucker, "The Music and Book Killers," *LewRockwell.com*, February 2, 2009, http://www.lewrockwell.com/tucker/tucker128.html.

24. Rothbard, *Man, Economy, and State*, 657.

25. Julio H. Cole, "Patents and Copyrights: Do the Benefits Exceed the Costs?" *Journal of Libertarian Studies* 15:4 (2001), 92, http://mises.org/journals/jls/15_4/15_4_3.pdf; Rothbard, *Power and Market*, 90.

26. Bell, "Indelicate Imbalancing in Copyright and Patent Law," 9.

27. Boldrin and Levine, *Against Intellectual Monopoly*, 87–88, 206–07.

28. Ibid., 1–5. George Selgin and John L. Turner question the details regarding Watt, though they don't necessarily support patents. See George Selgin and John L. Turner, "Watt, Again? Boldrin and Levine Still Exaggerate the Adverse Effect of Patents on the Progress of Steam Power," *Review of Law and Economics* 5 (3): 1101–1113, http://www.bepress.com/rle/vol5/iss3/art71.

29. Boldrin and Levine, *Against Intellectual Monopoly*, 246.

30. Ibid., 222–23.

31. Ibid., 229.

32. Ibid., 230.

33. Cole, "Patents and Copyrights," 93; Rothbard, *Man, Economy, and State*, 658.

34. Boldrin and Levine, 218–219.

35. See Murray N. Rothbard, "Toward a Reconstruction of Utility and Welfare Economics" in Mary Sennholz, ed., *On Freedom and Free Enterprise: The Economics of Free Enterprise* (Princeton, NJ: D. Van Nostrand, 1956), http://mises.org/rothbard/toward.pdf; Rothbard, *Power and Market*, 89–92.

36. James Bessen and Michael J. Meurer, "Of Patents and Property," *Regulation* (Winter 2008–09), 22, http://www.cato.org/pubs/regulation/regv31n4/v31n4-4.pdf.

37. Robert S. Boyton, "The Tyranny of Copyright?" *The New York Times*, January 25, 2004, http://www.nytimes.com/2004/01/25/magazine/25COPYRIGHT.html.

FURTHER READING

Boldrin, Michele and David K. Levine. *Against Intellectual Monopoly*. New York: Cambridge University Press, 2008. This is the utilitarian case against IP. The authors make the case that intellectual property is not necessary to spur creativity and innovation. Their evidence and arguments go far beyond what is presented in this chapter. This book is available at http://www.dklevine.com/general/intellectual/againstfinal.htm.

Kinsella, N. Stephan. *Against Intellectual Property*. Auburn, AL: The Ludwig von Mises Institute, 2008. This is the rights-based case against IP. Kinsella shows how intellectual property is antithetical to true private property rights. This book is available at http://mises.org/books/against.pdf.

Lessig, Lawrence. *Free Culture: How Big Media Uses Technology and the Law to Lock Down Culture and Control Creativity*. New York: Penguin, 2004. Lessig is not a libertarian, and he supports IP in principle, but his book shows how ever-lengthening copyright terms enrich powerful interests at our great cultural expense. This book is available at http://www.free-culture.cc/freeculture.pdf.

11

The Fight for Votes

For most people, the obvious way to advance a political cause is to run candidates for office and go after votes. But as noted in Chapter 1, this has not been the traditional libertarian way. Besides, most people are not libertarians and are not going to become libertarians overnight, so they are not going to vote for libertarian candidates. Libertarian political campaigns can educate people and bring them into the movement, as Ron Paul's did like no other, but even the best-run campaigns are unlikely to result in a win. Many more people will have to become educated about liberty, or persuaded to want liberty, before a libertarian could have a real chance.

For libertarians, there are more obstacles to the political success. Many libertarians refuse to vote at all, regardless of who is running, so a libertarian candidate will not even get their votes. Also, democracy by its nature leads people to vote for policies and candidates that make government ever bigger. So the whole endeavor may be futile.

Nonetheless, some libertarians are moving forward with efforts to directly advance the cause through political action. As we will see, one of them, the Libertarian Party, has been around for several decades and may be on the decline even as a vehicle for libertarian education as it attempts to attract a broader following. Another, the Free State Project, seeks to take a single state in a libertarian direction by moving 20,000 libertarians into it. It shows some promise. Yet another, Ron Paul's Campaign for Liberty, seeks to continue his success and advance the ideas through education, activism, and political organization.

LIBERTARIANS AND VOTING

Many libertarians refuse to vote at all.

Why won't libertarians vote? For one thing, even if they have no objection in principle, there is usually no one worth voting for. The Republican and Democrat are usually not too different from each other and are equally offensive to liberty, and even if one candidate *seems* like the lesser of evils based on his or her promises, there is no predicting who would actually do worse things in office. For example, probably most libertarians guessed in 2000 that George W. Bush was the lesser of evils, but in hindsight it is hard to imagine that Al Gore could have been worse. And even if you could determine who is the lesser of evils between two candidates, many libertarians would find it distasteful or even immoral to vote for them because the lesser of evils is still evil. To some libertarians who eschew voting for this reason, the occasional Libertarian Party candidate with no chance of winning does not sufficiently sweeten the deal.

Also, many libertarians decline to vote because it would imply approval of a system they reject. Lew Rockwell has stated this position well:

> Nonparticipation sends a message that we no longer believe in the racket they have cooked up for us, and we want no part of it. You might say that this is ineffective. But what effect does voting have? It gives them what they need most: a mandate. Nonparticipation helps deny that to them. It makes them, just on the margin, a bit more fearful that they are ruling us without our consent. This is all to the good. The government should fear the people. Not voting is a good beginning toward instilling that fear.[1]

Some economically minded libertarians do not vote because it is a waste of time—the benefits do not outweigh the costs. Voting is not free, after all. It takes time and effort to go to the polls, and even more time and effort to learn about the candidates and issues. And in return for paying that cost, a voter does not receive any tangible benefits—one vote will not decide an election, so there will be no payoff for having cast it. Obviously, millions of people *do* perceive a benefit to voting, otherwise they would not voluntarily go do it. Presumably this benefit is the good feeling they get for having done their "civic duty" or having expressed their preference, albeit in an anonymous, futile way. But many libertarians reject the idea that there is any duty to vote, so they do not get this benefit, and they find something better to do on Election Day.

Not all libertarians are so opposed to voting, though. Some would argue that voting for the rare principled libertarian candidate, such as Ron Paul, is justified and sends the right message to the government and to other candidates. In addition, if people who agreed with Ron Paul had not been willing to vote for him, he never would have received so much attention and advanced the movement as he has. Many libertarians also condone voting on ballot issues—against all bonds, taxes, and other increases in government—as a matter of self-defense.

THE TROUBLE WITH DEMOCRACY

Libertarian non-voting is just one reason why libertarians are not likely to see much electoral success anytime soon. There are also problems inherent in the American political system, and democracy in general, that will make it difficult for libertarians to advance very far in it. We will consider just a few of the most significant factors libertarian scholars have identified.

One problem is what economists of the "public choice" school call rational ignorance. For most voters, it makes sense to remain ignorant on most issues most of the time because the cost of learning about them exceeds the benefits. What is the point when you don't really have a say? Special interests, however, have a large stake in issues that hurt consumers: trade protectionism, farm subsidies, corporate welfare, and so on. By itself, each of those things hurts voters a relatively small amount that is difficult for a rationally ignorant voter to perceive. So the members of a special interest group, who have much to gain compared to what any given voter has to lose, lobby Congress successfully. Voters tolerate this both because of their rational ignorance and because, even if they are aware of the harm being done to them, the costs of organizing in opposition would outweigh the benefits of stopping any given piece of legislation. (This provides an argument in favor of promoting libertarianism as a comprehensive political philosophy instead of on an issue-by-issue basis because the combined costs of government interventions *as a whole* are enormous.)

Economist Bryan Caplan, in his 2007 book, *The Myth of the Rational Voter*, proposed another reason why people vote for candidates who support harmful policies: irrationality. There are some issues, especially economic issues, on which many voters hold views that are simply incorrect. For example, many voters believe that immigration imposes large costs on the economy, so they vote for candidates who would restrict immigration. But an overwhelming majority of economists, not limited to libertarians, would say that immigration benefits the economy, or at least does not hurt it much. Even when confronted with this evidence, voters stick to their beliefs. Caplan argues that people do this because it feels good to them to blame foreigners for problems (instead of blaming, say, themselves), so they indulge this belief because—well, why not? There is no real cost for holding an irrational political belief. People cannot afford to be so blind to reality in most other areas of their lives—ignoring the law of gravity would have swift consequences, for example—but they can afford to indulge their irrationality in the political realm, and they do.[2] Again, libertarians' best hope for breaking through and reaching such people may be to show them that their beliefs—in government, across the board—are costing them far more than they know.

In his book *Democracy—The God That Failed*, Hans-Hermann Hoppe has identified still more problems with democracy, of which we will consider just two here. Hoppe's work shows that democracy helps government maintain an appearance of legitimacy and creates incentives for democratic rulers to abuse their power. In earlier centuries, under monarchies, there was a clear-cut distinction between the ruler and the ruled—the king did not pretend to "represent" the people as modern politicians do. That meant if the king got out of line, the people would hold him to account, possibly by killing him. There was a "class-consciousness" among the king's subjects, and they knew very well that the king's interests were different from, and often opposed to, their own. Under democracy, though, people accept the myth that the government and "the people" are one and the same—that government is not a matter of one group of people (a criminal gang) using force to control another group of people (everyone else). This myth makes people less inclined to question their political leaders, or for politicians to feel threatened or constrained by those they rule over.[3]

Hoppe also points out that under monarchy, a king theoretically "owned" his kingdom and could pass it on to his heirs, so he had an incentive to mostly respect property rights and grow his kingdom over the long run, not to bleed it dry. Politicians in a democracy, however, are only in office for a short time, and cannot pass the "kingdom" on to their heirs. So politicians have an incentive to take all they can get while they can get it.[4]

All of these factors—plus, of course, the fact that most people are not libertarians and do not mind when government coerces their neighbors or even them—make success under our political system problematic because they work in favor of government growth and against people being motivated to do anything about it. Still, that is not stopping some libertarians from trying to use the system to make what gains they can.

THE LIBERTARIAN PARTY

As we mentioned in Chapter 1, the Libertarian Party (LP) began essentially as a vehicle for education—a way to get the word out to the large percentage of Americans that only pays attention to political issues during campaign seasons. As the LP was getting off the ground in the early 1970s, Murray Rothbard argued that it was an important project because it provided one of the only venues for libertarians to come together and meet each other. A political party also, in Rothbard's view, gave libertarians something they could *actually do* once they discovered the philosophy, to keep them active and interested. But Rothbard did not just see it as a social club; he also envisioned that the Party could eventually have "real political influence and leverage," even if it only elected a Congressman or two, serving as a "vanguard for the repeal of oppressive legislation, the whittling down of crippling taxes, and for a rollback of the State apparatus."[5]

Today, the Libertarian Party no longer seems necessary for any of those purposes. In the Internet era, libertarians have countless virtual meeting places. They do not need LP events to find fellow libertarians and exchange ideas, and websites such as *Meetup.com* help them organize to do things together in "real life," too. The Internet also provides a means of getting the word out to newcomers that reaches far more people far more effectively than the Libertarian Party's poorly funded campaigns ever have. (In the 2008 presidential race, for example, candidate Bob Barr managed to raise less than $1.4 million[6]—not much more than 2004's candidate, computer programmer Michael Badnarik, raised and considerably less than candidate Harry Browne raised in 2000.[7] None of these candidates appeared in major presidential debates, purchased any noticeable amount of advertising, or otherwise attracted significant public attention.) Ron Paul has proven true Rothbard's suggestions that a libertarian could use a presidential campaign as a means of bringing attention to the ideas, and that just one libertarian Congressman could influence the national debate. But the Libertarian Party was not necessary for this to happen, except perhaps in its early days as a precursor to these bigger and better things. It is little wonder, then, that the LP's membership was, after Barr's campaign, half of what it had been after Harry Browne's 2000 run for President; that the LP in 2008 appeared on the ballot in the fewest number of states since 1984; and that its 2009 budget was the lowest of any year since 1992 (even without adjusting for inflation).[8]

The outlook for the LP gets even worse. In an internal Party struggle between opportunists who want to maximize votes received and purists who want to stay strictly on message, the opportunists have lately come to dominate. That is how Bob Barr—a former CIA agent and then a conservative Republican Congressman—came to be the LP's nominee in 2008. (That, and his dazzling of LP convention delegates with talk of $40 million in fundraising and a record-smashing 5 percent of the vote.)[9] For the race, Barr recanted some of the positions he had taken in his days in Congress as a drug warrior, social conservative, and no one's idea of a libertarian. But even after his nomination,

Barr did not become a libertarian as movement libertarians have long defined that term (or as this book defines it). He did not call for an immediate withdrawal of American troops from around the world. He did not call for an end to the war on drugs, but only for federal tolerance of state medical marijuana programs—a position not too different from Barack Obama's. He did not call for an end to the Federal Reserve, saying this would be a distraction. When the 2008 financial crisis worsened shortly before the election, Barr did not blame the Fed for causing it, as other libertarians did, but issued a statement urging the government to prosecute private individuals for their alleged roles in it. With tepid, Establishment-approved stances like those, and not too much credibility as a recently "converted" politician, it was little wonder that Barr failed to excite the legions who had supported Ron Paul in the primary season, let alone anyone else.

The results were predictable. Barr's raw vote total was better than those of most past LP candidates, but his percentage of the vote, about 0.5, was typical, and less than those of past candidates Ed Clark (1980); Ron Paul (1988); and Harry Browne (1996).[10] Despite his national name recognition, despite his experience, despite his moderation (to say the least) of many of the LP's traditional "extreme" positions on the issues, Barr's campaign was a flop by any measure.

Yet the LP does not seem to have learned from this. Its platform remains essentially libertarian (far more so than Barr at his best), if softer than it once was. But the Party's tone and emphasis day to day tend to make the LP sound more like an organization for Reaganite conservatives than for libertarians. For example, the Libertarian Party has tended to criticize Democrats in much the same terms conservatives would do so for whatever the Democrats' latest big-government schemes are, rather than calling attention to more fundamental issues. Other times, the LP gets even further off track; for example, an inexplicable April 2009 press release urged President Obama "to more closely monitor border crossings" to prevent the spread of "swine flu." While some respectable libertarians, including Ron Paul, believe the government may properly restrict immigration (a position that is a deviation from libertarianism), urging a federal crackdown on *anything* is contrary to the LP's supposed purpose of educating people about liberty and reducing government across the board. Also, most libertarians who saw this scratched their heads because the supposed threat of a "swine flu" epidemic seemed to be the product of government and media scaremongering, not something worth harassing or detaining peaceful Mexican border-crossers over. The LP's slogan on its website at the time of this writing is "Smaller Government, Lower Taxes, More Freedom"—listing three things almost every Republican politician would claim to support. This conveys no information on what distinguishes a Libertarian from a Republican and gives no reason for someone looking for something different to proceed any further.

The opportunist "reformers" within the national LP advocate an incremen-talist approach, under which LP candidates would propose small, supposedly realistic reductions in government rather than large reductions in taxes and spending or outright abolition of programs. By asking for too much too soon, the reformers say, Libertarians give up too many votes and therefore, their thinking goes, have no impact instead of at least some minimal impact. Murray Rothbard identified the flaw in this approach some 20 years ago: even many Republicans will promise at least some small reductions like this. So why would voters choose the Libertarian, whom they reasonably believe has no chance of being elected and of making these small reductions, over the Republican, who has a chance of winning?[11] This strategy also defeats the original educational purpose of Libertarian campaigns because it does not tell voters that there is a real alternative to the statist status quo. In contrast with the LP opportunists, Ron Paul does not shy away from advocating radical goals (for example, abolishing the Federal Reserve) but also suggests immediately practicable steps toward those goals (for example, his bill to audit the Fed).

By becoming a Republican Party Lite, the LP destroys its reason for being, the only reason why anyone supported it in the first place. If it continues down that path, the Party will remain in existence, but only as a hobby for people with nothing else to do and for candidates who want to run vanity campaigns. It will not succeed at spreading ideas or winning elections, and it will be relegated to the margins of even the libertarian movement, let alone the larger political scene.

State LPs

We should note incidentally that each state has its own Libertarian Party organization, and many of these follow different paths from the national Party. Many have stayed more radical. Sometimes candidates backed by a state Libertarian Party have played a bigger role in elections for lesser offices, too. LP candidates' votes exceeded Republican margins of victory in two U.S. Senate races in Missouri and Montana in 2006, meaning that LP voters possi-bly swung those elections to the Democrats.[12] Whether the Democrat was bet-ter or worse than the Republican would have been is irrelevant, of course; the benefit is that this gives politicians a reason to pay attention to libertarians. Libertarians have racked up big numbers in Massachusetts races for U.S. Senate: Carla Howell received 11.9 percent in her 2000 bid against Senator Ted Kennedy,[13] and Michael Cloud received 16.7 percent in his 2002 run.[14] In 2008, Bob Barr received 0.6 percent of North Carolina's presidential vote, but Duke University economist Mike Munger received nearly 3 percent in his LP run for governor.[15] Because of these relatively strong performances, LP founder David

Nolan has urged the Party to shift its focus away from presidential elections, perhaps abandoning them altogether; it gets more "bang for the buck" in lower-level races.[16]

THE FREE STATE PROJECT

Fresher, more radical, and possessing a plan, the Free State Project (FSP) may show more promise. In 2001, Jason Sorens—at the time a Yale Ph.D. candidate—hatched the concept after he saw libertarians' political efforts failing and wanted to do something about it. He spelled out his ideas in an article published online.

The Plan

The problem, as Sorens saw it, was that libertarians comprise a very small percentage of the U.S. population, so their chances of winning a presidential race and beating back government at the federal level in the next 20 years are "virtually zero." For libertarians to create a freer society anytime soon, they would need to put all their efforts into one smaller place; for this, he suggested a single U.S. state. By moving to a low-population state and leveraging their influence, libertarians could "take over" the state government, "slash state and local budgets," and "eliminate substantial federal interference by refusing to take highway funds and the strings attached to them." Then, they could "bargain with the national government over reducing the role of the national government in [the] state."[17]

Sorens stuck with the idea and drew up more specific plans. People who wanted to join the FSP would take a pledge to move to a given state (to be determined later) and then do everything they could once they were there to advance the cause. No one would need to move anywhere right away. The target state would only be selected after 5,000 people signed up; then they would take a vote. After that, no one would be required to move to the selected state until the number of pledges reached 20,000.

What specifically would the 20,000 do to advance liberty once they arrived in the new place? Anything they want. The FSP's purpose is just to get them there. After that, it is up to the individuals to plan, organize, and take whatever actions they deem appropriate to persuade their neighbors to support more liberty and less government.

Moving to New Hampshire

Membership hit the 5,000 mark in September 2003, so it was time to choose a state.[18] Sorens outlined criteria a state would have to meet to be suitable for their purpose. The state would need a population of less than 1.5 million, and it would need to be a state where the Democrats and Republicans spent less in the 2000 election than $5.2 million—the amount the Libertarian Party spent nationally that year, when it had 40,000 members. (The thinking is that if 40,000 LP members would give $5.2 million in a year, 20,000 FSP members could do the same in a two-year election cycle.) Hawaii and Rhode Island met these criteria, but were eliminated from consideration because of their demonstrated support for centralized government. New Hampshire, Sorens's favorite, won the vote, beating out Wyoming by a 55 to 45 percent margin.

Why New Hampshire? There are numerous advantages.[19] New Hampshire is already relatively free, compared to most other states. It is the least-taxed state except Alaska. There is no state tax on earned income in New Hampshire and no sales tax. Open carry of firearms is allowed essentially everywhere, including the statehouse where the legislature meets. In fact, a recent bill seeking to ban guns in the statehouse was rejected overwhelmingly—and FSP members and other citizens openly carrying firearms were present to watch.[20] Concealed carry of handguns is allowed, too; permits are given out on a "shall issue" basis, which essentially means that all you have to do is ask, although that is still too much government interference by libertarian standards. (Incidentally, Dick Heller, of the *Heller* gun case, is an FSP member.) There is no seat belt law. There is no motorcycle-helmet law. There is no law requiring auto liability insurance. There is no regulation of raw milk sales.

These libertarian policies suggest that New Hampshire natives are already more libertarian than the average American. So do other facts. Sorens found that, controlling for "type of election (primary vs. caucus), turnout, and number of candidates . . . New Hampshire gave Ron Paul his highest vote share in the 2008 campaign."[21] The state government retains institutions left from the time of the American Revolution that are relatively conducive to limiting government. It has a 400-member legislature, and each member is paid just $100 per year. The large number of members means voters can hold politicians accountable relatively easily; most have only about 3,000 constituents.[22] The low pay means the legislature does not attract "career politicians." Local governments are held accountable, too, as town hall meetings are held and citizens vote directly on budget line items. Another remainder of the American Revolution can be found in Article 10 of New Hampshire's constitution, which explicitly affirms the right of the people to overthrow the government if it oversteps its bounds. That and the state motto, "Live Free or Die," may not have much legal force, but undoubtedly have helped maintain the state's liberty-friendly spirit.

Sorens has identified other historical factors that have helped shape New Hampshire into a relatively liberty-friendly state. It was never pulled to the left by Progressives and unions, as many states were, because those groups tended to be found in big cities, and New Hampshire has no big cities. The state was never pulled to the right by "socially authoritarian" religious groups, Protestant or Catholic, because those groups generally only impose their agenda where they predominate—and religiously diverse New Hampshire has no dominant group. There is also no large group of people in the state that depends on the federal government, either, so New Hampshire is ranked third for receiving the least amount of federal tax money for each dollar sent to Washington, which bodes well for future efforts to rebuff the feds.[23]

Finally, New Hampshire is many people's idea of a decent place to live. Winters may be harsh, but otherwise it is temperate and not subject to natural disasters that strike other states. It has mountains; it has seacoast; it has moderately sized cities; it has farms. What it lacks in big-city culture, citizens can make up for by traveling to nearby Boston, enjoying its benefits without bearing the burden of its taxes and government.

Despite all this, some people originally drawn to the FSP did not like the choice of New Hampshire. There has long been a "Western" subset of American libertarians who tend more toward rugged individualism and the distance from Washington, D.C. that living in the middle of nowhere provides. Many of these people strongly preferred Wyoming, the least populous state. Some, led by Kenneth W. Royce (a.k.a author Boston T. Party), formed their own group, Free State Wyoming. This effort appears to have attracted a significantly smaller, quieter following than the New Hampshire project, and its individualistic members seem to be okay with that.

Now What?

So the FSP has chosen its state, but it has a long way to go before anyone has to move there. The number of members at the time of this writing is approaching 10,000, the halfway mark. About 750 of those members have already moved to get a head start, with more early movers arriving in the state all the time. And New Hampshire is feeling their presence.

For example, one early mover, Matt Simon, became a leading voice in the push to legalize medical marijuana as executive director of the New Hampshire Coalition for Common Sense Marijuana Policy. A medical-marijuana bill passed in both houses of the legislature, but was vetoed by Democrat Governor John Lynch. An attempt to override the veto by a required two-thirds margin succeeded in the House, but failed in the Senate. Although this particular drive failed, the votes in the legislature show that libertarians worked effectively in persuading their neighbors and legislators, which provides hope for future efforts.

At the time of this writing, four FSP members have been elected to the New Hampshire House.[24] According to FSP President Varrin Swearingen, FSP members have been active and successful in, among other things, opposing a proposed statewide smoking ban in restaurants and bars, supporting laws to protect gun rights and homeschooling rights, and supporting a bill that removed New Hampshire from the federal Real ID program.[25]

Members of the FSP also came to dominate a government-created panel that was established to find redundancies in the state health and transportation departments. This happened because Republican former governor Craig Benson befriended LP gubernatorial candidate John Babiarz when they ran against each other in 2002. Benson then appointed Babiarz to chair a state commission seeking out government inefficiencies—a task to which a libertarian is presumably especially qualified and motivated because it presents opportunities to find ways to cut government. Babiarz, in turn, selected FSP members to fill eight of eleven seats on the health and transportation boards.[26] As libertarian journalist Brian Doherty observed, "Unusual as this might be on the national level, the head of the state Libertarian Party is a serious political player in New Hampshire."[27]

One problem for New Hampshire activists may be that New Hampshire is already so relatively "good" where other states are "bad" that it may be challenging to find winnable issues that will get activists and the public motivated enough to effect change. Some other states have decriminalized possession of small amounts of marijuana, so that is one potential opportunity. Probably there are occupational licensure laws they could effectively attack, and other areas in which the state has granted monopoly privileges and subsidies that could be repealed. Beyond that, there are surely spending cuts that could be made on numerous relatively small things, but these are the sort of issues that, due to voters' rational ignorance and each issue's smallness, could be difficult to get people worked up about. So libertarians may struggle to find the right issues unless they are going to challenge fundamental ones—such as government schools—and really strike at the root. A longer-term campaign of education will likely be necessary before the FSPers get their fellow New Hampshirites on board with such projects, which may frustrate some activists who were hoping to see nearer-term results.

In addition to political efforts and activism, FSP members are also creating their own media to spread the word. They have established a nightly nationally syndicated radio talk show, *Free Talk Live*; created weekly television shows; founded several print publications; and of course they provide ample media content online.

Originally, Sorens's plan suggested that secession was a possible goal, but the FSP today does not advocate this, presumably because it would be too poorly received by New Hampshire natives. Still, should the state lean ever more libertarian over time, while the federal government becomes ever more authoritarian, this remains an interesting possibility. At the very least, the potential threat of secession could force the federal government to think twice about its impositions on the state and its people.

In the meantime, a critical challenge for FSP activists will be to take a thoughtful, careful approach and not do anything to create a backlash against the FSP among natives who could view the newcomers as invaders and resent the effort to have their government "taken over." It is true: Libertarianism, as a movement outside the mainstream, attracts a disproportionate number of "fringe" characters—people whose lack of normalness goes beyond their views on the proper role of government—as does political activism in general. So it is easy to imagine a few loose cannons, or people more interested in attracting attention to themselves than in advancing liberty, creating big problems. Acts of civil disobedience that seem meaningful to FSP members could simply look like foolishness or pointless troublemaking to outsiders. The more responsible elements within the movement will have to manage public relations effectively without compromising their radicalism if the experiment is to have any chance of success. Time will tell whether that is possible.

Seasteading

We should note briefly that for some, a "Free State" will not cut it. For no-government libertarians, a "free state" is a contradiction in terms. Besides, no matter how relatively free New Hampshire becomes, it is unlikely to escape the grasp of the federal government's income tax, monetary policy, regulation, and foreign policy. Better, some libertarians say, to just go form a new libertarian country based on all the citizens' actual consent.

Some libertarians have thought they could achieve this by building or buying an ocean island. Past efforts to do this have failed—badly, and sometimes after taking substantial sums of people's money—but Patri Friedman has an idea, "seasteading," that he believes can succeed. Friedman brings some credibility to such a project as a successful former Google engineer, the son of libertarian anarchist legal and economic scholar David Friedman, and the grandson of Milton Friedman. To pursue this idea, he has created the Seasteading Institute with help from an initial $500,000 in funding from PayPal co-founder Peter Thiel. The first steps in this project are to figure out how a floating community would be technologically feasible and how it could establish its legal independence from existing governments. Friedman envisions that early "seasteading" projects would involve placing islands in existing countries' national waters. These could offer services that are not available on the mainland, or which are, but for a fraction of the price. But the ultimate goal is to eventually create fully libertarian islands offshore that are free of any countries' laws.[28]

In terms of libertarian radicalism, the Seasteading project rates highly, and it also wins points for seeking to advance liberty through purely private, entrepreneurial means rather than through politics. In terms of likelihood of success, it rates rather lower. And it also runs into this problem: many libertarians, no matter how much they love liberty, do not especially want to live in the middle of the ocean. After all, liberty is no one's *only* value. Still, Friedman has thought of answers to this and many other potential objections and addresses them on the Seasteading Institute's website for those who are interested.[29]

THE CAMPAIGN FOR LIBERTY

Ron Paul's campaign for the 2008 Republican presidential nomination was by far the most successful libertarian political campaign ever, in terms of funds raised (over $30 million); votes received (1.2 million); attraction of new members to the movement; and influence on the national debate. After he nonetheless failed to win the Republican nomination—no surprise there, as most Republicans are not libertarians—Paul did not attempt a third-party run because that would have required him to expend all of his energy just getting on the ballot (and states with "sore loser" laws might not have let him on, anyway), plus he wanted to continue to work within the Republican Party.

The campaign was so flush with cash, and managed its money so responsibly, that it had a substantial amount, nearly $5 million, left over at its end. So Paul used a portion of that money to help fund a new organization designed to advance his ideas after the election was over, the Campaign for Liberty, which got its start with the November 2008 Rally for the Republic in Minneapolis.

The Campaign for Liberty's first and foremost purpose is to educate both its membership and the public on the various issues Paul raised during the campaign, including monetary policy, free-market economics in general, non-interventionist foreign policy, educational freedom, and constitutional restraints on government.

As a 501(c)(4) non-profit organization, the Campaign for Liberty cannot endorse candidates, but it can still influence the political agenda—and is already doing so. So far, it has been hugely successful in promoting Paul's bill to audit the Fed, The Federal Reserve Transparency Act of 2009. The Campaign urged its members to send letters to their representatives asking them to co-sponsor and vote for the bill, and, as during the presidential campaign, Paul's supporters came through. A majority of House members signed on to co-sponsor the bill, including every Republican member and many Democrats. Will the bill ever pass in both Houses of Congress and receive the President's signature? Probably not. As we saw in Chapter 3, there is just too much at stake for the federal government for it to let that happen. But success in Congress right now is not the point. Campaign for Liberty Editor-in-Chief Anthony Gregory observes that these efforts really "are about education."[30] Not education for legislators so much—they mostly just do what it takes to get campaign contributions and votes—but for the public, by increasing the visibility of the issues. If the efforts eventually produce tangible political results, that is welcome, too.

Like Ron Paul's presidential campaign, the Campaign for Liberty does not direct grassroots members' activities from the top down much. The national leadership provides education and guidance on the issues, but the idea is to empower members to carry out campaigns on their own.[31]

At the time of this writing, it is too soon to say what the Campaign for Liberty's likely impact will be going forward. As Gregory notes, the bill to audit the Fed provides a perfect issue to rally around because it "inspires people," it transcends party lines, and it is timed just right to tap into people's frustration over the economic crisis. Whether circumstances will come together to help future issues get that kind of traction, and what exactly those issues would be, is difficult to predict.

The Campaign for Liberty's character has been fundamentally libertarian despite involvement by some conservative-leaning people in its administration. No doubt it has stayed on course because the people running the Campaign for Liberty know which issues animated Ron Paul's supporters in 2008 and will keep them engaged now. The organization is so radical on these key issues—war, the Fed, taxation, civil liberties—that any individual's personal deviations aren't noticeable. And the Campaign has pleased libertarians by avoiding those issues where Paul himself deviates from libertarianism, notably immigration. As a result, the Campaign is, in effect, more libertarian than the present national LP.

The Campaign for Liberty probably has some value in one way that the LP used to, in that it gives people who had been Ron Paul supporters during the 2008 presidential campaign something else to do to stay involved, and keeps them focused on the issues. Left on their own, these people certainly could find plenty to sustain themselves elsewhere in the libertarian movement, and many do so by reading, for example, the material available from *LewRockwell .com* and the Ludwig von Mises Institute. But to keep the movement hanging together, and to put it to use toward future efforts, some structure helps. The LP has not been effective at this, and purely educational organizations such as the Mises Institute and the Foundation for Economic Education are not designed for it. So the Campaign for Liberty may fill an important niche.

The Ron Paul campaign also inspired a student organization, Young Americans for Liberty, which at the time of this writing has 140 chapters at colleges and high schools across the country. It publishes a magazine, *Young American Revolution*, and promotes issue-oriented activism. Here, too, guidance from a national organization to keep momentum going, combined with significant autonomy for local chapters to do things in their own creative way, is likely to keep the energy of the Paul campaign alive.

RAND PAUL AND THE TEA PARTY MOVEMENT

As this book goes to press, the political process has put libertarianism in the news once again.

In May 2010, Ron Paul's son, ophthalmologist Rand Paul, received the Republican nomination for a U.S. Senate seat in Kentucky, thanks to strong support from the burgeoning "Tea Party" movement.

At first, the press pointed to the younger Paul's victory as a sign of the Tea Party's strength. But media coverage soon took a different turn after MSNBC host Rachel Maddow pressed Paul for his views on the 1964 Civil Rights Act. Taken by surprise, Paul stated unequivocally that he opposed racial discrimination but expressed reservations over the Act's provision that prohibited discrimination by private businesses that offer "public accommodations."[32]

Paul's objection to the second portion of the Civil Rights Act was a libertarian one: the law violated private property rights and freedom of association. Just as freedom of speech means we must tolerate people who say racist things, so freedom of association means we must tolerate people who discriminate in who they allow onto their property. As economist Walter Williams put it, "the true test of one's commitment to freedom of association doesn't come when he permits people to associate in ways he deems appropriate. It comes when he permits people to voluntarily associate in ways he deems offensive."[33]

Libertarians have also pointed out, in response to Paul's critics, that libertarian policies do not lead to widespread private discrimination because businesses generally do not want to turn away customers. In fact, as economist Donald Boudreaux explained, it was the "capacity of free markets to make people colorblind that obliged racists in the late 19th century to use government to achieve their loathsome goals" by enacting Jim Crow laws.[34]

Of course, Paul's political enemies ignored these theoretical and historical points and simply used the issue to suggest that he must be a racist. Libertarianism's enemies seized the opportunity, too. A *Salon.com* item declared that Paul's view demonstrates that "libertarianism is juvenile," and a *New York Times* piece claimed that the libertarian view championed "private businesses" while "ignoring the rights of just about everyone else."[35]

The incident illustrates the difficulties of advancing libertarian ideas through a political candidacy. In a sound bite of thirty seconds or less, it is much easier to say that we need government to fight bad things—terrorism, drug addiction, and so on—than to explain how government caused these problems and is not necessary to fix them. For race-related issues in particular, an especially nuanced explanation is required—and a political campaign may be the worst possible forum in which to provide it.

As for Rand Paul, although he has been criticized for taking a libertarian position, he does not actually appear (or claim) to be a libertarian. On many issues—such as the war in Afghanistan and the war on drugs, neither of which he would end—many libertarians have found his views unacceptable. Still, he leans libertarian on many other issues, and there can be little doubt that he would be, by far, the most libertarian U.S. Senator.

As for the Tea Party movement, it is a mixed bag. Its members want less taxation and government spending, but it is unclear what spending they would all agree should be cut, and many are staunchly opposed to the libertarian view on important issues such as war and immigration. The movement appears to be anti-Establishment in a way that many libertarians find encouraging, but mainstream Republicans are doing their best to co-opt it so they can use it to their electoral benefit and then return to business as usual. Whether the Tea Party will be able to resist such efforts—and whether it will prove to be a pro-liberty movement, rather than just an anti-Obama movement—remains to be seen.

NOTES

1. Llewellyn H. Rockwell, Jr., "The Right Choice?" *The American Conservative*, November 3, 2008, http://www.amconmag.com/article/2008/nov/03/00013/.

2. See Bryan Caplan, "The Myth of the Rational Voter," *Cato Unbound*, November 6, 2006, http://www.cato-unbound.org/2006/11/06/bryan-caplan/the-myth-of-the-rational-voter/; Bryan Caplan, *The Myth of the Rational Voter: Why Democracies Choose Bad Policies* (Princeton, NJ: Princeton University Press, 2007).

3. Hans-Hermann Hoppe, *Democracy: The God That Failed* (New Brunswick, NJ: Transaction Publishers, 2001), 21–26.

4. Ibid., 15–39.

5. Murray N. Rothbard, "The Need for a Movement and a Party," *Libertarian Forum* (June 1973), 6–7, http://mises.org/journals/lf/1973/1973_06.pdf.

6. "Summary Data for Bob Barr," *OpenSecrets.org*, http://www.opensecrets.org/pres08/summary.php?cycle=2008&cid=N00002526.M.

7. Bill Woolsey, "Libertarian Fundraising: Some History," *Barr HQ*, August 15, 2008, http://www.barrhq.com/general/libertarian-fundraising-some-history/.

8. "David Nolan: Whatever Happened to the Libertarian Party?" (audio), *The Lew Rockwell Show*, December 16, 2008, http://www.lewrockwell.com/podcast/?p=episode&name=2008-12-16_085_david_nolan_what_happened_to_the_libertarian_party.mp3.

9. Llewellyn H. Rockwell, Jr., "Hey, Wha' Happened to the Libertarian Party?" *The LRC Blog*, November 17, 2008, http://www.lewrockwell.com/blog/lewrw/archives/024050.html.

10. Brian Doherty, "Where Did the Libertarian Party Go Wrong?" *Reason.com*, Nov. 17, 2008, http://www.reason.com/news/show/130107.html.

11. Murray N. Rothbard, "Libertarianism" (video), May 1989, http://www.youtube.com/watch?v=ONS33ukkTtE.

12. David Boaz and David Kirby, "Libertarian Voters in 2004 and 2008," *Cato.org*, January 1, 2007, http://www.cato.org/pubs/policy_report/v29n1/cpr29n1-1.html.

13. Declaration of Carla Howell, *Paul v. Federal Election Comm'n*, Case No. 02-CV-781 (D.D.C. 2002), available at http://www.realcampaignreform.org/howell_dec.htm.

14. Jeff Trandahl, *Statistics of the Congressional Election of November 5, 2002*, available at http://clerk.house.gov/member_info/electionInfo/2002/2002Stat.htm#21.

15. North Carolina State Board of Elections, "NC-Election Results," 2008, http://results.enr.clarityelections.com/NC/7937/14537/en/summary.html.

16. Rockwell, "Hey, Wha' Happened to the Libertarian Party?"

17. Jason Sorens, "Announcement: The Free State Project," *The Libertarian Enterprise*, July 23, 2001, http://www.ncc-1776.org/tle2001/libe131-20010723-03.html.

18. Brian Doherty, "Revolt of the Porcupines!" *Reason*, December 2004, http://www.reason.com/news/printer/36415.html.

19. Most of the ones suggested here can be found, among others, in Jason Sorens, "What Can 20,000 Liberty Activists Accomplish in New Hampshire?" *FreeStateProject.org*, April 12, 2004, http://www.freestateproject.org/about/essay_archive/20000nh.php; Bill Walker, "Moving to the Free(er) State," *LewRockwell.com*, November 14, 2007, http://www.lewrockwell.com/walker/walker28.html.

20. "What Would Your Gun Rights Be Like in a Free State?" *FreeStateProject.org*, http://www.freestateproject.org/intro/gun_rights.

21. Jason Sorens, "Leveraging Institutional Change," *Cato Unbound*, April 10, 2009, http://www.cato-unbound.org/2009/04/10/jason-sorens/leveraging-institutional-change; Jason Sorens, "Which is the Most Pro-Ron Paul State? Assessing the Determinants of Paul's Primary and Caucus Support," http://www.acsu.buffalo.edu/~jsorens/rpvotes.pdf.

22. Doherty, "Revolt of the Porcupines!"

23. Sorens, "What Can 20,000 Liberty Activists Accomplish in New Hampshire?"

24. Associated Press, "For Members of Free State Project, Less is More," July 26, 2009, http://www.msnbc.msn.com/id/32145266/ns/us_news-life/page/3/print/1/displaymode/1098/.

25. Varrin Swearingen, "Successes Influenced or Caused by Participants in the Free State Project," *Varrin.com*, April 30, 2008, http://varrin.com/fsp-successes.html.

26. Daniel Barrick, "Panel Advising Benson Has Libertarian Leaning," *Concord Monitor*, April 14, 2004, http://www.cmonitor.com/apps/pbcs.dll/article?AID=/20040414/REPOSITORY/404140312/1031.

27. Doherty, "Revolt of the Porcupines!"

28. For more on seasteading and similar efforts of the past, see Brian Doherty, "20,000 Nations above the Sea," *Reason* (July 2009), http://reason.com/archives/2009/06/08/20000-nations-above-the-sea/singlepage.

29. "Seasteading FAQ," *Seastead.org*, http://seasteading.org/learn-more/faq.

30. Interview with the author, July 31, 2009.

31. Ibid.

32. For a transcript and some libertarian commentary, see David Weigel, "Rand Paul, telling the truth," *Washington Post Right Now Blog*, May 20, 2010, http://voices.washingtonpost.com/right-now/2010/05/rand_paul_telling_the_truth.html.

33. Walter E. Williams, "The Right to Discriminate," June 2, 2010, available at http://econfaculty.gmu.edu/wew/articles/10/TheRightToDiscriminate.htm.

34. Donald J. Boudreaux, "Which Institution Is More Enlightened?" *Cafe Hayek*, May 24, 2010, http://cafehayek.com/2010/05/which-institution-is-more-enlightened.html.

35. Gabriel Winant, "The lesson of Rand Paul: libertarianism is juvenile," *Salon.com War Room*, May 21, 2010; Sam Tanenhaus, "Rand Paul and the Perils of Textbook Libertarianism," *New York Times*, May 21, 2010, http://www.nytimes.com/2010/05/23/weekinreview/23tanenhaus.html.

FURTHER READING

Caplan, Bryan. *The Myth of the Rational Voter*. Princeton, NJ: Princeton University Press, 2007. Caplan shows why voters behave irrationally by favoring government interventions that actually harm their interests.

Hoppe, Hans-Hermann. *Democracy—The God That Failed*. New Brunswick, NJ: Transaction Publishers, 2001. Hoppe holds out no hope for attempts to advance liberty through the democratic political system. He systematically attacks democracy as the cause of ever-expanding government and ever-increasing "decivilization" of the world.

Conclusion

Several themes appear through this book about libertarianism today.
One theme is that, as a political philosophy, libertarianism today is not too different from libertarianism at any other time, for a good reason: Libertarianism is based on two unchanging fundamental principles, non-aggression and private property rights. The libertarian prescription—more freedom, less government—is the same regardless of time or place. Also, the laws of economics that libertarians emphasize do not change: For example, government money printing will have essentially the same effect in America today that it had in France in the late eighteenth century, Germany in the 1920s, Yugoslavia in the 1990s, or Zimbabwe in the 2000s. The historical details may vary, but the underlying ideas stay the same. In rare cases such as intellectual property, libertarians adjust their views, but they do so by going back to first principles.

Another theme is that libertarianism is not untried. Unsophisticated critics sometimes raise the challenge: "If libertarianism is such a great philosophy, why haven't any countries adopted it?" In fact, practically every libertarian idea has been implemented somewhere at some time, and most of them have been in place at some time within the United States. We saw examples of this with America's history of drug freedom, educational freedom, and gun freedom, among others. People who are unsatisfied by libertarian philosophy or economic theory can look at what happened when liberty was tried, and can see that it worked. They can also look to the vast areas of life where we still enjoy freedom, and see that this has not created chaos.

Although libertarianism has been tried here and there, liberty should not be blamed for problems it has not caused. As noted in Chapter 3, the financial crisis was not the product of libertarian policies. Likewise, most "privatization" or "deregulation" that occurs is not libertarian, so libertarianism should not be blamed for their failures, either. More often than not, these efforts involve granting government monopoly privileges to politically connected businesses. In promoting their actual ideas, libertarians will need to clarify confusion over these terms that have been hijacked by the State and its friends.

Along similar lines, this book has shown that big businesses are not necessarily friends of liberty. Businesses exist to make money. In a free economy, they could only do this by serving consumers. In our economy, businesses do make money by serving consumers, but they also obtain unfair advantages through government privileges. These privileges include, among many others, direct "corporate welfare" subsidies; regulation that imposes high costs that existing big businesses can afford, but smaller would-be competitors cannot (as with the Food and Drug Administration); intellectual-property laws (especially extensions of copyright terms); price supports (for agricultural products, for example); government contracts to produce war supplies and other things consumers have not demanded on the market; and, of course "bailouts" for failed firms. Thanks in part to prodding by so-called "left-libertarians" who emphasize these points, libertarians do not rush to the defense of big business or extol business leaders' virtues to the extent they once did.[1]

Another theme we have emphasized is that libertarianism is *only* a political philosophy, and is only concerned with aggression against peaceful people. This point seems critical to libertarians' success because, as Ron Paul emphasized in his campaign, "freedom brings people together." Libertarianism does not require anyone to alter his or her views on religion, lifestyles, charity, or anything else. It only requires people to agree to disagree *peacefully* about such issues. America may have the strongest libertarian tradition of any country, but it also has a strong Puritan streak (which eventually became its so-called "Progressive" streak), which seeks to use government to reform others.[2] If liberty is to triumph, Americans' libertarianism will have to overcome their Puritanism.

Another important theme is that libertarianism today is both radical and populist. During the 1980s and 1990s, the movement's public face trended in the opposite direction. Well-funded Washington, DC think tanks obtained a modicum (but only a modicum) of Establishment respectability by downplaying certain taboo issues (money, drugs, war) and pitching "public policy" solutions to the Washington elite. This strategy reached its pinnacle of "success" when the Bush Administration briefly embraced the idea of supposedly "private" social security accounts by proposing a program (long urged by the Cato Institute and others) that would have allowed Americans to put a portion of their Social Security contributions into individual accounts, investing the money in stocks and bonds.

Many libertarians outside Washington criticized this proposal for two main reasons. First, this would not remove the most offensive aspect of social security because government would still force people to give up part of their income now in exchange for an unenforceable promise of payment later; in fact, funding private accounts while paying current social security recipients would have required a considerable tax *increase*. Second, it would give the government far more influence over the economy, as the government would decide what stocks and bonds to buy on citizens' behalf and would therefore become a part-owner of many heretofore private firms. In other words, although the program would give citizens a small amount of "choice," it would expand government power and bureaucracy.[3]

It did not take long for Bush to drop this plan. It was not very popular and, besides, Bush's primary interests lay elsewhere.[4] So what did the Beltway libertarians gain from endorsing this scheme? Perhaps nothing, except association with an unpopular president's plan. Although it is good from the libertarian perspective to make Americans aware of social security's unsustainability, this campaign did little to educate anyone about a viable libertarian alternative in the form of true privatization.[5]

Ron Paul's success changed the focus and direction of the libertarian movement by returning to core issues such as money and war, and pitching them directly to ordinary people, not to his colleagues in Washington. In doing so, Paul drew enthusiastic young people's attention to the key thinkers who inspired the libertarian movement in the first place, especially Ludwig von Mises and Murray Rothbard, whom the Establishment-friendly libertarians had long downplayed.

Another theme in this book is that political action is not the only way to achieve liberty. Education must come first, and political activity is not necessarily even the second most important priority. Libertarians may also advance their cause by creating successful alternative institutions, of which home-schooling provides one impressive example. Some libertarians also focus on escaping government—"voting with their feet" by looking for places to go other than the United States where their rights and privacy will be better respected. As easy travel and communications (including the ability to tele-commute) only increase, governments may find themselves forced to compete for citizens by lowering taxes and other limits on freedom.

Finally, one point that should have come across is that there is much more libertarian literature readily available than ever before. It is deliberate that most of the recommended readings and works cited in this book are available online for free. I hope this introductory book has captured your interest enough to seek out those books and articles and explore libertarianism at the next level.

NOTES

1. For a debate among libertarians on the merits and problems of big business, see "When Corporations Hate Markets," *Cato Unbound*, November 2008, http://www.cato-unbound.org/archives/november-2008-when-corporations-hate-markets/.

2. On the history of Puritanism and Progressivism in America, see Murray N. Rothbard, "Origins of the Welfare State," *Mises.org*, August 11, 2006, http://mises.org/story/2225.

3. See, e.g., George Reisman, "Real Social Security Reform," *The Free Market* (May 2005), http://mises.org/freemarket_detail.aspx?control=537; Llewellyn H. Rockwell, Jr., "The Failed Compromise," *LewRockwell.com*, March 16, 2005, http://www.lewrockwell.com/rockwell/failure-of-compromise.html.

4. See Brian Doherty, *Radicals for Capitalism* (New York: PublicAffairs, 2007), 1–2, 573–74.

5. On possible steps toward true privatization, see, e.g., Reisman.

Index

About the Author

JACOB H. HUEBERT is an award-winning attorney and an adjunct professor of law at Ohio Northern University College of Law. His writing appears frequently in newspapers across the country and in academic and professional journals. He holds a bachelor's degree in economics from Grove City College and a juris doctor from the University of Chicago Law School, and he is a former law clerk to a U.S. Court of Appeals judge. He is also an adjunct scholar of the Ludwig von Mises Institute.